82

Rusden
5 Albert St
East Melbourne.
41-6274

PEOPLE
&
PLACES

PEOPLE
&
PLACES

Random Reminiscences
of the Rt. Hon. Malcolm MacDonald

Collins
ST JAMES'S PLACE
LONDON

To Marion with love

Contents

Introduction

This book contains some unimportant, light-hearted autobiographical reminiscences. If I wished to do so, I could write a serious and no doubt rather pompous story of my life, as some more or less eminent individuals in my generation have done. But I shall not do that. There are various reasons for this. Among others, I never kept a diary about my experiences in public affairs, my appreciations of celebrated contemporaries, or my personal reflections on current events; and such a work is a necessary foundation for any accurate memoirs. Quite apart from the fact that I always wished to spend my leisure hours escaping from official work and enjoying more pleasing recreations, I felt that such scribblings were liable to be too subjective, tending consciously or unconsciously to exaggerate the rightness of the author's own part in affairs, and sometimes at least to be unjust to colleagues or critics who disagreed with him. In such cases these records would be not a guide but a misguide to future historians—and so, I felt, they were better unwritten.

I naturally recognise the fine value of particular people's diaries. For example, men like Samuel Pepys and Harold Nicolson are diarists of genius, and their works are literary as well as historical classics which are precious to multitudes of readers. However, most daily scrawled records do not approach that class. Of course, the diaries or similar writings of certain other personalities besides diarists of genius are immensely useful to their fellow human beings. These are the reminiscences or memoirs not of men, but of supermen—figures like Winston Churchill among the Titans of the present century. Their commentaries are naturally often self-centred and prejudiced, but these very elements throw additional light on their grand authors, helping historians and students of mankind to understand better those rare, significant men of destiny. Their autobiographies have immense, and in each case unique, value. But the lighter screeds of smaller men are mostly unimportant.

Fortunately I learned early in life how comparatively insignificant all us lesser mortals are. This happened immediately after I left school. At my school—the well-known co-educational establishment called Bedales—I seemed to be an important personage. As a result of my varied interests and activities through eight years there, during my last twelve months I held several distinguished offices. I was the Head of the School, the Head-boy (with a Head-girl as my partner at that level of responsibilities), the Captain of the football XI, the Vice-captain of the cricket XI, the Editor of the school magazine, the Prime Minister of the government in our debating society (which was formed on a model of the House of Commons), the Captain of the fire brigade, the leading athlete in our annual sports, not only a principal actor in our annual Shakespeare plays but also the script-writer, producer and chief male star of musical comedies on our original stage—and various other characters besides. I was rather pleased with myself, and no doubt a bit conceited. I seriously wondered what on earth would happen to the school when I left it, assuming that its vivid life would decline when I departed. Yet I could not stay there to save the situation; I must go and continue my education at a university. I felt very sorry indeed for the place. . . . Six months later I returned to visit it, expecting to find the community, its leadership and its inhabitants all in rather a mess. I found the opposite. The school was flourishing; if anything, it seemed even more calm, genial and robust than during my tenure of various supreme offices. My successor as Head of the School had no problems on which he wished to seek my advice; he was serene, self-confident and happy. I learned my lesson. I realised that I was not in the least indispensable—that I was, indeed, expendable. From that moment I have understood that almost all us mere individuals are of little or no account in the great onward—or is it backwards or sideways?—march of Humanity.

Partly for this reason I have never kept a personal diary. From time to time I wrote for my own later use daily notes on some particular item among my hobbies, like bird-watching or exotic travels. It is true that through nearly half a century I have been connected with national and international affairs of great importance, and that now and then I played a distinct part in helping to influence them. My comments on these could therefore be of interest. However, many of those comments are already on record. They fill the voluminous pages of all the contemporary telegrams, memoranda, dispatches and other papers which I wrote at the time about every successive development in each of the various lands where I strove as a servant of the British nation—and of the human race—and these are presumably now locked up in secret official archives. There they can wait until the time comes for their study—little bits and pieces of the raw material of history. They record my spontaneous yet considered reflections on events and people at the moments when my opinions on these were fresh; and so they describe as accurately as is possible the essence of my thought, judgment and action in each given situation. No doubt they reveal not only such successes as I may occasionally have achieved, but also the mistakes which I made—without the intrusion of greater wisdom induced by later hind-sight. I am content to leave my personal comments at that; and so this volume does not contain any solemn reflections or afterthoughts on those affairs.

As I have already written, its contents are light-hearted reminiscences. They do refer here and there to this or that weighty political or diplomatic episode in which I was involved—but only incidentally. Some people may therefore regard the book as frivolous, and as treating with undue levity the rather grim and extremely significant period of world history through which my generation has lived. That, of course, is not my intention; I am very well aware of the remarkable importance of the revolutionary epoch in Mankind's story which has developed during the last half-century. No one in his senses would attempt to ignore this, and some day when I am free from official restrictions, and feel in the mood, I shall perhaps write a slim volume containing reflections on the subject. . . . But luckily there is a lighter side to life, the value of which is frequently under-estimated by too serious-minded people. Its trivial incidents are—thank goodness!—as common in our Earthly existence as ponderous ones, and the creative goodness of their qualities should not be under-rated. They produce laughter and good cheer and happiness, whilst the others encourage thoughtfulness, solemnity and often sorrow. All these various moods are important and constructively helpful in Mankind's efforts to solve its somewhat baffling problems. The gayer side of life is as vital as the more sombre if we are to keep a wise sense of perspective about our human failings, difficulties, attainments and aspirations.

Accident of Birth

The first surprising adventure of my life befell me at the moment of my birth. By a stroke of good fortune at that crisis in my career —in August, 1901—I became a child of two very remarkable people. Naturally I was not at the time aware of this circumstance; nor did it begin to dawn on me until many years later that my parents' marriage was one of those romances which might seem a figment of the author's wild imagination if it were related in a work of fiction.

Perhaps my father was the more unusual parent of the two. I never met his sire, but I knew his mother well. My brothers, sisters and I used to spend our summer holidays in her home in Scotland; and we loved her dearly. She was a handsome, grey-haired old woman usually dressed—like many aged dames at the start of this century—in a white lace cap, a shawl round her shoulders, and a prim black dress with its skirt reaching down to her toes. Her intelligent, lively and charming personality made her the most popular resident in the small fishing town called Lossiemouth where she lived. She stayed in a little cottage consisting of a "but and ben" downstairs and two attic bedrooms upstairs, with flowering fuchsia shrubs growing on either side of its door leading to a modest lawn and a patch of vegetable garden. She taught us children how to cook porridge and bake scones, instructed us genially in some of the simple truths of life, and took us on her gossiping, laughing visits to various fishwife friends. Naturally the respect in which she was held by our neighbours was helped by the fact that her only child—my father—was the well-known leader of the Labour Party in Parliament in distant London.

For some years it did not strike my childish mind as strange that whereas his name was Mr. James Ramsay MacDonald she was known to everyone as Miss Annie Ramsay. He was in fact the illegitimate son of this humble and poor but vividly characterful spinster.

I never learned the story of her tragic love affair, but I should not be surprised if a tale told me long afterwards by one of her female cronies was near the truth. Annie had been a young servant girl in a farmhouse near Lossiemouth, and she lost her heart to a ploughman named MacDonald working in its fields. In due course the couple became engaged to be married, and their banns were about to be published in the local kirk when they had an unhappy quarrel. She promptly told him that their betrothal was off, and that she would not become his wife.

He was astonished. "But you're going to be the mither o' my bairn," he said.

She replied that she was well aware of the fact—but that it made no difference. She refused to change her mind, and went to live with her widowed mother in a cottage near the Old Seatown of Lossiemouth.

When her son was born he was christened James and brought up by the two devoted women. For many years afterwards their friends and his playmates called him simply Jimmy Ramsay; but later he adopted his father's surname. His attractive mama received many proposals of marriage; but she refused them all. Miss Annie Ramsay she remained to her dying day more than forty years later—independent, gentle, witty and proud.

II

My mother was born of very different stock. A daughter of an impeccably respectable, well-to-do and indeed quite distinguished pair of Victorian worthies living in the fashionable West End of London, her maiden name was Margaret Ethel Gladstone. Her father was an eminent professional member of the Royal Institution, her mother was closely related to the great scientist Lord

Kelvin, and the family were distantly connected with the Grand Old Man, William Ewart Gladstone. Nothing could be more proper than all that.

Of rather saintly and yet practical disposition, young Margaret did a lot of charitable social work in various parts of London; and in this connection she first came in touch with some of the pioneers of the Socialist Movement who were starting their campaigning in Britain. She was attracted by their political doctrine, and not long afterwards fell under the particular spell of the eloquent oratory and good looks of a youthful Scots propagandist for their cause. When she broke the news of her love for him to her family most of them disapproved, but her widowed father met the young man, liked him, and with great good sense agreed to the match in spite of his poverty, his radicalism and his bastardy.

As if these circumstances were not unorthodox enough, the partnership also turned out to be a historic one, for the pair became two of the most important founders of the British Labour Party. My mother led a small group of devoted colleagues in organising the Women's Labour League of those early years, whilst my father did more than any other individual to create the political organisation and establish the Evolutionary Socialist philosophy of the Party. In due course he became perhaps the finest statesman that the British Labour Movement has yet produced. Some people would of course emphatically dissent from this judgment, but I am inclined to think that impartial future historians will agree with it.

A sense of adventure at being his son awakened in me during my childhood, and never afterwards left me. It started when I heard one day from my mother's lips (when I was only five years old) the astonishing news that he had become a Member of Parliament. This seemed to me a very illustrious position, and I felt filled with pride. Later I learned more about his distinction. Often famous personages came to our home to discuss public affairs with my parents, and I gathered from some of their remarks which I overheard as I sat quietly reading story books near-by that my papa was an outstandingly able, greatly admired political leader.

I was thrilled to get further evidence of this whenever we children went for tea with him on the terrace of the Palace of Westminster overlooking the River Thames, when many important looking people used to come and greet him with fervent cordiality. I realised that I was lucky to be a son of such a great man.

III

A further fact about my mother's and father's partnership deeply impressed me in my early years. This was the superlative affection which bound them together. Their profound love for one another made them ideal companions in their private life, whilst their zealous joint political work made them perfect comrades in their public lives. For a while the relationship caused me to suppose that human existence is invariably blessed with supreme life-long joy— and then it was suddenly revealed to me that this same existence can be damned with profound, perpetual sorrow. When I was ten years old my mother died very prematurely, and at a single blow my father was transported from infinite happiness to inconsolable sadness. I can never forget the terrible anguish which he suffered at her departure. He never really recovered from this throughout the rest of his long, publicly crowded and yet privately solitary life.

In his intense loneliness he nonetheless persevered as a champion of the human causes to which he and she had passionately dedicated themselves—and so one of the most dramatic real life stories of our time continued on its way.

IV

When my mother died in 1911 my father was, at the age of 44, the respected leader of the Labour Party in the House of Commons. Obviously a brilliant career lay before him. Yet three years later that prospect was shattered. The First World War broke out in

1914; he was reserved in his support for Britain's entry into it; and because a large majority of his Labour Party colleagues took a strongly different view he resigned their leadership. At once he was denounced throughout the length and breadth of the British Isles as a traitor, and his career appeared to have collapsed in ruins.

This judgment seemed to be confirmed when he lost his Parliamentary seat in the next General Election in 1918; and his virtual eclipse continued for a further four years. Then came another complete turn of the wheel of fortune. In 1922 he was re-elected to the House of Commons, and a few days afterwards—to everyone's astonishment—was chosen by a narrow majority of his fellow members to be again the Labour Party's captain at Westminster. Nor was that all: since Labour's team now for the first time attained the position of the second largest party in the House, he automatically became the Leader of His Majesty's Opposition.

Less than two years later he rose still further—to the top. After another General Election he became Prime Minister—incidentally the first Socialist Premier in Britain's history. His fine gifts as a Parliamentarian and a statesman made him universally admired at the time by friends and foes alike, whilst his charm as a man brought him widespread popularity. However, politics is an uncertain field of human endeavour where even powerful leaders have limited control over the national and international events which decide their fates. During the next seven years my father experienced the normal ups and downs of any outstanding politician, becoming after a comparatively short period in 10 Downing Street once more the Leader of the Opposition, and then for a second time head of a Labour Government. After that he experienced yet another unforeseen, dramatic reversal of fortune. I need not describe here the causes of this development, and shall merely state the facts. In 1931 his Labour Administration collapsed, he became the Prime Minister of a National Government in its place —and he was promptly thrown out of the Labour Party which he had done more than anyone else to create and carry into power. He became the most despised of men among most of his earlier colleagues, whilst his acclamation by an overwhelming majority of his countrymen reached new heights.

That was the beginning of the end. Within a year or two his abilities started to wane, and with them his influence and public reputation also gradually declined.

V

This remarkable series of events closely affecting my own personal life occurred from the time when I was a child less than ten years old until I was a young man of thirty. Its succession of strange, contrary occurrences naturally made a deep impression on my feelings and thoughts. As I have already indicated, in my infant years I felt proud of my father's illustrious and apparently assured position. When of a sudden in 1914 he became the most vilified man in Britain I was a youngster at school, and I felt sadly baffled, although my affectionate faith in him never wavered. When he recovered his popularity and distinction on being chosen Leader of the Opposition I was an undergraduate at Oxford, and was filled with delighted surprise. When he took office for the first time as Prime Minister two years later my emotions were elated; when he fell from that eminence nine months afterwards my pleasure turned to disappointment; when he recovered the Premiership in my young manhood I was once more exultant; and when a couple of years after that, on one and the same day, his Labour Government crashed in disarray and his National Government rose in triumph, I felt upset and approving, apprehensive and bold, sad and happy all at the same time. . . . But I need not write further on this theme, still less record here the many lessons which I learned about human affairs from watching at close quarters—and to some extent sharing—my parent's extraordinary changes of Fate. I shall only mention that it was a glorious adventure to be a son of one who started life as a poor, illegitimate baby, and who ended up by being three times Prime Minister of Great Britain.

VI

My own personal life was almost as incalculably and sometimes surprisingly affected as his own by the developments which kept either battering or exalting him—although, of course, on a much lower level of affairs. Insofar as I had any plans for a career in my youth they were very different from anything that subsequently happened to me. When I was at my kindergarten I wanted to be an engine driver. At school my interests took—as I have mentioned in the Introduction—a literary and theatrical turn; and for some unaccountable reason I conceived the idea that I would become the Shakespeare of the XXth century. This notion persisted at the university, where I still hoped that I might reign supreme in the world of literature by becoming the most accomplished and acclaimed Man of Letters of my generation. That aspiration stimulated one of the three ambitions which I then formed. The first was that I should write half a dozen books which would live for several hundred years, the second was that I should make half a dozen friends who would last through life, and the third that I should ride in the Grand National and last the course. I did not mind whether I won the classic steeplechase or not, so long as I reached the winning post still in the saddle of my trusty steed.

The first and third of those ambitions have of course been denied me; but the second I did achieve. Incidentally its results give me more pleasure than any other attainment could possibly do.

Only once in my life did I acquire any personal political ambition. That was in the years 1914-18 when my father was the most hated man in British public life. I then conceived the desire that I would one day become the son of Britain's Prime Minister— a virtually hopeless wish which was satisfied some years later. Otherwise I never had any particular hankering to get involved in politics. However, because of my parent's increasingly distinguished part in them after he became Leader of the Opposition, I somehow could not avoid a certain amount of implication.

Whilst I was still an undergraduate at Oxford his Labour Party colleagues kept offering me safe constituencies for the approaching General Election; but I thought it wrong that I should be given the privilege of a secure Parliamentary seat simply because I was a son of the Party's leader. Nevertheless, after rejecting several proposals I felt it would be inconsiderate to show complete indifference to their friendly thought, and eventually I compromised by refusing every safe constituency but suggesting that if they would find me an at present hopeless, strongly Conservative seat which I might conceivably gain for the Labour Party 10 or 15 years hence—if I should remain the candidate in it—I would go there to fight for our cause. They produced such a place in the aristocratic Dukeries in Nottinghamshire, and I contested it unsuccessfully in the General Elections of 1923 and 1924. Somewhat to my surprise I won it in 1929—and so I found myself at least temporarily committed to public life as a Member of Parliament.

Then my private Shakespearian plans began to go further awry. I naturally expected to remain a back-bench member of the House of Commons for several years whilst I made up my mind whether I wished to continue a political career, or preferred to devote myself to some other main interest. However, two years later that intention got upset. In 1931 the Labour Government fell from office, the National Government took its place, there was a shortage of candidates for Ministerial posts from my small National Labour group—and at Stanley Baldwin's and Herbert Samuel's insistence my father (not without pleasure) offered me the job of Under-Secretary of State for Dominion Affairs. I could not refuse it.

Naturally I felt flattered, and rather pleased with myself; but this was partly because my term of office as a Minister was expected to be extremely short. At that time we anticipated that the National Government would remain in power for only six weeks, solely to pass through Parliament the necessary legislation for overcoming the economic crisis which had arisen, and then to resign. Unfettered party politics would afterwards be resumed, another General Election would be held—and, since I had been dismissed with my father from the Labour Party, and entertained no desire to join any other party, I assumed that my life in politics would end. I remember strolling with friends through the garden at Chequers marvelling and laughing gleefully at the turn of events. I anticipated the brevity of my eminence as a junior Minister without any disappointment, and began to consider what other occupation I should adopt.

However, everything developed differently. To cut a long story short, a succession of National Governments continued in power for the next ten years, and I remained a member of every one of them. After the first four years I was promoted to being a Cabinet Minister. In Baldwin's, Chamberlain's and Churchill's Governments I became Secretary of State for the Colonies, Secretary of State for Dominion Affairs and Minister of Health in turn.

So the choice of my career had been taken out of my hands, although I of course acquiesced not unwillingly. Work in the Government during those fateful years was intensely interesting; and I began to settle down to the notion that I would stay in politics for the rest of my days. Then another unexpected somersault occurred in my prospects. Early in his wartime Premiership Churchill conceived the idea of sending Ministers to be his personal and official representatives with important allied or friendly Governments overseas. Unprecedentedly they would retain their Cabinet status and Membership of Parliament throughout their years of absence from Britain. Thus Lord Halifax went as Ambassador to Washington, Philip Cunliffe-Lister did duty in West Africa, Oliver Lyttleton was later sent to Cairo, Harold Macmillan went to North Africa, and other Ministers were posted elsewhere. In 1941 Churchill asked me to go to Canada as High Commissioner; so I departed to Ottawa.

That started several revolutions in my life. Although I was fond of occasional travels abroad, I did not intend to remain long overseas, for my main interests and affections were centred in Britain. Yet I have never lived in Britain since! Instead, for the last twenty-six years, I have stayed continuously in a succession of countries almost everywhere else round the Earth, with only brief returns now and then to London for official consultations in Whitehall. I lived for five years in Canada, ten years in South East Asia, five years in India, eighteen months in Europe, and six years in Africa. I have become a stranger in my native land.

Associated with that geographical revolution was a professional one. Before Churchill's appointment of me to Canada it never entered my mind that I would intrude into the world of diplomacy, still less of Colonial administration and related activities. Yet those have been my ceaseless occupations throughout the last quarter of a century. My successive posts have been very higgledy-piggledy. Starting with my unexpected appointment as a member of the British Cabinet in 1935, I have been in turn one Minister, two Secretaries of State, three High Commissioners, an Ambassador Extraordinary, three Governors-General, one Commissioner-General, a Governor, two Special Representatives, a couple of Special Envoys, and occasionally other highfalutin potentates as well. It has all been very unplanned, very odd, and very enjoyable.

Flo

The year was 1924, and the month was August. A few weeks earlier
I had ended my undergraduate career at Oxford; and I was now
making a brief motor tour through Aberdeenshire before setting
out on my first journey round the world. A friend had given me a
note of introduction to a farmer named Duncan Campbell who
lived somewhere on my route. Our mutual acquaintance warned
me that between Duncan and my family the traditional enmity
dividing the Campbell and MacDonald clans was further aggravated by the fact that Duncan happened to be a dyed-in-the-wool
Tory who hated the political faith of Britain's Labour Prime Minister—my father. Nevertheless the acquaintance expressed a strong
hope that I would drop in and visit Duncan, since he thought
we should take to each other. He believed Duncan would regard
me more in sorrow than in anger, and that our talk might achieve
something in promoting a better understanding in Scottish Conservative circles of the Labour Government's aims, even if it
could accomplish nothing by way of reducing the time-honoured
hostility between the Campbells and the MacDonalds.

He added that Duncan held an important place in northern
Conservative councils since he was the chairman of the Eastern
Aberdeenshire Unionist Association. I gathered that this Campbell
was a man of robust physical appearance, tough mental attitudes,
and gruffly charming personality. He was also a good breeder of
Aberdeen Angus cattle. Moreover, he possessed a quite distinguished wife who was a remarkable contrast to himself. Whereas
he stood huge and strong in body, she was of delicate "petite"
build; and whilst his mind was engrossed in earthy problems like
rearing fine dairy cows and promoting staunch Tory politicians,

her considerable intellect took flights of fancy into the realms of literature and art. Indeed, she was a well-known broadcaster for the B.B.C. on such topics as Robbie Burns's poems and Walter Scott's novels. They had one son and a daughter. The boy took after his father more than his mother, being a convinced Imperialist who was serving in the police force of some overseas Colony; whereas their girl—named Flo—was more in character with the mother, having recently won an Honours Degree at Aberdeen University.

My travelling itinerary had been so uncertain that I could give the Campbells no notice of the exact day or time of my arrival; and in the end I sent them a telegram one morning saying that I would call on them that afternoon.

It was a sunny summer's day, and the lovely Aberdeenshire countryside looked fruitful with ripening crops, green pastures and herds of lusty cattle. At about four o'clock I observed a white farmhouse perched on a hillside which answered to the description I had been given of my destination. Sure enough, when my car drew up before its front door a burly farmer hailed me with a loud shout of greeting, announcing that he was Duncan Campbell. I introduced myself, and he gave me a cordial if candid welcome. Saying that it was a privilege to meet a Prime Minister's son even though he strongly disapproved of this particular Prime Minister, he added that we should not discuss politics in case these caused us to come to blows, but that he would show me his farm and tell me anything I wanted to know about animal husbandry.

"Come ben the hoose, and ha'e a cup o' refreshing Tory tea," he said. "It'll no' poison ye; indeed, it micht do ye some guid."

He told me that unfortunately his wife had gone away from home for a few days, and that his daughter Flo was also absent, although more temporarily. She had motored to Aberdeen on an unavoidable errand, but would hasten back in about an hour's time. He then announced that immediately after her arrival he himself would have to leave for a while, since he must preside early that evening over a meeting of the local Conservative Party. He explained that it was a special meeting called to adopt a new

Parliamentary candidate for the East Aberdeenshire constituency, and that he therefore could not miss it. Remarking that I probably knew the individual concerned because he, like me, had just graduated from Oxford, he said the fellow's name was Robert Boothby. I replied that I knew Bob Boothby well, and that he should make a very effective candidate. My rabid host did not seem unduly deterred by this recommendation of his prospective choice by a political opponent, but on the contrary expressed gratified appreciation of my judgment.

We chatted amiably on various more or less inoffensive topics. In the course of the conversation Duncan asked whether I would stay the night on the farm so that we could continue our talk after his return from his political engagement. I explained that I had run out of clean clothes and new razor blades; but he dismissed the objection with a wave of his hand and a promise to lend me everything I needed. So I readily agreed to stay.

After tea we went out-of-doors to view the farm. Strolling across a yard, we visited his dairy and then inspected the herd of cattle. They were a truly impressive assembly of beasts.

"Now come and see the hay that keeps them sae fit," said Duncan.

We walked into a field sloping behind the farmyard, where a group of haystacks stood on the hillside basking in golden sunshine. Their owner led me up a ladder to the summit of the latest, half-constructed stack so that under his expert guidance I could examine the quality of the fodder. As I stood aloft listening to a lecture by him on the subject, a gay feminine laugh sounded from the ground below.

"So that's where you two have gone into hiding," a girl's voice called merrily. "I've been looking for you everywhere."

"Ah, that's Flo," said her father.

Looking down, I saw a young lady gazing up at us. Duncan shouted an introduction of me to her, and she and I exchanged polite smiles.

To this day—nearly half a century later—I remember vividly the youthful loveliness of her face. Her blonde hair was ruffled by a slight breeze as she tilted her head upwards to peer at us. Her rosy cheeks were features of a healthy country lass, whilst her broad brow, intelligent blue eyes and sensitive mouth were marks of an intellectual university student. Those qualities were combined in a visage so beautiful that it might have belonged to a Greek goddess.

Duncan and I descended the ladder, and I then noticed other details of her appearance. Her figure had athletic grace, with the strong limbs of one accustomed to working in fields; but it was dressed in a chic, pretty frock which would have attracted approving attention in any elegant drawing-room.

After a few minutes Duncan said that he must now hasten away to his political meeting; and he asked Flo to take good care of me until his return. She said she would do so with pleasure.

The sun continued to shine warmly, and for the next three hours Flo and I sat high on a hilltop conversing about all sorts of things. We discussed books by our favourite authors, and exchanged opinions about the paintings of several Scottish artists such as Allan Ramsay, David Wilkie and the great Raeburn. She was as enthusiastic an admirer of their works as I was. An undertone of zealous Caledonian patriotism animated all our talk, and led us into comments on various episodes in the history of our native land. In the course of the review we voiced a sentimental prejudice in favour of Mary Queen of Scots against her formidable and in many ways wiser rival, Good Queen Bess. However, we never mentioned the regrettable feud between the Campbells and the MacDonalds.

Time passed swiftly; and I felt sorry when—much sooner than I thought necessary—Duncan's returning motor-car appeared along a road in the rustic scenery spread like a map below us. Reluctantly I watched it climb the hill to the farmhouse, halt before the door, and eject his hefty figure.

Flo and I strolled down the hill to meet him.

II

When the three of us sat at their supper table in the farmhouse kitchen Duncan told Flo and me about the political meeting he had just attended. It had gone well, young Bob Boothby made a good impression on the assembled Tory leaders, and they unanimously adopted him as their prospective candidate. In the subsequent discussion Duncan had spoken vigorously about the incompetence of the Labour Government, the iniquities of its policies, and the need to overthrow it as soon as possible. Afterwards he startled his audience, and provoked a lot of light-hearted chaff, by announcing that he must leave the meeting early because he was to entertain Mr. Ramsay MacDonald's son as his house-guest that evening.

Our conversation then turned to other topics. During a pause in the talk I remarked that the name "Flo" must be a shortened form of something longer; and I asked my hostess what her proper name was.

"My full name," she answered, "is Flora MacDonald Campbell."

I caught my breath, and stared at her in astonishment.

"That's the most surprising, contrary and romantic name I've ever heard," I observed. "There must be some Highland legend attached to it. Do tell me the story."

Duncan laid down his knife and fork, and said, "I'll tell ye the tale. We've checked its authenticity, and it's the solemn truth."

He hesitated for a moment, and then continued, "In this case the name Flora MacDonald has nithing tae do wi' Bonnie Prince Charlie's girl friend. Our family records go a wee bit further back than that. Forgive me if I refer to the Massacre o' Glencoe. That's a sore point wi' ye MacDonalds; but the story began that nicht."

Then he related the following scrap of history.

When Campbell troops went into Glencoe one day in February 1692 to enjoy the MacDonalds' hospitality for a week, only their

officers knew that the secret purpose of the visit was to ingratiate
themselves with their hosts, and so put themselves in a secure
position to kill them all. The junior soldiers were ignorant of this
treacherous intent.

One of those troopers was a young Campbell named Duncan.
He happened to be billeted in a MacDonald cottage where a
daughter of the house was a charming lassie called Flora. At the
age of eighteen her eyes had a gentle glance, her voice a soft lilt,
and her step a maidenish grace which were enchanting. Within a
few hours of his arrival Duncan fell in love with her. He was
slightly perplexed, for hitherto he had assumed that all the Mac-
Donalds were contemptible creatures; but now he began to modify
that view. His sentimental inclination became all the more persuasive when Flora showed signs of reciprocating his feelings.
Apparently she did not resent his tentative mode of wooing; on
the contrary, she encouraged it subtly by her sweetness to him.
When each day's work was done the two used to climb to a high,
remote spot among the heather on a mountain-side where they
would talk and laugh happily for a while together. Yet he refrained from putting any romantic proposition to her because his
obstinate prejudice against her clan still lingered.

Then he received an appalling shock. After several pleasing,
friendly days in the glen his commanding officer confided to him
and his comrades-in-arms that on the following night they were
to slay all their hosts. He could not really disapprove of this order,
since he thought it right and proper that all the male MacDonalds
should be dead. But an awful fear stabbed at his heart. He felt
afraid lest, in the confused combats which might arise when the
killings started, Flora would get hurt. And he could not bear the
thought of her perhaps even being killed. Indeed, the more he saw
of her, and talked with her, and walked beside her, the more he
wished her not only to continue living, but to share the rest of her
life with him. Yet he now knew that he had come to Glencoe to hurl
her father and brothers into a grave, not to lead her to the altar.

A terrible conflict of rival claims arose in his mind—a struggle
between his old loyalty to his clan and his new loyalty to his love.

The fact that this affection was linked with the Campbells' traditional enemies, the hated MacDonalds, produced a painfully anguished dilemma. How strange, contradictory—and yet commanding—was the emotion of love gradually transforming and destroying the sentiment of hate!

For long he wrestled with his conscience. It was a bitter, agonising contest. However, youth's heart is usually stronger than its head; and in the end his heart won at least a partial victory. He could not betray the whole purpose of his fellow-clansmen's arrival in Glencoe, and so eventually he decided on a compromise. Waiting until it was too late for any other MacDonald to be warned, he did his best to rescue Flora. Not long before the appointed hour when the slaughter was to commence he made an excuse to lead her away towards their private trysting place high above the glen; and as the fatal moment approached he told her what was about to happen. He explained that it was inevitable, that he could do nothing to stop the catastrophe, and that if she were now to hasten home to try to save her kinsfolk the only result would be that she and he would both perish with the rest. He declared that he had brought her away because he adored her, and wished to protect her from possible death.

Then he pleaded passionately, "Flora, will ye run awa' wi' me? Will ye be my wife?"

It was an unfair situation in which to place a love-lorn maiden; but that was not his fault. At first she protested, and cried, and struggled to run home and warn her family; but he prevented her, clasping her to him, and holding her prisoner until a few instants later the first sounds of killings arose from the valley below. There were gunshots, and cries, and sounds of confusion.

Then in mixed fright and relief, horror and hope, sorrow and dawning joy Flora clung to Duncan as closely as he had clung to her, with all her devotion pouring forth in a torrent of desperate, earnest words.

He said they were now both in danger because Campbell sentries were posted at every pass leading out of Glencoe so that not a single male MacDonald should escape the cruel destiny awaiting them that night. Moreover, his clansmen might stay for the next day or two plundering their dead enemies' property. He and she must therefore remain unmoving in their hiding-place, in the hope that they would not be discovered.

Flora answered that she knew of a secret path leading out of the glen—a narrow, little-known, rarely used sheep track climbing steeply up a mountain-side which the Campbells in their ignorance would probably leave unguarded. It was a difficult, dangerous route; but if Duncan were ready to follow her, she might guide them both to safety before dawn broke.

He agreed; and they set forth. Slowly they ascended the height, and throughout the next few days fled across Scotland to the distant east coast near Aberdeen. There they settled, far removed from their MacDonald and Campbell relatives. As soon as possible afterwards they got married—and started to produce the line of descendants who ultimately included my friend Flo.

Romance in California

The reason for my starting on a journey round the world in 1924 was that I had been chosen a member of a team of representatives from Oxford University who would visit America and engage in a series of public debates against students in numerous colleges there. Each year in those days a trio of Oxford undergraduates or newly initiated graduates like myself went to the United States and Canada to join in such argumentative contests with their contemporaries in universities scattered across the North American continent. From September onwards my two colleagues and I were to travel from campus to campus throughout the Mid- and Far-West; and afterwards we would continue on our way to Hawaii, New Zealand and Australia for similar debates in their colleges. Those pleasant, friendly and garrulous contacts with the young generation in various lands were a liberal education for me which eventually lasted ten months.

Towards the end of the American part of our tour my Oxford companions and I fetched up in Los Angeles, to engage in public argument against a team of local college undergraduates. We checked in at the resplendent Biltmore Hotel, where we would stay during our three days' visit. On the morning of our arrival I unpacked my clothes in my room, and then descended to the hotel lobby to meet our young American hosts, who were going to take us out to lunch. We were about to leave when a page-boy started walking round the vast hall crying aloud repeatedly, "Calling Mr. Malcolm MacDonald . . . Calling Mr. Malcolm MacDonald . . . Calling Mr. Malcolm MacDonald . . ."

I went to him, and told him that I was the person he mentioned. He handed me a scrap of paper on which was scribbled a hotel room

number with an intimation that the apartment's occupant was
Lord Charles Conyngham, who would like to speak to me on the
telephone.

I had never heard of Lord Charles Conyngham; but I supposed
I should comply with his request. I therefore excused myself
for a few moments from my companions, went to a telephone
booth, and rang the stated number.

A voice responded at the other end of the line, and I asked
whether Lord Charles Conyngham was there.

"This is Lord Charles speaking," answered the voice in a
lackadaisical, aristocratic English drawl.

"I'm Mr. Malcolm MacDonald," I observed. "I believe you
wanted a word with me."

"Oh, Mr. MacDonald, how kind of you to ring," came the reply.
"I just wanted to welcome you to Los Angeles. I wasn't at Oxford
myself; in fact I'm a Cambridge man. But we graduates from the
rival English universities should unite in any contest against our
cousins in the American Wild West. I'm so glad you've come here;
and I wish you success in your debate."

"That's very kind of you," I commented.

"I don't believe we've ever had the pleasure of meeting?"
the voice said in non-committal enquiry.

"No, I don't think we have."

"I thought not; but it's a pleasure I look forward to."

"I look forward to it too," I answered politely.

"I met your father once," continued His Lordship. "It was on
board ship crossing an ocean."

"Really!" I said.

"Yes; we struck up a delightful sea-voyage friendship—playing
deck-quoits and all that sort of thing. I hope he's well."

"Very well," I replied.

My father had just ceased to be Prime Minister of Great Britain,
and was now Leader of the Opposition. I basked in his reflected
glory.

"Are you free to come upstairs and have a drink with me?"
asked Lord Charles.

"I'm afraid not," I said. "Some friends are waiting in the lobby to take me out to lunch."

"I'll only keep you a few minutes; I'm sure they'll understand. Do come up."

I repeated that I must rejoin my American hosts, but suggested that I could call on him at some mutually convenient time later in the day.

"Oh, do come for just a moment, Malcolm. I'd like to introduce you to a very charming lady."

I changed my mind. One should never be so discourteous as to refuse to meet a very charming lady. I therefore agreed that I would excuse myself for a further short while from my friends; and I went and explained the situation to them.

As I ascended in an elevator to an upper story in the hotel, I wondered what the charming lady would look like. Was she an English girl, or an American? Would she be sweet seventeen, or round about twenty, or a few years older? I was myself a susceptible bachelor aged twenty-three.

A uniformed valet met me as I stepped from the lift, and directed me to the right room. When he knocked on its door the same highfalutin' voice with which I was becoming familiar called, "Come in."

Entering a pleasant chamber, I saw at its farther end a rather stout, bald-headed, middle-aged man wearing pince-nez spectacles reclining with his feet up on a sofa. Dressed in a neat dark suit, with a pearl tie-pin stabbed into his necktie, he looked every inch a member of the aristocracy. If I had not been already aware of that noble distinction, I would have guessed it from his manner, for he did not trouble to rise at my entry, but stayed nonchalantly stretched on his couch where with languid gestures he was manicuring his finger-nails.

"How nice of you to come upstairs, Malcolm," he observed. "I'm delighted to see you." And he graciously interrupted his occupation for a moment to extend a hand in friendly greeting to me. No actor on the stage could have given a more true-to-life representation of an idle, blue-blooded scion of a Ducal house.

I glanced round the room for any glimpse of a charming lady; but none appeared.

"What would you like to drink?" asked His Lordship. "In this dreadful land of Prohibition it's difficult to find the right refreshment before lunch; but I've got a goodly array of bottles tucked away in my cupboard."

I said I could only stay for a minute, and that I therefore had no time for even a sip.

He stopped paring his nails, swung his feet off the sofa on to the floor, and smiled affably at me.

"Your father's a great man," he remarked. "I hope he'll soon be our Prime Minister again."

I thanked him for this kindly good wish.

"How is he?"

I repeated that he was in excellent health.

"And how are Philip Snowden, Arthur Henderson and Jimmy Thomas?" he asked, mentioning the three other principal leaders of the Labour Party.

I replied that they were all well.

Lord Charles said he knew every one of them. Then he mentioned again his meeting with my father on board a ship, saying it had been on a long sea voyage a few years earlier. I recollected my parent making a trip at that time.

"Haven't you really got time for a drink?" he enquired.

In the absence of the promised female I answered "No," and added that I must now take my leave since I had already kept my American hosts waiting too long.

He declared that he looked forward to talking with me about politics and mutual friends in England during my few days in Los Angeles. Then he added, "I'd like you to meet a very charming lady before you go downstairs."

I replied that I would gladly do so if the introduction did not take too long.

"It won't take a minute. She's staying a few suites away on this floor."

He picked up a telephone, asked for a room number, and afterwards told whoever answered the call that he would bring Mr. Malcolm MacDonald, the son of his friend, Britain's recent Prime Minister, at once to meet them.

We went into the corridor, and strolled to a door a few yards away. When Lord Charles tapped lightly on the door a lady's maid opened it. She ushered us into a lavish drawing-room. Its furnishings were elegantly feminine, with decorative chintz curtains flanking long windows, engravings of paintings by Watteau and Fragonard hanging on the walls, pleasant tapestries covering gilt Louis Quinze chairs, choice posies of flowers standing here and there on antique French cabinets, and a plutocratic ostrich-feathered fan and diamond-studded handbag lying casually on a table. Otherwise the place was empty.

The lady's maid tripped across the room, disappeared through a half-open inner door, and gently closed it behind her.

"Mrs. Graham's a very cultured lady," Lord Charles remarked as we seated ourselves. "She's got exquisite taste."

I expressed approval, although I felt a stab of disappointment at the intimation that she was already married. But perhaps she was a young divorcée, or a very premature widow.

"And she's very well read," His Lordship continued.

My pleasurable anticipation at the prospect of meeting the enchantress increased, since she was evidently a paragon of all the virtues.

For another few minutes we sat in silence, like expectant devotees of some sacred matriarchal sect awaiting an appearance by the goddess. I kept glancing at the door through which the maid had departed. Presumably her mistress was within, putting finishing touches to a ravishing make-up.

Then the door opened, and I heard a rustle of silk in a room beyond. A moment later an unforgettable apparition entered our presence. She was dressed in a fabulously rich gown, with gorgeous jewellery sparkling in her ears, round her neck and on her fingers. Her head was capped by a wig of golden hair, her face was that of an ancient witch, and she hobbled into the room with almost audible creaks of her joints.

I presumed that she must be the charming young lady's grand-mother.

Lord Charles rose with a beaming smile, advanced to greet her, and bowed over her extended hand as he gently kissed it.

Turning to me he said, "Malcolm, may I have the pleasure of introducing you to Mrs. Graham?"

As I shook her wrinkled, bony fist I reckoned she must be well beyond man's (and woman's) allotted span of three-score years and ten. Hiding my surprise as best I could, I expressed great pleasure at meeting her, and then stayed for a few moments of polite chitter-chatter before putting into suitable words my profound regret that our interview must be so fleeting—but I should return to my friends downstairs.

She favoured me with a grinning display of expensive false teeth.

Lord Charles remarked that he hoped we would all meet again for more leisurely converse on some further occasion; and with grimaces of mutual regard Mrs. Graham and I took leave of one another. I hastened from the room.

II

During genial conversation with my Californian student acquaintances at lunch I asked whether any of them knew a Mrs. Graham who occupied a grand suite of rooms in the Biltmore Hotel.

"What does she look like?" one asked.

"Rather like a raddled old hen," I replied.

"With a diamond tiara on its head, and precious rings on all its claws?"

"Exactly," I said.

My questioner remarked that he had not the honour of personal acquaintance with the lady, but that he knew about her. She was a widow; her husband had died a few months earlier; he was an oil magnate from Texas; and he had left her a fortune reputed to be worth 55,000,000 dollars.

"Are you interested in her?" one of the other young Americans asked with a sly grin.

I pleaded innocence, and explained that a mutual friend had merely introduced me to her. I modestly refrained from mentioning that the friend's name was Lord Charles Conyngham.

III

When I returned to the hotel that afternoon a message awaited me in my room, inviting me to take a drink with Lord Charles before dinner. I sent a reply accepting the proposal.

At the appointed hour I went to his apartment. Dressed in an immaculate black tie and dinner-jacket, he greeted me with his usual easy, gracious manners; and for the next hour we sat sipping whiskies-and-sodas and discussing various aspects of the world, the flesh and the devil. He spoke interestingly about such things as English university life, salmon-fishing in Northern Ireland, and British politics. We exchanged opinions on several contemporary statesmen. Apparently he knew most of them personally, and he showed entertaining familiarity with their assorted human strengths and weaknesses. Our talk wandered also to the foibles of various celebrities in other fields. I felt that Lord Charles was rather concerned to emphasise his acquaintance with famous people not only in Parliamentary circles, but also in journalism, the arts and high society; and I recognised that he was perhaps a tiny bit of a snob. But he was well informed, his opinions on intellectual matters seemed impressive, and his judgments about people were clever.

Let me confess that when I entered the room I had tentatively entertained an unworthy suspicion about him prompted by the intelligence which I had gleaned about Mrs. Graham's enviable wealth. The thought flitted through my romantic imagination that he might be a fraud, a regrettable impostor who had invented his aristocratic name as a decoy to attract the little duck called Mrs. Graham into his net. Possibly he would even be ready to suffer the penalty of marriage with her if that proved necessary to achieve the privilege of sharing her riches—although this seemed unlikely, since he must be at least thirty years her junior. His interest in her was obvious, and it did seem to be graced by a touch of sentimentality. Yet to my vulgar—not to mention Scottish—mind there appeared no conceivable attraction about her except the very useful sum of 55,000,000 dollars.

I therefore went for a drink with him deliberately to ply him with questions, to test whether he in fact enjoyed the familiarity with eminent statesmen in Britain which he claimed. His conversation quickly reassured me. To all my enquiries in an apparently casual, yet secretly purposeful, cross-examination he gave correct answers, making none of the little slip-ups which I felt would be inevitable if he were really a bogus personage. Now I felt ashamed of myself. I had evidently done him a gross injustice; and when I left his room that evening I bade him "Good night" with sincere respect.

IV

His relationship with Mrs. Graham nonetheless continued to intrigue me. The wide difference between their ages made it a fascinating riddle. What was the answer to the conundrum? Was his motive romantic or mercenary, serious or flippant? Did His Lordship really contemplate matrimony; and if so, was she inclined to respond? Two or three passing references that he made to her during our conversations did hint at an especially friendly sentiment. And why not? It was true that he could not be more than forty years old whereas she must be in her seventies; yet surely (I thought to myself—a trifle dubiously) differences of age are irrelevant between two people whose remarkable charm, exquisite taste and distinguished intellectual attainments unite them in bonds of mutual affection.

There was also, of course, the magnetic element of her money. Why should I assume that a well-bred British aristocrat would be any more indifferent to good hard cash than men of commoner mould? I seemed to remember two or three instances of Dukes, Marquesses or Earls who chased upstart American heiresses at least partly because of their wealth. After all, those men had stately homes and large estates to maintain, and in times of heavy taxation this was not easy. Nor had I ever heard of any age limit being set for heiresses who were regarded as fair game in such hunting. Fifty-five million dollars were fifty-five million dollars whether their owner was sweet young seventeen or sour old seventy.

I therefore became intensely interested in the problematical courtship of Lord Charles Conyngham; and whenever I got half-an-hour to spare during the next two days I went to chat with him in his room. If any obstinate shred of my earlier mischievous suspicion about him still lingered at the back of my mind, it soon disappeared altogether. His manners, his knowledge of affairs, his acquaintances with distinguished people were all faultless; and except for his understandable trait of snobbery he showed every civilised grace to be expected from a lordling, even if he had been educated at Cambridge instead of Oxford.

One afternoon he and I enjoyed the privilege of taking tea with Mrs. Graham in her sitting-room; and this experience made me realise that I had partially misjudged her too. On further acquaintance I found her a gentle, unassuming, undistinguished and yet rather endearing old dame. If she betrayed no signs of the refined taste, wide reading and profound culture with which Lord Charles credited her, she nonetheless possessed some social graces and displayed an agreeable, harmless nature. And if those other qualities were mere figments of his imagination, they did appear significant evidence of a certain degree of genuine infatuation on his part.

She was very considerate towards me. Obviously she was pleased to meet me, probably not so much for my own sake as because I was a Prime Minister's son. Lord Charles took advantage of that mood to invite her and me to a dinner party which he proposed to give in my honour on the next—my last—evening in Los Angeles. It would be a small, select company. He hoped my

two Oxford debating colleagues would join us, and he offered
some snippets of bait in the form of three attractive American girls
whom he would ask to meet us.

Mrs. Graham and I gladly accepted the proposal; and later my
two travelling companions did likewise.

V

The evening of the party happened to be a Saturday, when each
week in the Biltmore Hotel's grand ballroom a sumptuous banquet
with dancing was held. Many celebrated, glamorous film stars
from near-by Hollywood always attended it, with countless other
lovers of feasting and gaiety from Los Angeles and miles around.

When I went downstairs to greet our host and the rest of his
party I found that all the apartments on the hotel's ground floor
were transformed as if by magic into the grottoes of a fairyland.
Everywhere fabulous decorations adorned the ceilings, walls and
floors; and the ballroom itself was cunningly devised to look like a
spacious frozen lake amidst sparkling snow-clad Christmas trees
and mountains. Round its shores were laid the tables for merry-
making diners, who in between bouts of eating and drinking
would sally on to the lake's smooth surface to dance. To stimulate
this activity a Negro jazz-band sat in a grove of incongruous tropical palm trees at the arena's edge, periodically breaking into the
soothing or throbbing, gentle or fierce rhythm of some popular
jig time.

We found our table set beside the lake, decorated with a pyra-
mid of small Union Jacks and Stars-and-Stripes in its centre
to celebrate Lord Charles' and Mrs. Graham's respective native
lands, whilst coils of dark-blue and light-blue ribbons intertwining among the crystal and silverware did honour to his lordship's and my sister universities.

Mrs. Graham presided at the table, with me on her right hand
and Lord Charles at her left. On my other side sat one of the trio
of decorative flappers who had been invited as dancing partners

for my Oxford colleagues and myself. All three of them were enchanting damsels as pretty as spring flowers; yet I could not muster up any particular interest in them because my attention was so fascinated by the Mrs. Graham and Lord Charles Conyngham affair.

Our meal had not proceeded far before I sensed that a crisis had arrived in their relationship. She had dolled herself up with such beauty-parlour cunning that she looked like a young miss of fifty rather than an old dame of near octogenarian vintage; and she was in rather skittish, even flirtatious mood. His Lordship was evidently gratified by this seductive temper, and responded with a facetious, daring courtliness which sometimes made her blush. Behind his spectacles his eyes shone with the glee of a huntsman in sight of his quarry, and at any moment I expected to see him lift a horn to his lips, toot it loudly, and cry "Tally-ho!" The pair behaved like a couple of somewhat senile teenagers in love.

I felt that they had now reached a mutual understanding—perhaps not yet expressed in precise words—that their destinies were to be intermingled. The Graham millions would purchase the Conyngham title, and "vice versa"; and each party would be satisfied that the transaction was a fair exchange with no robbery. I thought there was a glint in my fellow countryman's eyes which hinted that he might propose marriage that very night.

By now I had decided that I positively liked this presentable and refined member of the British aristocracy; and I felt glad that my two friends were so happy, both seeming about to achieve their hearts' desires. In between occasional sorties on to the ball-room floor with one of the young ladies in our party, to perform a fox-trot, a two-step or a tango, I dallied with the pair of elders at the table, joining pleasurably in their light-hearted, sentimental conversation.

Then the orchestra struck up an old-fashioned waltz. Lord Charles leaned across to Mrs. Graham and murmured, "May I have the pleasure of this dance with you?"

She smiled with coy delight, and answered, "Yes, my lord."

They rose and walked to the dance floor. He took her in his

arms with the care of a fireman about to carry a particularly fragile
and precious package to safety through leaping, perilous flames.
I saw him bend his head and whisper something to her, and noticed
a seraphic smile spread across her lips as they disappeared into
the mob of waltzers.

I did duty by the charming young neighbour on my right, and
as we pirouetted round amidst the throng she excitedly pointed
out to me this well-known film actor or that heart-throb movie
actress. But I had eyes only for the most ancient performers in
the crowd. Now and then I caught a glimpse of them, Lord
Charles clasping his partner round her waist, and she holding herself primly away from him in the manner of waltzing in her girl-
hood whilst she gazed into his eyes with a rather faded, worse-for-
wear but nonetheless ecstatic look. It seemed to me that they
were the leading stars in the most enthralling romance being
enacted that evening.

When the music ceased we all returned to our table. Mrs.
Graham was rather breathless, and she trembled a little. Did her
quivering have any hidden significance? Had Lord Charles proposed to her during the dance? And if so, had she consented to
become his bride?

From the light, conspiratorial gaiety of their talk when we resumed our seats I gained a distinct impression that the answer
to both those questions was in the affirmative. Their chatter was
lively, carefree and gleeful; and, as if they wished to share their
felicity with others, they included me in their conversation. They
asked whether I was enjoying myself, and whether I agreed that
the dance floor was perfect, and whether I liked the jazz-band,
and whether I did not think the saxophonist in it was an absolute
wizard. Mrs. Graham said he made her feel like swooning—as if
Lord Charles were not responsible for that dizzy state of her
health. She even began to hum one of the orchestra's intoxicating
refrains in a somewhat cracked, out-of-tune voice.

I was all attention, wondering whether they would honour me
by confiding their secret to me. Since I was due to leave Los
Angeles early the next morning, this would be my last chance

to learn; and if they had exchanged their vows, I was eager to be the first to congratulate them. Responding to their infectious mood, I declared that the party was going with a bang, that we were all grateful to our host for inviting us to it, and that we should like to drink to his health, wealth and happiness. I raised my champagne glass to him, and Mrs. Graham did likewise with a brightly beaming smile.

However, if there was a cat in their bag, they did not let it out. Our talk skipped from topic to topic, persisting through the next dance when most of our table companions disappeared into a whirlpool of jiggers performing a Charleston. Trying, no doubt, to recapture an atmosphere of lost youth, Mrs. Graham asked me about the famous Eights Week Balls at Oxford. Did the undergraduates and their young partners really dance all night, and then motor at dawn to the Isis to eat breakfast in boats along the river, still dressed in their ravishing ball-dresses, white ties and tails?

I confirmed that I had recently followed that hallowed ritual several times; and I enquired of Lord Charles whether he and his contemporaries did the same during their festive May Week at Cambridge. He replied jocularly in the affirmative.

I realised that I had never asked him which college he had attended.

"What was your college?" I enquired.

"Oh, I was at The House," he answered.

I could scarcely believe my ears. I felt staggered, shocked, appalled! With difficulty I betrayed no sign of any of these emotions, for I must not reveal a hint of my stupefaction. I should not let my mouth fall wide open in astonishment, nor my hair stand on end with bewilderment, nor my eyes pop out on to my plate with dumbfounded incredulity. I must not let Mrs. Graham see that Lord Charles had unwittingly made a foolish, damning *faux-pas*.

So I switched the conversation to another subject, asking her where she had been to school. But I did not pay any heed to her answer. Her whole world seemed to me to be crashing around us.

"The House" is not a college at Cambridge at all; it is the

familiar name of a college at Oxford—famous Christ Church. No one who had truly been an undergraduate at either of the great universities could possibly make such a silly mistake.

So Lord Charles was a phony—a shameless, lying, greedy impostor after all.

VI

I lay awake for a long time that night, wondering what I should do about my discovery. At the party I had given no indication of my disillusionment with the knave who was trying to deceive Mrs. Graham, and incidentally me. My leave-taking with both of them was very affable; I wanted a little leisure to ponder on the problem.

I must leave Los Angeles at crack of dawn the next morning to go to San Francisco, where my Oxford colleagues and I would take part in a debate at the University of California. If I was to expose "Lord Charles Conyngham," I should therefore act quickly. I was unlikely to see either him or Mrs. Graham again. It was tempting to make that latter circumstance an excuse for inaction and to dismiss them and their odd romance from my thoughts.

Yet could I do this? If I were completely irresponsible in the matter, such indifference might have been conceivable; but I could not ignore, or shed, my share of responsibility. I had made a distinct if unintentional contribution to their affair. Thinking over the events of the last three days, I assessed the bogus Lord Charles's motive in summoning me to play a part in the drama he had plotted.

I reckoned that he was anxious to impress Mrs. Graham with his importance, and that when he heard of my arrival in the hotel he seized on this as a Heaven-sent opportunity to parade a supposed acquaintance with a Prime Minister by a cunning exploitation of that Premier's son. Probably at first he did not feel sure I would in all innocence co-operate; and possibly this was the reason why he arranged to speak to me first, invisible, on a telephone instead of confronting me in person—to test from a safe distance whether I might be the sort of naïve individual who would accept him without question as the scion of nobility which he claimed to be, who would refrain from querying his assertion of friendship with my father, and who would thus be an easy, if unwitting, accomplice to his conspiracy. Then, having recognised from our phone conversation that I was likely to satisfy these requirements, he took the further precaution of inviting me alone into his room for a personal look at me—to confirm this first impression before taking the risk of introducing me into the presence of Mrs. Graham. Only when he had done that did he let me loose on her. No doubt after observing how amenable I was to all his little trickeries, he felt free to exaggerate to her the intimacy of his association with my father and with various other celebrities in Britain.

He had thus used me as a handy tool for the achievement of his aim. Naturally a silly, common, money-spoilt old woman would be impressed by all the renown in which her allegedly titled suitor seemed to bask; and therefore I would be partly responsible for the unfortunate liaison, subsequent disillusionment, and perhaps ruin which now awaited her. In addition to wishing to repay the self-styled Lord Charles for his unscrupulous misuse of me, I should also desire to undo the damage I had done her. From that point of view I should expose His Lordship forthwith, telling Mrs. Graham why I knew he was a fraudulent scoundrel out to lay hands on her millions.

Yet (I thought to myself) I must be fair. I should consider "Lord Charles's" side of the question too. He was a lonely Briton in a foreign land seeking by his wits to make his way in a difficult world. Of course, the method he had chosen to achieve this end was morally deplorable; but the same could be said of many other men accepted in respectable society, such as certain types of business tycoons who likewise made millions by means which were extremely shady. And possibly in return Lord Charles would give to another individual a degree of pleasure which most of those characters never gave. He might make Mrs. Graham fantastically happy, if his intention was to remain her partner and maintain the fiction of his title during her few remaining years. After all, she probably would not last longer than two or three further twelve-months, so the strain on him should be tolerable, whilst she would feel divine delight at being a Ladyship through the evening of her life. I did not know whether his further intentions were thus partly honourable—and I now had no time to find out. If I were to intervene impetuously and destructively, I might ruin her happiness as well as his; and I believed there were already quite enough unhappy people in the world without my adding unnecessarily to their number.

Moreover, I reckoned that whereas the crook was probably alone in this match of wits between himself and Mrs. Graham, she was almost certainly not alone. A woman of her wealth doubtless possessed many relatives and cronies who watched jealously over her interests—including her vast fortune. It was their duty to keep an eye on her conduct, and to advise her against indiscretions. They had a right to interfere with counsel in her private life—but what right had I? None. I was a chance intruder, an interloper whose influence in the affair was in any case probably only marginal. Again, even if my unexpected appearance had presented the fellow with an opportunity to press his deceit more potently, it had also stimulated Mrs. Graham to display with similar force an equally despicable human failing—snobbery. It was her own fault if the circumstance that I (a complete stranger) happened to be the son of a Prime Minister (an irrelevant consideration) made her feel that Lord Charles (the man, title or no title) would be a more agreeable husband. This seemed to me to be a demonstration of inexcusable stupidity.

At that point in my ponderings as I lay in bed in the dark small hours of the morning I thought to myself, "But supposing Providence, on finding that neither Mrs. Graham's own intelligence nor her friends' perception was sufficient to protect her against a villain, had deliberately introduced me on to the scene to utter a warning to her, should I not be failing in my duty if I stayed silent?" However, I had sufficient confidence in Providence's resourcefulness to believe that if it had indeed chosen me as its instrument, and I failed it, it would quickly find some other, more reliable agent to do its bidding.

Nevertheless, after reflection on every aspect of the matter, I felt that I could not ignore altogether Lord Charles's knavery. Even if I should make no immediate decisive intervention, I should not do absolutely nothing. I therefore resolved on a typical British compromise, deciding to place on record with some appropriate authority the facts of the Conyngham-cum-Graham situation as I knew them, so that if necessary that authority could initiate suitable action.

Having taken this decision, I fell asleep. And when I arrived in San Francisco later the same day I called on the British Consul-General, Mr. Gerald Campbell, whose duties concerning British subjects covered the whole of California. I told him that if a certain Mrs. Graham or any of her acquaintances came to enquire into the credentials of an individual who claimed to be Lord Charles Conyngham, he could take it from me that the fellow was a fraudulent scoundrel. I related my tale to Campbell, finishing up with the rogue's assertion that he had been educated at a college called "The House" in Cambridge.

The Consul-General agreed that this latter piece of evidence was completely damning.

VII

Two days afterwards my Oxford colleagues and I left San Francisco to keep a debating engagement elsewhere; but later the same week I returned for twenty-four hours to San Francisco. Soon after my arrival Campbell telephoned me, and invited me to come for a talk with him since he had an interesting piece of news to give me.

Over cups of coffee he told me that on the previous afternoon two strangers had visited him, saying that they were friends of a lady called Mrs. Graham. They apologised for bothering him, but said they felt troubled about a certain delicate, very confidential matter. Explaining that Mrs. Graham was a septuagenarian widow with an immense fortune, they added that she was being wooed by an Englishman who declared himself to be named Lord Charles Conyngham, and that she had succumbed to his ardent courtship, and promised to marry him within the next few days. Her relatives would have no objection to this if they felt sure Lord Charles was a genuine British bachelor peer—but their suspicions were aroused by the fact that he was more than thirty years her junior. Could he by any chance be either an intending bigamist who was already married to another, less sumptuously rich wife, or else an impostor with no claim to call himself Lord Charles Conyngham at all? Campbell's two interviewers begged him to excuse them for their impertinence in expressing these probably unjustified doubts; but they repeated that they felt it their duty to ensure that old Mrs. Graham was not about to be monstrously swindled. They therefore asked the Consul-General whether he could satisfy them that Lord Charles was in every way a genuine article.

Campbell informed them at once that he knew unofficially that the gentleman concerned was a fraud. He promised to telegraph immediately to the Foreign Office in London, to secure authority to take appropriate steps against the pretender; and he advised them to warn Mrs. Graham in the meantime to cancel the ringing of her wedding bells.

They expressed deep gratitude for his help, but ventured the opinion that, since three days must still elapse before the marriage took place, they should not give Mrs. Graham any warning before decisive action could be launched against the false Lord Charles; otherwise the silly old girl might give her crafty fiancé an unintentional hint of approaching events—and he might escape the clutches of the law. Campbell concurred with this; and they therefore agreed to meet again as soon as he received the expected message from London.

Campbell told me that after my earlier talk with him—and before their visit—he had in fact begun his own researches into the question of Lord Charles by consulting *Burke's Peerage* and other reference books concerning the British nobility. He had learned that a real Lord Charles Conyngham did actually exist, that he was a son of a Marquess in Northern Ireland, and that he seemed to be an elderly man living somewhere in obscure retirement—further evidence that the middle-aged whipper-snapper in California was a pretender. Campbell explained that he must, however, be extremely careful not to make a mistake; so he had telegraphed to the Foreign Office asking them to ascertain the present whereabouts of the veritable Lord Charles, and then to authorise him to take suitable action against the bogus substitute.

Campbell informed me that his reading of the various reference works disclosed that the character in Los Angeles was acting in a way typical of certain master-craftsmen in his criminal profession. The fellow evidently knew that a real, little known, fairly ancient and therefore probably harmless Lord Charles Conyngham was alive, if scarcely kicking, in some remote corner of the earth. Having decided to masquerade as this individual, he had studied painstakingly all the available information about him, and had adopted the other man's life in its every detail as his own. An actor of skill, he became almost word-perfect in the part, and related all the experiences which had befallen the true Lord Charles as if they had happened to him, thus securing himself against exposure by any chance intruder who might be acquainted with the Conyngham family history—short of a personal friend of the true Lord Charles.

But as sometimes happened in such cases (Campbell continued) the impostor was not completely word-perfect in his part. He had made a slight slip-up on one occasion—the error about "The House" which he perpetrated during a talk with me. Campbell explained that the genuine Lord Charles had indeed been an undergraduate at Cambridge, where his college was Christ's College. My fake lordling in Los Angeles had got confused; during some earlier conversation he must have heard Christ Church, Oxford referred to as "The House," and in a careless moment muddled that reference with Christ's College, Cambridge. So in his chatter with me he thought he was being very smart,

and unmistakably undergraduatish, in describing his college as
"The House."

Finally, Campbell told me that he expected to receive a message
from the Foreign Office later that day. He would then contact
Mrs. Graham's guardians, arrange for them to warn her, and himself organise the detention of her intended spouse. The betrothed
couple's hours of mutual bliss thus seemed to be numbered.

VIII

As I stepped from Campbell's office into Market Street a torrent
of traffic was pouring along that ever tumultuous thoroughfare.
Joining a group of pedestrians assembled on a kerbstone, I awaited
an opportunity to cross the road in safety. Before long a policeman
blew a whistle, the stream of vehicles stopped, and we foot-
sloggers sauntered across.

As I walked over the highway my attention was attracted by
a large, plutocratic-looking automobile in the front row of waiting
cars. Its vast, black chassis glistened ostentatiously in the sunshine, and its hood was down so that its occupants could enjoy
the pleasant warmth. I glanced at them—and almost whistled in
surprise. There sat Mrs. Graham and His bogus Lordship side
by side, so close together that they were probably holding hands.
Her look came as near to bridal radiance as is possible on an old
crone's face; and he wore an air of beaming satisfaction. They
were talking amicably together, so absorbed in each other's company that they had no eyes for others.

I hastened on my way, and when I arrived on the opposite pavement turned to catch another glimpse of them. The road was now
clear of pedestrians, and their car was about to continue its
journey. A few moments later it disappeared from my view in the
swift-moving flood of traffic, like a raft carrying them onwards
along the swirling, incalculable river of life.

IX

Next morning I left San Francisco on board ship for Honolulu; and I did not learn the end of the story until almost ten years later. I happened then to be visiting Naples, and went one afternoon with the local British Consul to see the fabulous remains of Pompeii. Whilst we wandered among its sad, vivid ruins we reconstructed in imagination the busy life that filled it nearly 2,000 years ago.

As we conversed I asked my companion where he had been stationed before he came to Naples.

"I was in the Consulate at Los Angeles," he replied.

My thoughts leaped from Pompeii two millenia ago to Los Angeles a decade earlier.

"Were you there in January, 1925?" I enquired.

"Yes."

"Do you remember a gentleman who called himself Lord Charles Conyngham?"

"Very well," he said with a reminiscent laugh.

"Can you tell me," I asked, "whether he ever married the multi-millionairess Mrs. Graham?"

"No; he didn't. We caught him a few hours before their wedding was due to take place."

Medical Service

During a break in the debating tour through North America I went to spend a holiday with some friends in Canada. My host was that passionately eloquent Presbyterian preacher, rather sentimental novelist and wholly admirable man, Dr. Charles Gordon, whose pen-name was Ralph Connor and, whose books *The Sky Pilot* and *Glengarry Schooldays*, were at the time best-sellers which brought him world-wide fame. His son King was a friend of mine at Oxford; and I went to stay with the Gordon family at their summer home on an island in the Lake of the Woods a hundred miles from Winnipeg.

One evening a group of us sat talking beside its shore. The night was windless and balmy, a crescent moon gleamed with eerie brightness in a star-strewn heaven, and the lake waters lay darkly calm. We were in reminiscent mood, for two or three members of our company had set an example by relating adventures which had befallen them with Eskimos, Redskins, moose or bears in the Canadian wilds.

A young friend of the Gordons took up the tale. He was a freshly qualified doctor who a few weeks earlier had graduated in Medicine at Manitoba University.

"Last winter," he began, "I was studying hard for my final exams, but I was afraid I wouldn't pass them. Three of my fellow medical students were in the same predicament, and we wondered what we could do to make sure of gaining our Degrees. Shortly afterwards a boy in Winnipeg hospital died of a rare and little understood brain disease. Hitherto the medical profession had been almost helpless in its presence; and they wished to discover any facts they could about it. One of our lecturers in surgery, who enjoyed a good reputation as a budding brain specialist, was particularly anxious to perform a post-mortem operation on the corpse; so he visited the boy's parents to make a respectful request that, in the interests of science and humanity, they would permit investigations to be conducted on their dead son's brain before he was committed to a grave. To that suggestion the bereaved mother and father returned an unqualified refusal. The incident seemed to be closed."

The narrator continued that the boy's funeral was held on the following day, his mortal remains being buried in a cemetery on the prairie just outside the city. The four prospective candidates for doctor's Degrees attended the ceremony, and carefully noted the position of the grave.

Immediately afterwards they called on the lecturer in surgery.

"Sir, were you very keen to get that corpse?" one of them asked.

"Yes; very," he replied.

"Do you really think you'd have learned some useful things from it?"

"Without any doubt; I might have made a very important discovery."

"If we get you the body, sir," remarked the spokesman of the quartet, "would you do us a favour in return?"

"What's that?"

"See that we pass our final exams next term."

The don looked shocked.

"Of course not," he said. "As a bribe for body-snatching? What do you think I am—a criminal fool?"

"No; not a criminal or a fool, sir, but a great servant of Medicine."

The surgeon smiled wistfully, but observed, "I admire your enterprise in thinking up such a proposition, but I couldn't contemplate it. It would be wrong for me to enter into any understanding of that sort."

"Okay, sir. We thought we'd just ask you."

"I tell you straight, I couldn't be a party to such a bargain. I'm not a great servant of Medicine, but I'm an honest one. If you young asses can't pass your exams, you shouldn't be admitted to the medical profession in any circumstances—and you won't be."

After a few moments' reflection he added, "Besides, think what would happen to us if we were discovered. Body-snatching's a serious offence; the punishment for it is several years' penal servitude. So you couldn't even sit your exams, let alone pass them, if you were caught. Your lives as well as your careers would be ruined. . . . Talking of lives," he continued reflectively, "it's a thousand pities I couldn't perform a post-mortem on that corpse, for it might have enabled me to save other lives in future. And it would have suited me well to work on it to-night, for I have to stay very late in the operating theatre anyway, doing an experiment. But I refuse to consider your proposal. Go home to bed— and sweet, innocent dreams."

"All right, sir," said the leading student.

The pupils hastened away, and took council together.

At Winnipeg in mid-winter the sun sets very early, and the nights are long. The four youths had little time to make their preparations—but most of them were already made. Their car was waiting in a back-yard with chains on its wheels for driving over snow; some shovels, pick-axes, chisels and screwdrivers were packed into its boot, and a bottle of rum lay on its seat. As good medical students they recognised that this refreshment might be useful medicine to keep them warm and energetic during a perishingly cold night's heavy toil.

They thought it prudent to delay their expedition from the noisy city of the living to the silent city of the dead until long after darkness fell, since some motor traffic might still be passing to and fro, and one of the drivers might catch sight of ghostly figures among the tombstones, and be sufficiently unsuperstitious to report those spectres to the police. So they waited impatiently until all such busy-bodies were likely to be tucked up in bed. Then they set forth. When they noticed that the sky was cloudless, and that an almost full moon illumined with pale brightness the snow-covered earth, they felt partly glad and partly apprehensive—glad because this providential lantern would shed clear light on their difficult labours, but apprehensive lest it should reveal their activity to unfriendly eyes.

The graveyard lay behind a wall stretching alongside a road some distance from the city. Beyond it the highway continued its thousand-mile journey across the vast, flat prairie. The youths had already agreed on their plan of action, and as soon as they arrived at the cemetery gates they put it into operation with silent efficiency. Two of them hastened into the dormitory of eternal sleepers, carrying pick-axes and shovels in their arms; a third stayed at the gateway to act as sentry; and the fourth began driving their car slowly to and fro for half a mile in each direction in order to spot any traffic which might be approaching. If he sighted a vehicle he would give two hoots on his motor-horn—at which the trio doing duty at the cemetery would promptly down tools and disappear into hiding until the intruder was safely past. They agreed to exchange their respective jobs at regular intervals throughout the next few hours, so that the couple currently acting as grave-diggers would always feel fresh to work with tireless energy.

The pair who started that task had little difficulty in finding the correct grave. No fresh snow had fallen since the funeral, and the lately dug soil appeared as a dark patch amidst the surrounding white sheet of ground. On it lay a bunch of flowers. Removing the posy and placing it respectfully on one side, they raised their pick-axes and let them fall with sharp bites into the earth. The implements did so with resounding clangs which gave their holders an initial fright. The North American prairie stretched as flat as a pancake to the horizons, and the wintry silence reigning over its deep covering of snow was profound. Even the slightest whisper seemed to echo so loudly that it could be heard by everyone else within hailing distance—including all the citizens of Winnipeg. However, the two diggers were tough young Canadians accustomed to taking risks in outlandish circumstances, and they were now also dedicated servants of the noble profession of Medicine. After a breathless few moments they therefore subjugated their fears, and started to rain a succession of sharp blows with fanatical fury on the ground.

The temperature was several degrees below zero, and most of the earth was frozen hard. Fortunately the hunks of soil in the grave had been crumbled so recently that they were not yet settled back into stiffly obstinate solidity. Nevertheless their extraction required a long spell of hard labour, and only gradually did a vigorous onslaught by pick-axes and shovels make a significant impression. Slowly but surely, inch by inch and then foot by foot, the level of ground in the trench descended.

Several times the quartet exchanged their jobs. Twice un-invited cars hove into sight along the road; on both occasions a couple of toots from the guardian motor uttered the agreed warning; and at each signal the youths in the cemetery quickly disappeared into temporary concealment. Otherwise the work proceeded without cease for an unconscionable time—until eventually one of their pick-axes uttered a dull thud when it struck the wooden top of a coffin below. The diggers permitted themselves grunts of prospective triumph, took swigs of rum, and redoubled their efforts.

In due course they had heaved out all the remaining clods of earth, exchanged their shovels for screwdrivers and chisels, wrenched off the coffin's lid, and found themselves gazing at the figure of a recumbent youth lying wrapped like an Egyptian mummy in its tomb.

One of them stretched an arm into the cavity, inserted his fist beneath the corpse, and with gentle tugs urged the boy to rise from the dead. The youngster offered no resistance, and quite quickly his two resuscitators lifted him up to the earth's surface.

At that moment in the episode the narrator at the Lake of the Woods was doing sentry duty at the cemetery gate. Hearing a muffled commotion behind him, he looked round and, to his consternation, saw three men rapidly approaching him. For a fraction of a second he felt alarmed, thinking them strange intruders. Then he realised that two of the apparitions were alive whilst the other was dead, and that these were his colleagues bringing their coveted prize.

"Good work!" he muttered. "But dammit, the car's just passed, and won't be back for five minutes."

So for what seemed an interminable period the quick and the dead huddled on the ground together, awaiting transport into town. To the deceased this was a matter of little account in the infinite passage of eternity; but to the living each minute seemed an endless, intolerable age. At last, however, they saw the car's headlights approaching, and one of them stepped into the roadway to beckon it onward more rapidly. At once it accelerated, then halted at the gate, took aboard its incongruous troupe of passengers, and started at top speed towards Winnipeg.

They broke the speed limit all the way through the city's streets to a group of buildings housing the Medical Faculty at the university. Its rows of windows were starkly black—except for one where a glimmer of light shone behind discreetly pulled curtains. Those occupants of the car who had eyes to see were relieved to notice that the illuminated space punctured a wall of the surgical laboratory. Someone inside must be working late, for the hour was already three o'clock in the morning.

The car stopped in front of a door leading into the building; and one of them jumped out. He tried the handle of the door, which immediately opened.

"Good; it's unlocked," he said, in his tense relief emphasising the obvious.

Carefully they lifted the corpse from the car, and carried it indoors. Hastily they bore it along a corridor, round a corner, and towards the room where they hoped to find their medical tutor at work. Sure enough, when the students entered the place they saw the surgeon bending over a specimen of a human brain exposed on a table. As he glanced up at them they raised their captive at arms' height above their heads in proud demonstration of the gift which they brought him.

He did not flicker an eyelid, nor betray any other sign of surprise.

"What have you lunatics been up to?" he asked in a matter-of-fact tone which concealed any element of emotion.

When they told him, he gasped half-helplessly, shrugged his shoulders, and pointed to an operating-table in the middle of the room. Strolling away from the brain which he was examining, he pulled a pair of rubber gloves on his hands, and picked up some surgical instruments which lay conveniently near-by.

The body-snatchers placed their burden on the operating-table whilst he switched on an arc-lamp which at once threw a flood of light on the swaddled corpse.

None of them spoke a word as they got to work. One student freed the dead boy's head from its wrappings, another filled a basin with water from a tap, a third uncorked a bottle of antiseptic fluid and poured it into the water, and the fourth fetched a large pair of scissors from a drawer and handed them to their teacher.

He nodded a silent expression of thanks, and began to cut the dead patient's hair with the nonchalance of a barber giving a customer a trim. But he did not stop the shearing until his client was as bald as a Buddhist priest. Then he laid down the scissors, picked up a knife, and started to remove the youth's scalp.

With studious fascination his pupils watched the operation. Their teacher began to speak to them quietly as he dissected and examined the diseased brain, as if he were giving them a lecture on surgery in the normal course of their doctorial training. They observed him spell-bound, for his professional skill was deft. As he cut and dug he uttered an occasional exclamation of satisfaction; and soon he pointed out certain interesting discoveries which he was making.

His neat, infinitely careful excavations continued for a long while; but he and his audience were so absorbed that they did not notice the passage of time. They were astonished when a clock out-of-doors on the University campus suddenly struck five o'clock.

"We must be off, sir," said one of the students in alarm. His companions, too, showed awakened consternation.

"There are still several hours of darkness," the surgeon commented coolly.

"But it'll take us all that time, sir, to get the body back in its grave."

In matters medical the don was a master of practical considerations, but in other affairs he was a rather vague, absent-minded academic type.

"We mustn't spoil the success of our work at this crucial stage," he muttered. "I'll be as quick as I can."

He continued making cautious probings into the exposed brain before him, every now and then turning to scribble notes in an exercise-book lying close at hand. The students looked at each other anxiously, making poor attempts to hide their growing agitation. They seemed to have lost interest in the important service they were helping to perform for medical science. Their master, on the other hand, appeared indifferent to their new, worried preoccupation.

Half an hour passed. Then he murmured, "Splendid! I think I've discovered what the real trouble is."

"Can we go now, sir?" asked the students in unison.

He looked at them with surprise, as if he had forgotten their existence.

"Oh, yes!" he observed, glancing at his wrist-watch. "Yes, yes; you'd better run along."

Hurriedly he put the fragments of a human brain and skull back into their proper places, and re-closed the scalp above them. Then his eager aides wrapped the head once more in its funeral shroud, lifted the body from the table, and retraced their steps at a run to their waiting car. After the bright lights inside the laboratory, they were relieved to find that out-of-doors the moon had disappeared behind clouds, causing deep darkness to obscure their movements from any prying eyes.

They raced their vehicle at a most unfunereal pace through the city's empty streets, and careered fast and furiously into the countryside beyond. At the cemetery gates two of them leaped out with the corpse clasped in their arms, and ran stumbling into the graveyard. A third resumed sentry duty at the entrance, whilst the fourth re-started the motor and drove it slowly along the road —exactly as they had all been doing a few hours earlier.

The pair who went into the graveyard were horrified to see the chaos they had left there. One grave yawned open with a pilfered coffin lodged within, an untidy mass of earth sprawled alongside the pit, the coffin's broken lid lay abandoned near-by, and pick-axes, shovels and other tools were scattered at random across the snowy ground. The scene clearly betrayed an act of indescribably squalid robbery—but it seemed that no strangers had yet arrived to discover it.

The body-snatchers set to work to repair the damage. No robbers of Pharaohs' tombs in ancient Egypt ever strove more zealously to conceal their handiwork. Hastily but respectfully they laid the corpse back in its everlasting bed. Then they replaced the lid on the coffin, although they did not bother to screw it down. Instead they began shovelling the loose earth hurriedly back into the grave; and before very long the job was finished.

Nevertheless the site remained an awful mess, bearing many unmistakable bits and pieces of evidence of the grim work which had been performed there. And although the moon had not re-emerged from behind clouds now spreading more thickly across the sky, and this evidence therefore remained for the moment unrecognisable, as soon as the sun rose and daylight returned it would become evident to every passer-by.

The young men picked up all their tools, and ran to the cemetery gate. Rejoining their colleagues, they jumped into the motor-car, and started along the road back to the city. As they went they kept gazing anxiously into the heavens, hoping the clouds gathered there were heralds of a fresh, violent snow-storm which would blot out their footprints and every other sign of their night's activities.

As they re-entered Winnipeg the first rays of dawn began to lighten the eastern horizon. A few cocks in back-yards uttered preliminary crows, and early workpeople stepped from their houses into the streets. Then, of a sudden, a few feathery snowflakes started to float silently down from the sky. Before long a howling, blinding blizzard of snow was tumbling to the earth.

II

Several months later a Canadian University don aroused interest at an international Congress of Doctors by describing some new discoveries he had made concerning a certain rare brain disease. In the course of his lecture he paid warm tribute to a quartet of medical students who had conspicuously assisted him in his research work on the subject, although he did not mention the precise nature of their aid.

A few weeks afterwards those students sat for their final examinations in Medicine. When the results were announced two of the heroes had passed, but the other couple failed to obtain Degrees.

Cannibal Fare

After leaving Honolulu during that round-the-world debating tour my Oxford colleagues and I separated for a month's holiday before resuming our oratorical contests in the Antipodes. I spent the four weeks in the Fiji Islands.

For me this was a thrilling, novel experience. Except for our few days' stay in Hawaii on the way there, it was my first glimpse of an exotic land inhabited by members of the human race very different from the white-skinned Western peoples to whom I was accustomed in Great Britain, Canada and the United States. In any case Honolulu was then already so Americanised that, apart from its lush tropical scenery, it was not very convincing as a slice of life totally different from that lived in those other countries. But Fiji was like a new world to me.

As my ship edged towards the wharf in Suva harbour on the main island called Viti Levu I observed with fascination the crowd of Fijians watching our arrival. With their near-black bodies, fuzzy hair like mops, and white eye-balls surrounding dark staring eyes they looked like a bevy of animated golliwogs. Among them were several brown-skinned Indians who in those days were also almost completely strange beings to me. Only a few individuals on the quay were white-faced Colonial Government officers wearing topees, doing official duty in connection with the boat's docking or waiting to meet passengers aboard her.

I looked with excitement upon the tropical South Sea coast crowded with palm trees, and at a more distant prospect of jungle-covered hills. With deep pleasure I inhaled luscious scents of strange flowers and fruits gorgeously ripe in the brilliant sunshine.

To my eager, inexperienced, enquiring mind both the landscape and the characters in it were like apparitions in some fictitious theatrical romance. I looked forward to entering for a while into this, to me, unprecedented drama of real life.

Even in those days, however, the world was becoming so small a place that one could hardly ever escape entirely from familiar associations. When the ship cast anchor, and a gangway was stretched from the shore to its deck, the first man to climb aboard was a small, spare, deeply sunburnt Briton with a wizened face and a goatee beard who came to where I stood, scrutinised me inquisitively, and asked in a broad Scots accent, "Are ye Ramsay MacDonald's loon?"

I confessed that I was.

"Weel, weel!" he said. "I'm gey glad tae see ye. I was at school wi' your dad at Drainie fifty years ago."

I expressed astonishment, and asked him what he was doing in Fiji.

He answered that he would tell me the story of his life when he delivered me at my lodgings in Suva, and added that he had brought his old Ford car to convey me to Mrs. Brown's boarding-house, where I was booked to stay. So a cabin steward carried my trunk into the motor-car, my kindly, self-appointed one-man reception committee and I jumped in after it, and we drove to Mrs. Brown's modest establishment.

As we sipped cooling glasses of lemonade on its lawn my new acquaintance introduced himself to me in greater detail. He told me that his name was Alec Ross, and that when he was a lad eighteen years old a ship on which he was sailing round the world in search of his fortune stopped in Suva for twenty-four hours to unload some cargo. He went ashore to catch a tripper's quick glimpse of Fiji—and had never left the islands throughout the subsequent forty years. In the tropical sunshine of that day a generation ago he suddenly decided that this was the place where he wished to spend his life; and he only returned to the ship to fetch his luggage, say good-bye to the captain, and cancel the rest of his voyage round the Earth.

"Maybe ye'll decide tae do the same when ye've been here a few more minutes," Alec said to me with a laugh.

He reminisced for a while about his youth in Fiji, when he joined the Government service as a humble clerk and played a pioneering part in the establishment of the Colony's administration. Now he was postmaster in a township up a river called the Rewa, where he lived with his wife and children. He told me that when he happened to hear that I would be a passenger on a boat berthing in Suva that day he hastened down-river especially to greet me. He added that, since he had no adequately qualified assistant in his post office, he would have to hurry home again that evening. "Ye must come and stay wi' me ae day, and meet my wife and bairns," he said just before he left on his long return journey.

I replied that I would do so with pleasure.

II

I enjoyed many refreshing, enlightening experiences during my initial fortnight in Suva. Thus, for the first time in my life I slept under a mosquito-net to protect me from the bites of pestiferous insects; for the first time garrulous lizards scampered up and down the walls of my room, as rightful residents in it as I was myself; for the first time I ate luscious tropical fruits like paw-paws for breakfast; for the first time courteous black servants waited on me hand and foot; and for the first time I lazed sun-bathing all day long on beaches beneath a scorching blue and golden sky.

I also made some fascinating exploratory journeys to various parts of Viti Levu. Yet, much as I enjoyed those glimpses and tastes of a strange new existence, none of them made me want to follow Alec Ross's example, cancel my plans for further travels, and settle in Fiji for the rest of my life.

One day I kept my promise to visit Alec in his distant up-river home. He and his wife and children gave me a cordial welcome.

I found that she was a buxom, handsome, dusky-skinned half-caste woman who now spoke English with almost as broad a Scots accent as Alec himself. Her size was considerably larger in both height and width than his; and her still good-looking features showed that in her youth she must have been a voluptuous Beauty Queen type. Their offspring were a troupe of engaging youngsters who showed in their features variegated signs of their mixed breeding.

Alec was an utterly unrepentant Scot in all his characteristics, thoughts and habits. A voracious reader of serious books, the walls of his small office were covered with bookcases crammed with volumes of history, biography, literature and politics which he had amassed through the years; and presiding over them all was a plaster bust of Robert Burns. His manners were precise, canny and efficient; and his conversation was rather solemnly intellectual. His blousy wife was more harum-scarum in her mental processes, but she could mix earnest-minded commentaries on life with gay, scandalous gossip about local society. The pair fed their children on oatmeal porridge every morning, and led them to the local Presbyterian church each Sabbath day.

I still had no desire to settle in Fiji for life. Indeed, I felt a trifle disappointed. A callow, romantic young traveller, I was seeking the South Seas of fable. I longed to visit a desert island—some tiny sliver of sand crowned with elegant palm trees and marooned in a blue lagoon encircled by a white coral reef, where I might discover, at least in fancy, the footprints of Robinson Crusoe. I told Alec of my ambition.

He answered that exactly such a place existed a few miles out to sea beyond the mouth of the Rewa River, and he added that the name of the uninhabited little coral isle was Toberua.

III

Next morning I hired a small motor-boat and went with a native fisherman as my pilot to guide me to Toberua. The voyage down-river and out to sea was very pleasant beneath a cloudless sky emblazoned with a scorching sun. Soon after we began to rock gently on the smooth, slightly swelling ocean a tiny speck of green vegetation appeared on a distant horizon where the infinite heavens met the boundless deep. It floated like a mirage in the atmosphere several miles away. My nautical companion screwed up his eyes in the sunlight, pointed to it, and announced "Tober-ua."

As we chugged towards it during the next two hours I watched its features slowly reveal themselves. For a while they shimmered vaguely like an unsubstantial hallucination; but then they gradually assumed more material shape. The place seemed exactly the earthly paradise that I wished to visit. In its centre a cluster of tall palm trees posed with languid grace, its beach gleamed silver along the edge of an aquamarine sea, and the flying spray of break-ing waves glistened in the air above an encircling coral reef. My pilot knew where to steer our craft to enter a mirror-smooth lagoon—and a few minutes later I jumped overboard and waded through shallows to the shore.

Strolling up the beach, I approached the shelter of a coconut-palm grove. To my surprise I saw some old, sand-blown footprints on the ground ahead of me. Could they be antique relics of Robin-son Crusoe himself? Was my dream coming true?

Then I observed a small grass hut raised on stilts in the shade beneath the trees. For a moment I felt cheated, suspecting that inhabitants lived on this supposedly uninhabited isle. But I re-membered that Alec Ross had assured me firmly that Toberua was a desert island where no creatures except crabs, turtles and sea-birds lived, and where Man set only an occasional fleeting foot. And the hut did appear to be neglected. My spirits revived. I could now see beyond the palm grove to the atoll's farther shore—and no one was there. So even if the shack were not Crusoe's own still surviving, dilapidated home, it had no doubt been the retreat of some similar extinct character.

Then my doubts were renewed as I noticed several tracks of obviously freshly-made footprints leading towards the hut, and saw a clothes-line stretching between two bamboo poles with a shirt hung out to dry. A moment later I caught sight of a rowing-boat coming across the lagoon. The craft nuzzled into the beach, and out of it stepped three people. They seemed an incongruous trio. The first was a short, ivory-skinned Japanese man, the second was an even smaller Japanese woman, and the third was the tiniest of them all—a coal-black Fijian female child.

They walked towards me, the Japanese gentleman wrinkling his wizened face and baring his teeth in a broad grin as he approached. When he arrived within a few feet of me he halted, placed his hands flat on his thighs just above the knees, and made a series of low ceremonial bows. The lady did the same. He was naked except for a pair of ragged shorts, but she was neatly dressed in a kimono, obi and sandals. The little Fijian girl made no bow, but stuck a finger in her mouth and stared shyly at me. She wore a white European frock covered with a pattern of red roses.

I smiled and bowed in return to the newcomers. When sufficient polite physical jerks had been exchanged between us I cocked a thumb in the direction of the hut and asked the man, "Your house?"

He grinned again, and nodded in silent affirmative.

Then he pointed with a gesture of introduction to the woman, beamed broadly once more, and announced "My wife."

She and I performed additional courteous obeisances to each other.

After that he turned to the small golliwog girl and declared with the most sublime grin of all, "Our daughter."

I thought this statement a considerable biological inexactitude; but I let it pass.

My boatman had by now arrived ashore with a picnic basket for lunch, which he placed on the ground in the shade of some feathery-topped coconut trees. I asked the Japanese gentleman whether he would like to taste a glass of beer, and he drew in his breath through his teeth with a sharp hiss of delight at the suggestion. His spouse and alleged daughter accepted offers of less potent liquids; and we all settled on the ground to refresh ourselves.

The old boy's English was tolerably good if one overlooked an excruciating accent; and as we sipped our drinks he told me his story. He had been a sailor in the Japanese Navy who somehow got stranded in Fiji at the end of the First World War. Here he took to deep-sea fishing in his own small boat, an occupation which he found so pleasant and profitable that he resolved to settle permanently in this archipelago. He sent to Tokyo for the wife from whom he got separated during the war; and they made their home at the mouth of the Rewa River. There they stayed until only a month ago, when they decided to move further out to sea, and came to squat on Toberua atoll. With typical Japanese skill at imitative work, they built a native grass hut, completing it very recently.

I pointed to the Fijian maiden, and asked when she was born.

"So far as we know," he answered, "about five years ago."

"You don't know for certain?" I enquired, smiling. "Then she's not really your very own daughter?"

He chortled, and confessed that she was not.

Then he explained that he and his wife were very happy together, but that there had been one sadness in their lives. They failed to produce a child. They eagerly wished for a baby—and suddenly they found one. It was at a time when an epidemic of Spanish 'flu swept through Viti Levu soon after the war, killing large numbers of the inhabitants. One morning the Japanese fisherman chanced to land at a remote coastal village where a scene of horror met his eyes. Corpses lay scattered among the huts; and when he anxiously inspected them he found only one body in which a breath of life still stirred—a baby girl apparently not more than a few weeks old. He picked her up, and took her home to his wife. They saved the hapless orphan, and later gained permission from the authorities to adopt her.

I looked at the now robust youngster, who was smiling with satisfaction at finding herself the topic of conversation.

"What's her name?" I asked.

"Fiji," he answered.

"No, not her nationality," I said. "Her name."

"Her name is Fiji," he retorted.

"Just plain and simple 'Fiji'?" I said, rather charmed.

He nodded, with a proud semi-paternal grin.

He told me that he and his spouse had tried hard to discover the infant's name, but that, since there were no survivors in the community where she was born, this proved impossible. Being ignorant of Fijian customs concerning the christening of children, they left her for some time anonymous. Later they began to require some description by which to address her, and they decided that it would be safest to call her just "Fiji."

We picnicked together in the grove of palm trees, and afterwards went in my motor-launch for an expedition across the lagoon. By now the tide had risen high, and no breakers were splashing on the coral reef. Instead it lay deeply submerged beneath a smooth ocean surface. Cruising slowly several fathoms above it, we gazed through transparently clear waters at a fabulous, scintillating submarine world. The reef stretched a few feet wide, extending as a solid yet delicate rampart of different types of coral. Many forms of animal life inhabited that fantastic ocean-bed architecture. Crabs in plenty skedaddled across mosaic-like floors, sea-slugs wormed their way in and out of numerous nooks and crannies, assorted species of shell-creatures climbed up and down crenellated walls, starfish lay dormant, water-beetles paddled to and fro, and sea-snakes wriggled hither and thither through the corally pleasance. Many shoals of tiny, variously-hued fish cruised here, there and everywhere. Some were striped black and white like nautical zebras, others gleamed with variegated shades of blue, yet others were speckled by gorgeous splashes of red or green or yellow, whilst extra lots seemed to be clad in silver armour. There was no limit to the vivid contrasts of their decorations, which ran the whole gamut of the colours of a rainbow.

The Japanese fisherman asked me whether I would like to be introduced personally to some of those lovely creatures; and I replied that I would. He promptly fitted on a pair of diver's goggles, and plunged overboard into the briny. Little Fiji clapped her hands with glee as he descended like a gigantic frog with flinging arms and kicking legs through the depths. Eventually we saw him arrive on top of the reef, grasp a globe of bristling stag's-horn coral, wrench at it with both fists until it was uprooted from its moorings, and then turn turtle in the water, kick himself upwards from the rock-crystal wall, and shoot towards us through the mirror of the ocean. When he broke its surface he held up the hunk of coral for our inspection; and Fiji stretched down her hands, took it from him, and passed it delightedly to me.

Lo and behold! Inside its intertwining branches several tiny fish were caught, like singing-birds in a cage. At the human sea-monster's sudden appearance they had taken fright and fled into its coils for protection, only to find that they had chosen the very fragment which he selected for upheaval. They were then too confused to dart out again before he conveyed them swiftly to the upper air; and so they now huddled, gasping, behind their coral prison-bars. We studied them hurriedly, admiring their varied exquisite hues, and then dipped the fragile stone into the water again so that they could make good their escapes. One by one they dashed from their confinement, and swam with the gusto of liberated convicts back to their accustomed homes.

We spent the whole afternoon afloat in the lagoon, and then returned for tea on the idyllic isle of Toberua. My kind host and hostess asked me to stay a few days with them, and I wished I could accept their suggestion; but I already had commitments elsewhere. So I was forced to depart before sunset.

Momentarily I was tempted to feel as Alec Ross had done on the day of his first arrival in Suva. When I took my leave of the Japanese couple I said to them, "If I decide to stay in the South Seas, and never to leave them, can I come to live with you? I'll be your adopted son and Fiji's brother, and I'll help you with your fishing. You can christen me plain and simple 'Scotland'."

They gave glad grins of consent.

IV

On the following day I went to visit another small island. Unlike Toberua, it was not reputed to be deserted; on the contrary, it had been for generations the home of the most famous community of natives in the whole Fijian archipelago.

This isle's name was Bau. A relic of an ancient volcanic eruption, it lay alongside Viti Levu, separated from that principal land mass by only a narrow channel of water. Yet, although it was a tiny speck of earth compared with its gigantic neighbour, it had been through most of the nineteenth century an impregnable fortress. That was because the slim straits between it and Viti Levu were staked with rows of deadly, submerged defence-works, whilst its seaward side was protected by the coral reef. Its strategic strength made it the capital of a grim dynasty of renowned cannibal chiefs which culminated in the mid-century with the most celebrated, if not the bloodthirstiest, of them all, King Cakabau.

In its hey-day the small, grass-hutted capital of Bau was the site of some hard-fought battles followed by triumphal orgies in which the victors feasted on their defeated enemies. Even in interludes of peace its inhabitants watched spectacles scarcely less sanguinary—the solemn strangling of widows at the funerals of their late husbands, the burial alive of men holding upright in deep pits the corner-posts of any chief's new house, the launching of the king's war canoe across a long ramp of prostrate, still-quivering bodies of sacrificial human beings which reached from the top of the beach into the ocean—and many similar antique rituals.

During his reign Cakabau occasionally got into trouble with Western governments concerning a rather delicate matter. Increasing numbers of their citizens were sailing on voyages across the Pacific Ocean, and every now and then one of them failed to return home, not because he had been drowned in a shipwreck amidst the ocean waves but because he had been boiled in a cooking-pot along Fijian shores. The embarrassing diplomatic consequences for Cakabau sprang from his difficulty in asserting his authority effectively throughout his widely scattered realm, which consisted of some 250 islands. In spite of being the most powerful ruler yet known in Fiji's history, he could not always prevent his subjects in outlying atolls from indulging their hitherto unexceptionable taste for "long pig"—the name by which roasted human flesh was known to them—when rash white sailors unintentionally presented themselves as novel delicacies for their menus. More than once the authorities in Washington in particular threatened dire action against the Fijian people when reports of such excesses involving American mariners or missionaries reached them.

In desperation King Cakabau appealed for help from his royal sister, Her Majesty Queen Victoria of England. He promised grateful loyalty to Britannia—who in those days still ruled the waves—if she would become Fiji's Protecting Power. The proposal was not tempting to the British Government, since the Fijians' notorious love of swallowing "long pig" did not accord with the prim tastes of Victorian England. However, this difficulty was overcome after Cakabau announced that he had decided not only to forswear cannibalism, but also to become a Christian. British honour was satisfied, and in 1870 the Government in London assumed responsibility for the administration of Fiji under the nominal sovereignty of that notorious ex-devourer of human flesh.

So authoritative did Cakabau (sustained by British administrators) become among his simple people that in the end his writ put a virtual stop to cannibalism, and subsequently he led his bewildered but faithful subjects in a life of Christian piety. Dying at a ripe old age in the odour of sanctity, he was buried on the summit of a hill dominating his little capital at Bau—the very height from which in earlier times his sentinels kept an eager, hungry lookout for enemies. There his bones still lie under an imposing tombstone.

I went to Bau to pay my respects to his grave, and to view his

historic island. In appearance the place had changed little since
his day. A deep peace reigned over it. The fiery midday sun
burned scorchingly from a cloudless sky; no breath of wind stirred;
and even the natives accustomed to tropical heat had retired for
siestas in the shade inside their huts. When I landed from my boat
the cluster of buildings looked like a deserted village—or rather,
like a deserted farmyard, for all the houses were made of reeds
and grass, appearing like a group of haystacks. Their oblong walls
were of grass, their sloping roofs were of grass, and none of their
grassy exteriors were broken anywhere by windows. Even a
tiny aperture would have admitted a little sunlight indoors, and
that would prejudice the comforting coolness of the shadowy interior. So the only breach in each dwelling's defensive straw
shield against the sun was a small doorway for entry through one
wall.

The haystacks were mustered round a central open space of
rough greensward. On a terraced mound at its farther end stood
a super-haystack several times the size of any other edifice. It was
the Council Chamber of Chiefs, built several years earlier to
replace the antique Heathen Temple which formerly graced that
same eminence. Other relics of bygone times still survived near
the Council Chamber—the Killing Stone and the Hanging Tree—
but they were now preserved as mere museum pieces. Palm trees
grew in groups here and there. In the afternoon stillness their
lofty plumes of vast tropical leaves hung motionless, as if carved
in stone. Beyond them stretched a shore of gleaming sand edging
a slumbering ocean; and on the beach reclined a fleet of slim
canoes like a school of sea-serpents sunning themselves on dry
land before slipping back into the deep.

The village wore an aspect of profound quietude and emptiness;
but as I walked among the huts I soon realised that the place was
far from deserted. Through every doorway I glimpsed pairs of
human eyes staring at me from the floors inside dark rooms. Their
owners lay full stretch on the ground, collapsed in utter laziness
in the midday heat, naked except for grass skirts. They scrutinised
me interestedly but dumbly. Then some children's curiosity got

the better of them, and these ventured out-of-doors to gaze more closely at me. Bau was disturbed by few tourists in those days, and a white stranger was a rare phenomenon.

I sought the residence of King Cakabau's grandson, Ratu (or Chief) Pope, to whom I carried a note of introduction. When I enquired of the youngsters "Ratu Pope?" as I pointed at this or that hut they understood my meaning, and waved me towards a dwelling which I then noticed to be rather larger than any other except the Council Chamber of Chiefs.

As it happened, the Ratu had been called elsewhere on duty that day; but one of his male relatives was expecting me, and at the sound of my approach he came to the door to greet me. Dressed in an open-necked shirt and a knee-length Fijian man's skirt with a zig-zag hem, he was a portly, smiling fellow. He led me indoors, and introduced me to the Ratu's wife. Their living-room was as stately as the interior of any haystack could be—which is saying quite a lot. Filling an outer shell of grass walls and gabled roof, it differed from the other village houses not only in its bigger size, but also in being lit by two windows inserted beneath deeply overhanging eaves. Iron sockets to hold lighted torches were fixed on timber pillars, a few comfortable cane armchairs stood around, several examples of beautiful Fijian tappa-work mats— made of tree-bark beaten to parchment thinness, and adorned with stencilled patterns—lay upon the floor, and some decoratively carved antique war-clubs hung on the walls.

We settled in seats as we sipped the local brew called kava and discussed Fijian affairs. After a while I asked my host about the history of Bau. He related some little bits of it, but remarked that a much greater authority on the subject resided a few huts away. That person had not acquired his knowledge by reading books at school, but by living the history himself. A veteran chief named Ratu Akuri, he had witnessed with his own eyes all the memorable events and changes in Bau throughout the last century—for he was more than a hundred years old. If I would be interested to meet him (said my new acquaintance), we could go and call on him.

I answered that I would very much like to see the grand elder; so we rose, and I followed my guide out of the house and across the village green to a small dwelling standing beside the sea.

As we entered it my companion spoke a few words aloud in Fijian, and then motioned me to sit down beside him on the floor. No response came to his utterance, and I assumed that we were alone in the room. After the dazzling glare of sunlight out of doors my eyes took some time to adjust themselves to the shadowy interior, which seemed impenetrably black. Gradually, however, the shadows began to assume shapes, and I started to distinguish this or that feature in the chamber. It contained no stick of furniture, nor any article of utility or adornment. Only the bamboo poles sustaining its grass-woven walls, and the cross-beams supporting its roof were dimly visible. Then I detected at the far end of the room a long object lying motionless on the ground. Slowly I recognised it as an emaciated human body stretched prostrate on its back, clad in nothing but a loin-cloth. Gazing at it, I took it to be a corpse laid out for burial; and I thought my guide also regarded it as that, for he continued to sit absolutely silent, contemplating the figure in the respectful attitude of one paying homage to the dead. I felt a sharp emotion of sadness, for apparently the venerable Ratu Akuri had by some odd coincidence died that very day.

Of a sudden the body emitted a feeble grunt. I saw one of its hands grope on the floor beside it, pick up an article lying there, raise what turned out to be a fan above its face, and start wafting this implement to and fro before its nose.

My companion made a low guttural reply to the grunt.

Slowly the body came more to life, muttering a short phrase in its native tongue.

The man at my side answered with a whole sentence in the same, to me, incomprehensible gibberish.

Then I saw the prostrate human form roll its head sideways in our direction so that its face turned towards us. Opening one eye, it scrutinised me carefully. The second eye remained shut; nor did the figure move another muscle.

The old, old man—for this was indeed Ratu Akuri—murmured something.

My interpreter translated the remark to me, observing, "He says welcome to his home."

I expressed great pleasure at being there; and our go-between conveyed this sentiment to the chief.

Another period of silence followed. Then the recumbent body twitched for a while, slowly gathered its strength, gave itself two or three heaves, and sat up facing us. By now my eyes were accustomed to the obscure indoors, and I looked with admiration on the bald-pated, bony and yet vividly aristocratic features of the semi-death's head gazing back at me.

My two acquaintances exchanged several sentences in their native speech.

"The Ratu says he's very glad you've come to Bau," said my guide.

I replied that I felt especially happy to meet the historic island's renowned oldest inhabitant; and our interpreter translated this remark.

It stimulated a surprisingly lively burst of monologue from the ancient patriarch. After a while my companion interrupted his speech to turn their talk into a dialogue, and later I intervened to make it a conversation *à trois*. Ratu Akuri responded by starting to speak hesitantly in English; and before long he was launched on a flow of racy reminiscences. He talked of King Cakabau, telling us various personal anecdotes about that revered worthy.

At one point in his stories I asked him, "How old are you, Ratu?"

He gave a toothless grin and answered, "I'm a hundred years old."

A grey-bearded youngster of about seventy summers, who had joined a group of villagers standing in the doorway eavesdropping on our conversation, guffawed and remarked, "He's much older than that!"

Ratu Akuri's memory began to probe further back into the past, and he related episodes in the lives of Cakabau's two predecessors on the throne. Soon he gave an account of a battle which the first of these fought against a rival claimant to the crown near the very spot where we now squatted. Pointing a skinny finger through his door, he indicated the exact place beside the shore where the fighting occurred. He himself had been an eye-witness of the contest, watching it as a child clinging to his mother's grass skirt.

His narrative was a picturesque description of a savage skirmish between two hosts of primitive warriors—and from my recent reading of Fijian history I knew that the battle had actually been fought in the year 1829. So the first-hand account of it which I now sat hearing in 1925 from the sole survivor of the scene seemed to establish his boast that he had passed a hundred birthdays.

The old boy went on talking. A gleam of reminiscent pleasure lit his eyes as he described the banquet with which the victors celebrated their triumph on that memorable night. Amidst the fierce light of bonfires the king had entertained his followers to a feast consisting of cooked remains of their vanquished foes.

For some time I had wished to ask the centenarian a certain question, and after a pause I ventured to put it.

"Ratu," I said, "have you yourself ever eaten human flesh?"

Without a flicker of an eyelid he replied, "Oh, yes; in my youth many a time."

"What does it taste like?" I enquired.

"Like good roast pork."

Recognising his utter lack of embarrassment, I pursued the subject further.

"Which are better to eat, black men or white men?" I asked.

The elder considered the problem for a few moments, and then observed, "Most of us preferred black men. We thought they were more tasty because white men had too much salt in their flesh."

I put one more question. "Have you yourself ever eaten a white man?" I said.

He gave a wry smile and answered, "No, only an American."

Hey-ho! Those were the days nearly half a century ago when British Imperialism still held unchallenged sway, and when many simple, dependent peoples in the Empire assumed that the only veritable white men on Earth were the pukka sahibs from old Britain.

V

Incidentally, a few years later in a speech to an important luncheon club in New York I quoted word for word that conversation with Ratu Akuri. When I spoke the last sentence a deadly hush fell upon my vast American audience. For a moment I was not sure whether they would rise as one man and fling me out of the room. Or possibly, I thought, they might send me captive to the kitchen, to have me roasted there. Then a burst of laughter rent the air and continued for several minutes. I breathed again.

Dancing Girls

I made my first acquaintance with the Far East in 1929, when I sailed to Japan as a secretary to the British delegation attending an international conference. After a few days in Tokyo our party travelled onward to Kyoto, where the gathering would take place.

Kyoto was the capital of Japan for over a thousand years before it yielded pride of place to Tokyo in the second half of the nineteenth century. In many ways its antique appearance was still unchanged when I arrived there from what it had been in its heyday, for after the Imperial Court with its regal splendours departed to the new centre of Government, Kyoto relapsed quietly into history, remaining untouched and unspoilt by all the changes which the recently opened intercourse with foreigners began to bring in various other regions of the ancient Land of the Cherry Blossom. The old city's narrow cobbled streets, houses built of light timber and rice-paper, miniature Nipponese gardens, and aged Shinto shrines, Buddhist temples and princely palaces appeared much as they had done when the place was the national capital. Most aristocrats, scholars and other citizens residing amidst these remnants of bygone days still wore with pride the austere male and brilliant female kimonos which from time immemorial had been the native dress of their race. The place's traditional arts, too, were still practised by its craftsmen with the same flawless skill as had been maintained by their forebears for countless generations. In hundreds of little workshops lovely porcelains, silks and lacquers were being perfectly produced. And although the pomp and glory of the Royal Court had been withdrawn, the city was periodically a stage for gorgeous pageantry and historical festivals. Kyoto was a vivid, enchanting relic of traditional Japan, like a coloured woodcut by the artist Hirosige come to life.

In one of its byways stood an inn of romantic renown called the Ichiriki Tea-house. This establishment's fame blossomed after it was the scene of a popular episode in Japan's national story; and it had been a place of fashionable resort every since. In it for several months through the year 1701 heroic Oishi Yoshio, the leader of the celebrated Forty-seven Ronin (or lordless Samurai) spent convivial evenings pretending an interest only in light-hearted gaiety in the company of local geisha girls, whereas he was in fact plotting the assassination of one of the Shogun's highest officials. Oishi's prospective victim had aroused his and his followers' enmity by forcing their own feudal lord to end his life by committing hari-kiri, thus depriving their knightly group of its leadership.

In truth Oishi Yoshio's parties at the inn must have been as beautifully gay as they were conspiratorially earnest, for the love-liest women in Japan lived in Kyoto—and the loveliest women in Kyoto were the geishas at the Ichiriki Tea-house. That tradition also was maintained when I arrived in the Orient more than 200 years later. The ladies of Kyoto were still reputed to be the most deliciously easy on the eye in all Japan. The waters of the Kamo-gawa rivulet flowing through the city's centre were said to be partly responsible for that. Their fluid possessed a special virtue which gave the complexions of those who washed in it a soft, perfect purity, just as it also lent a well-known touch of brilliance to the local textiles dipped into the stream for dyeing.

I am no authority on the subject of feminine good looks, but during my stay in the old capital I was prepared to lay down my life in defence of the judgment that if Japan's loveliest women came from Kyoto, Kyoto's loveliest girls were the geishas who en-tertained guests in the Ichiriki Tea-house. That house of good fame stood amidst its courtyards and garden on the same spot which it occupied when Oishi Yoshio honoured it by his presence. I dined there with friends on several evenings after our daily conference sessions ended. The inn's plump, dignified, middle-aged proprietress would greet us with beaming smiles and courtly bows as we arrived on an outer verandah; and we responded in kind. That impeccable ceremony over, we slipped off our shoes, donned soft slippers which she provided for us, and entered the building with silent tread, like pilgrims venturing into sacred precincts. She ushered us into the long, low room reserved for our party, a chamber almost empty of furniture and yet full of character. A single old Japanese woodcut hung on one wall, and a bowl of decoratively arranged flowers stood on a solitary table; but otherwise the place was featureless except for flimsy timber-and-paper walls enclosing it, rush-matting covering its floor, and a row of cushions arranged on the ground at its far end as seats where we would squat for dinner at low stool-tables.

We sat on the cushions in the cross-legged style of Buddhas— and at once all the cares and controversies of our international conference fled from our minds. We had been transported into another world, where peace reigned. A few moments later that world appeared like some Earthly paradise when a troupe of its customary inhabitants entered. They were eight geisha girls. Their exotic prettiness was as breath-taking as that of a flock of butterflies. As they came tripping towards us on soft shuffling feet, their eyes were modestly lowered to gaze not at us but at the floor, their mouths were artificially curved into formal smiles, and they fluttered little fans in their hands. That, at least, was their well-trained demeanour on the evening of my first visit; but on every later occasion as they advanced into the room their eyes glanced gleefully at me and my guests, and their lips parted with laughter as they uttered in sweet voices phrases of gay greeting. For at our initial meeting—as I shall tell—they and I established a true friendship which made us always very happy to see each other again.

A Japanese gentleman making a first visit to the tea-house would of course have found nothing extraordinary in their entry. For him the scene would be part of every day reality; but for us strangers from the Western hemisphere this novel encounter did not appear reality, but romance—as if we had stepped into some

fabulous fairyland. Even when I had sat there for an hour, with a
little flesh-and-blood geisha at my side teaching me how to convey
snippets of fried fish, sukiaki and other foodstuffs from my plate
to my mouth between a pair of chopsticks, I had to pinch myself
occasionally to make sure I was awake. Yet there was little chance
to dream. My tutor in the task of manipulating chopsticks was an
earnest young lady who kept me hard at work at my lesson. She
burst into giggles whenever I chased a bean for a long time fruit-
lessly round and round my dish and eventually managed to pick
it up between the long, thin implements, only to drop it by mistake
on to my lap or into my cup of saki-wine before it reached my lips.
Afterwards she resumed her instruction with redoubled zeal, as if
the sole purpose of her life was to make me a master of the art of
wielding chopsticks. And when every once in a while I showed
myself an apt pupil, she clapped her hands and uttered cries of
delight.

My fellow guests were undergoing a similar tuition. That was
the most enjoyable classroom in which I ever studied. Except
through an interpreter we could not exchange a word with our
school-ma'ams, since they and we spoke different languages. But
that seemed at first irrelevent. We were not so much concerned to
talk with our mouths—which in any case were preoccupied with
their efforts to capture titbits of food—as to gaze with our eyes.
We could still scarcely stop staring at those lovely, smiling maids
beside us. Every feature of their persons was intriguingly exotic—
their elaborately coiffeured black hair glistening with oil and glittering with flowers and jewellery, their dark slanting eyes and
quaintly rouged lips on oval faces so thickly white-powdered that
they looked like exquisitely pretty masks, their delicate, long-
fingered, eloquent hands, and their kimonos and obis coloured as
gorgeously as any rainbows. No bevy of Oriental princesses could
appear more entrancing.

They became even more theatrical when we finished our meal.
After congratulating us on our budding prowess with chopsticks,
they rose to perform songs and dances for us. A Japanese geisha
is a young lady carefully trained to exercise various talents. In a

tea-house she is not only a waitress who attends the customers at their meals, but also an actress who beguiles them with music and dancing, an entertainer who amuses them with parlour tricks and games, and (for those who speak Japanese) a conversationalist whose chatter is intelligent, witty and, if need be, intellectually accomplished. In the days that I write of they were not prostitutes —though I believe habits may have changed to some extent since. At any rate none of my friends at Ichiriki Tea-house was that kind of a girl. Moreover, I was not the kind of boy who wanted that kind of a girl. A rather shy Scots bachelor in his late twenties, I was of course blessed with a liking for pretty young members of the opposite sex; but I lacked any carnal knowledge of them. Nor did I feel in any particular hurry to make that acquaintance. Harlots and brothels held no attraction for me beyond a mild and slightly frightened curiosity which I never satisfied; and I did not wish to risk offending, still less insulting, any of my own respectable flapper friends by making suggestions which I feared they would regard as improper. Possibly times have changed since those somewhat prudish days. Anyway, I attached sincere, sentimental importance to my friendships with pleasing members of the fair sex, and already had an inkling that these could be truer and richer if they were more concerned with a comradeship of the minds, the spirits and the characters than with a conjunction of the bodies—although I naturally hoped that some day one of those companionships would embrace all these experiences together.

That is a diversion; yet perhaps it helps to explain why my chief desire at my introduction to marvellously attractive young Japanese womanhood was to become better acquainted with their individual personalities. I wished to win their respectful confidence, to avoid their assuming that I was just another of those tedious, boring men with only one interest in feminine society, and so perhaps to establish with them a sensible relationship in which we could exchange opinions and ideas. Thus possibly I would gain a more intimate insight than I possessed hitherto into the Japanese way of life.

In that mood I observed the girls as they performed a slow-motion, unexciting dance from a traditional "No" play and sang falsetto songs which aroused in me no enthusiasm. As I watched I noticed what seemed to me to be two different types among the actresses. There were eight in the group; and five among them looked distinctly older and more mature than the others, who appeared more childlike. In addition, although the senior quintet were exceedingly lovely, that younger trio were in some ways even more decorative. For instance, they wore more scintillating jewellery in their hair. Indeed, their comely heads might have been show-cases for a jeweller's shop, for each had many gorgeous gold-topped pins, flower-like brooches, tinkling silver bells, and other fluttering knick-knacks adorning her coiffure. Their faces were also more engagingly doll-like, their smiles more generously spontaneous, and their movements rather free-er. The elders' steps and gestures were disciplined by a self-conscious, well-regimented restraint which gave them an appearance of professional formality, whereas the other girls' actions had a rather relaxed, even amateurish air.

On enquiry I found that my analysis was correct. The five older damsels were fully-fledged geishas each about twenty years old, whilst the others were juvenile apprentices still in process of being trained in the duties of geishadom. They were early teenagers not yet qualified as proper geishas, and were in fact not entitled to be called by that honourable name. Their correct description in most parts of Japan was "*Hangyoku*," which being interpreted means "Half-pearl." The whole pearl is the finished geisha, and the half-pearl is an as yet semi-taught pupil. These latter young jewels have to undergo many years of strict tuition before they can graduate as geishas perfectly polished in all the accomplishments expected of their exacting profession. An ancient tradition declares that a little miss will be most successful if she starts her training on the 6th day of the 6th month (June) of her 6th year—and it is generally reckoned that she will take a dozen years before, at about the age of eighteen, she is sufficiently proficient to become a geisha proper.

In Kyoto the youngsters were not called "*Hangyoku*" but "*Maiko*," which means "Dancing girl." The three dancing girls at

Ichiriki that evening were all in their earliest teens. Partly because of their even more fetching fantasy, and partly perhaps because I was instinctively cautious not to become too familiar with their fully trained elders lest I should lose my head as well as my heart with one of them, I became most friendly with those juniors. By the end of my first visit to the tea-house they, the geishas and I were all on first-name terms. I have long forgotten the names of the geishas, but to this day I remember those of the dancing girls. One was called Komomo, which means "Little Peach"; another was addressed as Tokiko, which means "Child of Time"; and the third answered to the name of Matsumoto-tsuyu, which in English denotes "The Dewdrop under the Pine Trees."

II

After their programme of songs and dances all the girls rejoined us guests on the floor to perform their next set of duties. Since we could not understand more than a few words of Japanese it was useless for them to engage us in clever, witty conversation; so they proceeded instead to teach us a Japanese game which was comprehensible without speech. They produced small sheets of thin tissue paper which had been tucked inside their obis, rolled each one deftly into a length of string-like texture, and then curled it round to form a circle the size of a bracelet. Sitting in a row in front of us, they tilted their heads sharply backwards until they were looking up at the ceiling; and then every girl balanced one of the paper bangles flat on her brow. At a given signal they all began twitching their skins, wiggling their noses, frowning, grimacing and making other wobbling facial movements without changing the upward thrust of their heads. That induced the light tissue rings to start shifting gradually forward from their fore-heads to their eyebrows, then across the bridges of their noses, afterwards along the nose until they slipped over the tips of their nostrils, and thence on to their upper lips, whence they finally reached their mouths. It was a race to see which competitor could manoeuvre the paper quoit most quickly from her forehead into her mouth, where she had to catch it between her lips. If one dropped, its owner was disqualified. The winner held her bangle protruding firmly from her teeth with a triumphant grin.

After that they plucked another set of flimsy sheets of tissue-paper from their obis, fashioned them into similar bracelets, and asked us to tilt back our heads so that they could place these on our manly brows. They told us that when they said "One, two, three—go" (which seemed to be their sole command of the English language) we should start a similar contest between ourselves. We complied with good grace; and they screamed with laughter at our inexpert facial contortions which caused all our bits of paper to tumble from our countenances on to the floor. That was a challenge to our Western pride; and we demanded a fresh set of bangles with which to improve our techniques. In our efforts to perfect our skill we received every encouragement from our teachers, for they demonstrated on their own faces how we should twitch this eyebrow and wiggle that, wrinkle that nostril and quiver this, purse this lip and wobble that, so as to hasten the short journeys of the small paper quoits. Gradually we became masters of the art; and then we challenged our tutors to a contest— Japanese Geishas versus European Diplomats. They beat us every time—until they themselves engaged in a little diplomacy, and let us win.

I then said that in return for their gift of this Oriental game we must present them with an Occidental sport. They welcomed the notion, and with eager expressions awaited my instructions. I took a handkerchief from my pocket, and proposed that we should teach them how to play Blindman's-Buff. My travelling companions heartily approved.

One of my colleagues happened to be John D. Rockefeller the third, then a young man acting as a secretary in the American delegation at our conference, just as I was a similar functionary with the British team. He was—as he still remains—a person of high intelligence, sincerity and charm. Modest and unaffected, he entered into the spirit of our party at Ichiriki with quiet gusto.

After a while in the game he was captured by the current blind-man, a handkerchief was bound round his eyes, and he began to play the part of chaser.

Standing over six feet tall in his stockinged soles, he had to crouch as he groped sightlessly through the room, so as not to hit his head with a bang against one of the low beams supporting the ceiling. However, his every other movement was remarkably carefree. Different blind-men adopt different techniques to catch their prey; some move around slowly and cautiously with out-stretched hands feeling here and there, high and low in the atmosphere in the hope of contacting someone's head or body, whilst others dart swiftly hither and thither with constant sudden changes of direction in the expectation of knocking into some unprepared victim who will forthwith scream, shout or laugh with surprise, and so give away his or her identity. John's method was the latter. Like some lanky spider operating from the centre of its web, he dashed to and fro after the insects and butterflies flitting erratically around him in attempts to evade his clutches. As his sorties became more vigorous, so the high-pitched giggles and cries of the girls became ever more excited; and he grew increasingly bold in his offensive tactics. At one point he ran so precipitately in one direction that he struck the room's fragile wall, and his fists broke holes through its flimsy rice-paper partitions. Ricocheting away from this collision, he swerved at an angle—and hit an adjoining wall with the same result. It seemed as if all the walls might collapse one after another, and that our private party would become a public exhibition of a robust English nursery game. Fortunately, however, the damage was done on the garden side of the house, where only a moonlit rockery with some goldfish swimming in a pool could witness our revelry. John is an abstemious person, and he was as sober as a judge. His excessive zeal was just the intoxication of sheer fun with which we were all inebriated.

When we felt like a change from that energetic exercise I introduced our hostesses to another English game—Grandmother's Paces. The long chamber was an ideal pitch for this, and the Japanese girls took to it like ducks to water. Indeed, their customary gait consisting of smooth, inch-by-inch shuffles forward of each foot in turn was just the right means of making a surreptitious approach towards the target-person. They were very successful players.

A few hours sped by. When our watches told us that the time was already past midnight my conference colleagues announced that they must go home to bed. But I wished to remain longer with our new friends if that were convenient to them, to talk with them about themselves, their families and their customs, and so to catch further glimpses of Japanese manners. They expressed glee at the suggestion, and a member of the Japanese delegation at the conference who was in our party agreed to stay as my interpreter.

The geishas and maikos called "Sayonara" (Good-bye) to my companions as they withdrew to the veranda to recover their shoes and depart in their motor-cars; and then the rest of us once more settled on the floor for a gossip about things Nipponese.

In answers to my questions the girls told me many interesting facts about feminine habits in their native land. For instance, they explained the tradition by which their kimonos and obis must always be adorned with designs harmonious with the current season of the year. Thus in winter the patterns must have topical decorations congenial to the time of snowflakes, in spring they must be bright with representations of the foliage and flowers of the earth's rebirth, in summer they should be ablaze with the sunshine and blooms of this lusty period, and in autumn they must reflect the mood of that fruitful yet fading moment. It would be wrong, for instance, to wear a dress displaying chrysanthemums in spring, or to sport sprays of cherry blossom in the fall.

My tutors told me, too, about their families. Some of them had been born as country lasses whilst others were little city brats; but they all alike said they were not considered by their parents to be of equal importance with their brothers. Indeed, several of them had only left their homes and adopted the profession of geishadom in order to earn money to provide for their brothers' schooling and university education. The male sex was absolutely dominant in Japanese society. They expressed no complaint at that, accepting it as entirely natural and proper.

Then they told me about the famous Tea Ceremony, describing its rites and significance. And they spoke of other deeply-rooted Japanese manners, answering all my questions. We kept our interpreter busy translating my queries and their replies. The girls were lively in their chatter, often interrupting each other, sometimes arguing animatedly together, and occasionally talking two, three or more at the same time. They spoke without shyness, often jesting and laughing gaily. Not until the small hours of the morning did we break up our discussion, and separate.

The more I observed the little maikos, the more I felt enchanted by them. Their pretty persons, vivacious characters and sweet humours were entrancing, like those of a lot of story-book princesses—or rather, like a group of adorable out-of-this-world beings. The geishas also had winning ways; but custom decreed that they should be not quite so fabulously decorative or informally spontaneous.

III

I made several later visits with parties of friends to the Ichiriki Tea-house. The geishas and maikos did not work only in that establishment, for they must always be ready to go as entertainers in other similar places. But whenever I went to Ichiriki they clamoured to be there also, and cancelled all their other engagements.

One evening as I was leaving the tea-house after midnight, standing beside my car in the courtyard and bowing low in Nipponese fashion to the row of similarly bowing young ladies on the veranda, I wondered whether the trio of dancing girls had ever seen the inside of the grand, Western-style Miyako Hotel where I was staying. My interpreter was still handy, so I asked him to put the question to them.

He did, and they answered that they had not.

"Would you like to?" I asked.

When that sentence was translated to Komomo, Tokiko and Matsumoto-tsuyu they caught their breaths in astonishment, their slanting eyes widened with excitement, and they clapped their hands with delight.

"*Hai*" (which means "yes") they cried in high-pitched voices in unison.

They looked enquiringly at the proprietress of the tea-house who stood beside them, to learn whether she would consent. I asked her if I might take them then and there to view a Kyoto sight which they had never seen; and I promised to deliver the youngsters back to her within an hour.

She smilingly consented. The old dame knew by now that she could trust me—or perhaps she felt no such confidence, but did not worry unduly because she recognised that her juvenile charges were quite capable of looking after themselves. Moreover, there was safety in numbers; they were three to my one.

Anyway Little Peach, Child of Time, The Dewdrop under the Pine Trees and I climbed into my car, one of them sitting on the front seat beside the chauffeur and the other pair flanking me on either hand in the back. They were very impressed at the grandeur of riding in such a vehicle—apparently a new experience for them. Through the first several seconds they sat in unaccustomed prim, awed silence with their eyes almost popping out of their heads as we began to speed along the streets. Then they could suppress their excitement no longer, and all began to talk at once, standing up and examining the clock and other illuminated instruments on the dashboard, asking innumerable questions of the Japanese driver, and maintaining a ceaseless jibber-jabber of amazement. Without my interpreter I could not follow the contents of their chatter, but I needed no help to comprehend that my action in inviting them on this jaunt met with their unqualified approval. And once more at the sight of them jumping about so close around me in their gorgeously theatrical costumes—like a troupe of beautiful puppets come to life—I had to pinch myself to make sure I was awake.

Our car raced along Kyoto's main thoroughfare and climbed

the hill at its farther end to the Miyako Hotel. The hour being late—or rather, extremely early in a new morning—the city was sunk deep in slumber, and only an occasional belated reveller appeared along its dark, otherwise empty streets. When we arrived at the hotel's front door I asked my chauffeur to wait, as he must drive us back to the tea-house before long. The three children and I then entered the building.

Its lofty hall was brightly lit, but deserted by humanity except for a night porter standing behind the registration desk. He looked at me, gave a smile of recognition, and then glanced at the three dancing girls. He blinked with astonishment, must have thought me either crazy or else very crafty, and seemed on the point of making a protest. On second thoughts, however, he let the matter go, perhaps realising that in any case an objection would be unavailing since I did not comprehend his language. Not until the next day did I learn that it was strictly contrary to all custom in Kyoto for geishas or maikos to enter a modern hotel, and that I was breaching a hallowed rule.

A vast lounge alongside the entrance hall was plunged in darkness at that hour. I wanted my guests to view it; so I led them through glass doors into the huge chamber, where they stood for a moment nonplussed by its pitch-black gloom. Of a sudden, using every finger and thumb on both my hands at once, I switched on all the lights simultaneously—and the girls cried aloud with joyous surprise. Half a dozen scintillating chandeliers suspended from the ceiling revealed a sight the like of which they had never seen before, with plush armchairs, sumptuous sofas and gilt tables galore, a grand piano on a gaily curtained stage at the room's far end, and potted flowers and palm-trees standing all around.

I switched off the lights, returned to the hall, and motioned to my friends to enter an elevator waiting to convey me to my bedroom. The lift-boy looked with dubious enquiry at the hall porter, who shrugged his shoulders with helpless resignation. Meanwhile the girls clustered together in the lift's confined space, holding each other's hands in excited anticipation at what might happen next. When the boy pressed a button, and the door closed upon us, they gasped with fright. But a moment later that emotion gave way to delicious, wondering pleasure as they felt the sudden sensation of floating swiftly upwards into the air. They looked at the floor beneath their feet to see if it was still there, examined each other with quick, searching glances as if to discover whether they had all sprouted wings, and then jumped, clapped their hands, and screamed with excitement.

"Oh, Mac San!" (which is Japanese for Mr. Mac) they cried at me gratefully, as if I were some magician giving them a Heavenly experience.

They felt perplexed, however, about the cause of the miracle, and in noisy cross-examination sought enlightenment from the lift-boy. He was an impeccably courteous but woefully ignorant youth who evidently had no notion how to unravel the mystery for them; so he hid his lack of knowledge beneath a show of superior masculine contempt for their stupidity, merely pointing to the button which he had pressed as if it were the sole, obvious, well-known explanation of all the achievements of modern mechanical civilisation.

Soon we arrived at the top story where my room was situated, the lift slowed gradually to a halt, and its door opened to let us emerge into the corridor. However, my little friends were clearly so entranced by their first journey into upper space that I thought it a pity to end the experience for them at once. I therefore asked the boy to close the door again, and to convey us abruptly downstairs. He did so; and as soon as the floor began to drop beneath their feet the girls expressed their renewed happiness in laughing glee.

"Oh, Mac San! Oh, Mac San!" they kept repeating whenever they could stop to draw breath.

When we reached the hotel's bottom story I signalled to the lift-boy not to open the door, but to go immediately into reverse, and ascend promptly once more to the top floor. And when we arrived at that summit I asked him again to do the opposite, and descend to the nether regions. Afterwards we made those journeys a dozen times in quick succession, shooting upwards and downwards without hesitation. The sounds of mixed screams and laughter inside the lift were somewhat reminiscent of the noise in a gaily panic-stricken parrot house at a zoo.

The youngsters' thrills of pleasure never ceased. On one occasion when we were momentarily stationary on the ground floor I drew the lift-boy away from the button which controlled our cage, and suggested that Little Peach should work it. I showed her how to press her finger on the knob; and she responded with ready zeal. So did the elevator. We nearly went through the roof that time, and would have done so—and all really gone to Paradise —if Little Peach had got her way.

I decided then that we should abandon the lift, and continue our tour of the hotel. The boy therefore let us out into my bedroom corridor. The girls were amazed at the long succession of numbered suites which we passed before we arrived in front of mine at a far corner of the building.

When I reached it I stood still. Putting a finger upright against my closed lips, I signalled to my guests to be quiet. With touching obedience they immediately fell silent. I explained the situation to them by dumb-show. Pointing first at the door and then at myself, I indicated that this was my room. They understood, and made hushed grimaces of satisfaction at the prospect of seeing where I lived. Then I pointed at the door again, and whispered, "Mac San to Coke San," which meant "Mr. Mac and Mr. Coke." I held up two fingers to convey that Coke San and I inhabited the place together; for it was indeed a double room which I shared with my friend Gerry Coke. As I write this account of the incident thirty-eight years later he is Mr. Gerald Coke, the distinguished Chairman or Director of the Glyndebourne Arts Trust, The Royal Opera House in Covent Garden, and the Royal Academy of Music, as well as of other important organisations. At that time in Kyoto he was a young, unknown fellow secretary of the British delegation at our international conference.

The dancing girls knew him because he had attended two or three of our parties in Ichiriki Tea-house; and so they understood my meaning.

I then held up both my hands clasped together, bent them sideways, laid my face on them as if they were a pillow, and closed my
eyes. I murmured "Coke San," and pointed again to the door. My
intelligent audience comprehended that Mr. Coke was now lying
asleep in the room. They nodded their heads sagely, and one of
them opened her mouth wide and held a fist against it in mimicry
of somebody suppressing a yawn. They all giggled at her act, and
I could not help joining in their laughter.

Afterwards I held up a finger against my pursed lips again to
enjoin silence as I started to open the door. They caught their
breaths with excitement; and when I tiptoed into the room and
beckoned them to follow they entered ever so quietly. I closed the
door behind us.

Within the chamber a bedside lamp shed a gleam of light from
a table standing between two beds. The first couch was mine, and
its blankets and top sheet were turned down invitingly to receive
me. I ignored it, and crept to the farther bed. On its pillow lay
Gerry's handsome, blond-haired head with his eyes closed in
slumber. I motioned to my conspiratorial companions to join me
close beside him; and they did so soundlessly. But it was all they
could do to smother gasps of delight when they saw him stretched
unconscious there. Almost noiselessly I held a council of war with
them. Remembering from our games at Ichiriki that they understood the meaning of the English words "One, two, three—go,"
I conveyed to them in whispers and gestures that a pair of them
should take up positions on the farther side of Gerry's bed whilst
the third and I stayed on its hither side, that they should then all
bend their faces low above his, and that when I mouthed quietly
the order "One, two, three—go" they should promptly exclaim
aloud in unison, "Coke San!" They understood perfectly, nudged
each other in playful approval, and eagerly took up their allotted
posts. Gerry was lying on his back, and his countenance peered
sightlessly towards theirs as they bowed over him.

I said very softly indeed, "One, two, three—go."

At once the angelic choir called in sing-song voices, "Coke
San."

Gerry's eyes opened sleepily—and then abruptly dilated wide. To say that he looked astonished would be a considerable understatement. He stared like a man who is seeing a vision—and few visionaries can have experienced a more delicious dream than that trinity of maidens gazing down at him.

The girls burst into irrepressible laughter. Gerry then caught sight of me, and his mouth extended into a broad grin. I must say he took our rude intrusion very courteously.

I explained to him that I was giving our friends a conducted tour of the Miyako Hotel, since they had never been inside the place before. Meanwhile the youngsters chattered vivaciously together as they shuffled around exploring every nook and cranny in the room. They inspected our dressing-table, wardrobes and suitcases, toyed with our hair brushes and combs, peered into the bathroom, and examined themselves amusedly in reflections in a long mirror.

However, we had no time to waste if we were to see more of the hotel's sights; and my guests and I soon took our leave of Gerry. Issuing into the corridor again, I led them to the top of a staircase and down its steps to the floor below. They followed me as confidently as a litter of kittens. As we approached the door of another bedroom I once more laid a finger against my mouth to command silence. I knew that the apartment was occupied by two pleasant young females called Margaret and Rachel who were members of the Canadian and the British delegations respectively at our conference. They were acquainted with Komomo, Tokiko and Matsumoto-tsuyu because they had attended some of our parties at the tea-house, and had become friends with all the geishas and maikos there.

It was now past one o'clock in the morning, and I did not wish to compromise Margaret and Rachel by entering their sleeping quarters myself. On the other hand I did not want them to miss the pleasure of a visit from Little Peach, Child of Time and The Dewdrop under the Pine Trees on this auspicious occasion. I therefore gathered that trio round me, pointed to the door, and whispered softly, "Margaret to Rachel." They nodded smiling comprehension. Then I noiselessly opened the door, and motioned to them to tiptoe into the room. They trooped inside; and when they were within I closed the door, remaining myself in the corridor outside.

For a few moments the deathly hush of the small hours of the morning persisted; and then I heard pandemonium break loose inside the room. Margaret and Rachel were of course both fast asleep in their beds, and naturally they had not left any lamp burning. Equally naturally the three little dancing girls felt alarmed when they suddenly found themselves shut into a strange chamber in pitch-darkness; so they began to scream in high falsetto. As I had anticipated, that woke the two slumberers, who shouted in reply. The tragic chorus lasted only a brief while, for one of the damsels in bed switched on a light; and the competing sets of yellers quickly recognised each other. They exchanged exclamations first of surprise, then of pleasure, and finally of hilarity. The maikos must have explained by pointings to the door and cries of "Mac San" that I was outside, and responsible for their escapade, because soon Margaret came through the doorway in her dressing-gown to summon me within for a reprimand and a gossip. However, I declared that I must deliver the visitors back at Ichiriki Tea-house immediately, since their hour of truancy was almost up and we could therefore dally no longer.

As the maikos and I strolled along the corridor towards the lift I felt tempted to make another diversion. A few rooms from that of Margaret and Rachel a honeymoon couple were lying abed—none other than the Lord Chancellor of England and his bride. The first Viscount Hailsham was the leader of our British delegation; and since he had recently wedded his second charming wife, she accompanied him. I thought that a two o'clock in the morning invasion of their nuptial chamber by Little Peach, Child of Time and The Dewdrop under the Pine Trees would be a novel, and perhaps unique, honeymoon experience in the annals of the English Bar—but on prudent reflection I desisted from creating the precedent.

I rang the bell for the elevator, and when the lift-boy opened its door all four of us entered to descend to the ground floor. However, the little misses were not content with only one swift drop down the lift-shaft. They wished to spend a lot of time careering up and down, up and down, and up and down again, as if our vehicle were a jaunting car on a mountain railway in a World Fair. Moreover, Tokiko and Matsumoto-tsuyu indicated that it would be unfair if they were denied the opportunity, which Komomo had enjoyed earlier, of testing their skill at pressing the machine's button, and making it speed aloft into the sky and down into the bowels of the earth at their own sweet wills.

We therefore spent the next several minutes repeating that journey over and over again, to the accompaniment of shrieks of joy from the teenagers.

Afterwards we re-emerged into the entrance hall, where the night-porter looked at us with inquisitive dubiety. We hastened to our motor-car waiting out-of-doors. I asked its chauffeur to drive as fast as possible through the streets, since I had promised to deliver my friends back at the tea-house within the hour, and the sixty minutes were almost up. His skill as a potential racing motorist was considerable, and it enabled us to keep my promise.

IV

A few days later I gave a large luncheon party in the hotel for the principal delegates to our International Conference, and I also invited the proprietress, geishas and maikos of the Ichiriki Tea-house as honoured guests. For this reason the eminent diplomats and their wives all attended with enthusiasm. I was told by the local Japanese that such an official gathering to meet some of Kyoto's most gorgeous and yet humblest citizens was unprecedented in all the thousand years of history in the ancient capital. I felt very proud at adding a new notable episode to Kyoto's long and glorious records.

In the meantime I had been strongly criticised by many distinguished members of the conference for not introducing Ko-

momo, Tokiko and Matsumoto-tsuyu into their bedrooms during
the small hours of the morning a few nights earlier—and among
my severest critics were Lord and Lady Hailsham.

When I left Kyoto the next day all the geishas and maikos were
among the friends who came to see me off at the railway station.
Each one presented me with her photograph and decorative visiting
card printed in Japanese; and with long-drawn mutual ceremonial
bows we said our sad farewells.

                                        V

Two years later an English friend called to see me in London
immediately after his return from a visit to Japan, saying he brought
me a special message from Kyoto. He reported that he had attended a party at a famous restaurant called the Ichiriki Tea-house,
and that as soon as the geishas and maikos there heard he hailed
from Britain they crowded round him to ask whether he knew
"Mac San." On further enquiry he was astonished to discover
that the individual so named was me.

When he told them that he was acquainted with me, they asked
for news of my health, my activities and my prospective travel
plans. In particular they wished to know when I would reappear
in Kyoto; and they begged him to tell me that they were all waiting
impatiently to see me again.

Alas, I never did see them again. I had no opportunity to return
to Japan until nearly twenty years later, when in 1948 I went there
to visit a certain recently risen star shining in the Oriental firmament. He was General Douglas McArthur, who was in effect the
latest of the Japanese Shoguns. At that time I was the British
Commissioner-General in South East Asia, with my headquarters
in Singapore; and I flew to Tokyo to discuss the Far Eastern situation with the General.

After two days in the capital I intended to motor to Kyoto, to
call at the Ichiriki Tea-house and learn if possible the latest
whereabouts of Komomo, Tokiko and Matsumoto-tsuyu, so that

we could all meet and renew our friendship. Unfortunately the plan got knocked on the head by news of some critical developments in South East Asia which required my immediate presence there. I had to fly at once back to Singapore.

Nor have I managed to visit Kyoto during any of my subsequent travels to Japan. Perhaps that is a good thing, and in one way I am glad. No doubt Little Peach, Child of Time and The Dewdrop under the Pine Trees are by now not only wives and mothers, but grandmothers as well. It would be good to meet them as such honourable elders—and yet there is something to be said to the contrary. In my memory they still live vividly as I knew them forty years ago, staying for ever enchanting, gay and decorative maikos in their earliest teens—vivacious, adorable, immortal children. So, to me, they will always remain.

> *They shall not grow old as we that are left grow old;*
> *Age shall not weary them, nor the years condemn.*
> *At the going down of the sun and in the morning*
> *I shall remember them.*

Tally-Ho!

After that sojourn in Japan I travelled onwards through Korea and Manchuria to China. Two years earlier Generalissimo Chiang Kai-shek had made his famous March north, established mastery over most of the Chinese mainland, and set up the Kuomintang Government in Nanking. In due course I went to pay my respects to him there; but on my way I visited first the ill-starred "Young Marshal" Chang Shiu-liang in Mukden, and afterwards Sir Miles Lampson, the British Minister in Peking.

It was my first visit to fabulous Cathay. For four days I stayed in the gracious mandarin's palace in Peking's Legation Quarter which was then the British Envoy's residence. From it I made fascinating excursions to the Forbidden City, the Temple of Heaven, the Altars of the Sun and the Earth, and the Terrace of the Moon, as well as to the Ming Tombs, the Great Wall of China and other near-by places steeped in history. During those days was born my high admiration for the members of the human race who have been more continuously civilised than any other people on Earth. But that is another story.

Sir Miles and Lady Lampson were a charming host and hostess. Their children Mary and Graham lived in Peking with them; and they all made me feel at home as a member of the family. During dinner on my first evening His Excellency told me that on the following day they would go on an expedition to the Western Hills, where he owned a country house in which they were to entertain some members of the Diplomatic Corps to lunch. He asked whether I would like to accompany them.

I readily accepted the invitation.

Lampson then suggested that following the luncheon party we could visit the Summer Palace beside its lovely lake if I would like to do so. I replied with enthusiasm that I would greatly enjoy this. Lampson thereupon remarked that he would order an extra pony for me to ride. I caught my breath—but shyly held my tongue.

He then explained that he, Mary and Graham planned to trot across the several miles of plain to the Western Hills, viewing one or two interesting places on the way. For example, they might call at a Buddhist temple where some of the surviving eunuchs of the old Imperial Court now lived in retirement. Would I like to visit those notorious characters?

I commented that the trip should be very interesting—and if there was a note of uncertainty in my voice it was not caused by any distaste at the prospect of chatting with a group of eunuchs.

"We'll go on Mongolian ponies," Lampson said. And he added, "Have you ever ridden one?"

"No," I replied.

"You'll enjoy it," he observed. "They're engaging, lively little brutes."

I nodded my head somewhat dubiously.

"I'm afraid I haven't brought any riding clothes with me," I hastily remarked with as professional a cavalier's tone as I could counterfeit, hoping to open an escape route for myself.

"That doesn't matter," Lampson answered. "It's a very informal party, and any old trousers and shirt will do."

"I *am* glad you can come," said Mary with a most friendly smile.

"But . . ." I began.

"We'll start at nine o'clock in the morning," Lampson interrupted.

I felt flabbergasted, and stayed speechless with shock. They took my silence for consent.

And, indeed, I did seem to have committed myself. At that late stage of the conversation I was too ashamed to confess that Mongolian ponies were not the only breed of horse-flesh with which I was unacquainted. I had never so much as mounted, let alone ridden, any kind of horse in my life, except a rocking-horse in my nursery.

At nine o'clock the next morning I presented myself at the front door, and was ushered into a courtyard where a quartet of frisky-looking ponies awaited our pleasure. Lampson and his two youngsters appeared like smart competitors in a fashionable Horse Show in their neat riding-breeches, trim jackets and black velvet fox-hunting caps. I felt very out of place in my tweed plus-fours and tartan stockings designed for golf, which were the only sporting kit I carried in my travelling wardrobe. A jersey discreetly hid a pair of braces which I wore to keep my trousers up, even if I myself was fated to tumble disastrously down.

Lampson introduced me to the steed which had been mobilised for me. The little creature eyed me with friendly curiosity.

"It's probably smaller than anything you've ridden before," my kind host remarked, "but it's a sportive little animal."

"The smaller the mount, the shorter the fall," I retorted with a brave attempt at a laugh.

Mary and Graham were ready to start.

"We'll ride in single file through the streets until we get out of the city," their father proposed.

"You'd better all go ahead," I said. "I'll bring up the rear."

"Wouldn't you like to be in the middle of the party?" one of the children asked.

"No, you all know the way, and I don't. I'll follow you."

So they led their ponies to the front of mine. Whilst their backs were turned as they adjusted stirrups, arranged bridles and mounted their horses I clambered into my saddle. Fortunately a nimble Chinese stable-boy helped to heave me into place, smiling encouragement at me through his evidently perceptive, amused narrow eyes. As I peered from my lofty perch to the ground below me it seemed an unconscionably long distance away, and I felt relieved that my vehicle was to be a Mongolian pygmy rather than an Arab giant.

We set out. As our little cavalcade paraded slowly through streets thronged with pedestrians, rickshaws, carts and motor-cars I tried to adapt myself to my unaccustomed situation. The saddle gave me some measure of comforting support, but every now and then one or both of my feet slipped out of the stirrups, and I had great difficulty in recapturing those elusive, vivacious objects. Again, when the pony once suddenly shook its head in disapproval of my tight hold on the bridle, I lost my grip of the reins and almost collapsed to the ground with fright. Just managing to save myself by grabbing the saddle-front, I gradually restored my position from a spread-eagle sprawl to a more or less upright poise. I patted the pony's neck with false nonchalance, took the reins more lightly into my grasp, and uttered up a prayer of thanks—and hope.

That preliminary interlude of equestrian ambling through the streets was a useful period of reprieve from whatever sentence awaited me when we left the crowded city and emerged into the open country beyond. Riding at the tail end of our troop, I had time to make a few mistakes and learn their lessons unobserved by my companions. I became slightly used to my novel seat, teaching myself how to grip my heels clumsily yet securely into the stirrups. Thus I contrived to stay erect until we reached the magnificent wall of the old Tartar City which is Peking's boundary, and passed through a splendid gateway on to the threshold of the plains outside.

Lampson's pony in the lead of our party broke into a trot, and Mary's and Graham's mounts followed suit. Without any instruction from me mine promptly did the same. In all my subsequent political, diplomatic and pro-consular careers I have never received such a shaking as I suffered during the next several minutes, which is saying quite a lot. Bumping uncontrollably up and down, swaying irresponsibly this way and that, and now and then slipping almost over the edge of one of the precipitous slopes yawning on either side of me, I realised that I was helpless. I sat in the lap of a strange, four-footed god who could do whatever he liked with me. The divine little creature was the master of my destiny. Nevertheless, within myself a tiny scrap of obstinate human self-assertion strove to establish a degree of influence, if not control, over events. I nursed a firm resolve to stay on the horse at all costs, and to avoid the humiliation of being hurled to the ground. So I gripped and clung my way through our jolting advances across several hundred yards of ground.

My fellow cavaliers trotted briskly ahead without looking round, and thus fortunately remained unaware of my tribulations. But another audience had now appeared on the scene to witness them. Meandering along the road towards us came parties of peasants with vegetable baskets dangling from their lengthy shoulder poles, troupes of children riding bareback on water-buffaloes with a carefree air which put me to shame, and caravans of camels apparently arriving from the Gobi Desert with merchandise for the city. I had scarcely any eyes for them as they passed, my attention being concentrated on the pony's anatomy just in front of me; but I felt conscious of their astonished stares. I could almost hear the camels, buffaloes and people all guffawing.

Yet, again, that period of trotting violence served a useful purpose. It enabled me to collect my wits and discipline my limbs in the face of danger, to analyse the chief elements in the problem of how to remain upright on a moving horse, and to improvise some possible solutions to my precarious situation.

At one point Lampson glanced round and called to me, "How do you like your pony, Malcolm?"

Fortunately I was posed more or less erect at that moment, and he did not detect my uncomfortable embarrassment.

"It's a nice little animal," I answered appreciatively. And it had indeed treated my defects—of which it must have been painfully aware—with charity, refraining from any action that exposed them to public gaze.

As we progressed into the countryside the land became more open, and the riders and their steeds ahead of me grew friskier. Of a sudden they turned off the road into adjacent fields, and at once increased their pace from a casual trot to a smart canter. In vain I tried to restrain my eager charger from doing likewise. Tugging at the reins in an attempt to explain to it that it should stand still whilst I pulled up my stockings—which had gradually slipped down until they now hung in folds round my ankles—I hoped it would first halt, and then continue along the road at a prudent, dignified walk. My inexpert jerks at the bridle, however, conveyed no coherent message to it, and its colleagues' example was too infectious to be resisted. After one or two impatient, protesting stamps of its feet it took the law into its own hooves, and chased after those others. For a while its pace was a canter, and I rose and fell in the saddle with erratic abandon. Every second I expected to be hurled off sideways, and to crash to China's ancient earth. However, I somehow contrived to maintain a posture near enough to the upright to avoid disaster. In the process I lost all effective grip on the reins, which hung loose from my hands. The pony mistook this for permission to break into a gallop—and suddenly it charged away like a streak of lightning.

For a few moments I thought my last hour had come. Then I suffered one of the most astonishing, pleasant surprises of my life. My body ceased to bump up and down, my legs stopped swinging helplessly to and fro, and I sat unmoving in the saddle as comfortably as if I were lolling on a sofa. The pony's motion was as smooth as it was swift; it raced forwards with as serenely steady an action as that of a wooden horse on a merry-go-round. I felt entirely at ease—and I waved with jocular glee to the Lampson family as I sped past them. The Minister shouted "Tally-ho!" and gave chase with fervent gusto.

I learned later that a Mongolian pony's gallop is as unshaking a movement as that of any animal in the world because of the manner and order in which it then employs its legs. I forget the exact sequence in which it stretches its front and hind limbs in unison; but I am told that their co-ordination differs from that of other breeds of horses, which undulate wildly when they let themselves go at top speed. Nor did I understand this explanation at the time. I simply thought a miracle had happened; and I felt tempted to stand up in imitation of a circus trick-rider on my gallant mount's back, balance on tiptoe and utter yells of triumph.

My fear now was that the pony would stop galloping; so I gave it a few kicks of encouragement. It was delighted, seeming to approve at last of my prowess as a jockey. Careering onwards at a spanking pace, it appeared intent on beating every horse-racing record in the world whilst I sat in thrilled comfort on its back.

In due course, however, it tired, and slowed abruptly to a canter. At once I felt again as if I were sitting in the crater of an active volcano. Earthquakish eruptions kept shaking me up and down and to and fro, almost flinging me like a spew of lava over my vibrating little mountain-side. Nevertheless I managed to cling on until I induced the beast to subside into a leisurely walk. Then I contrived to recover some sort of presentable simulacrum of a cavalryman's poise.

After that I tried to alternate the pony's activities between a very fast gallop and a very slow amble. The obliging animal was not unwilling; and we crossed the plain in successive spasms of those two extremes. We would have appeared unsociable if we had sped in a straight line out of sight of our colleagues, who seemed content to spend much of their time cantering or trotting; so whenever we indulged in a bout of galloping I managed by judicious manipulation of the reins to induce my mount to career in wide circles around them, as if they were a herd of game which I was rounding up. They mistook this antic for a demonstration of ecstatic *joie de vivre*.

At one point we called at the temple where a group of eunuchs had retired. They were old men with bald pates, ivory complexions and high-pitched voices. Delighted at receiving a visit from His Britannic Majesty's Minister, they chattered and laughed merrily. I could not understand a word of what they said, but their venerable faces and antique, courtly manners were in themselves very eloquent of the past. The troupe were faded relics of the countless centuries-old Imperial régime of China during its last erratic, brilliant and yet shattering episode presided over first by the fabulous Empress Dowager Tsu-shi—familiarly called "Old Buddha"

—and then briefly by her successor, the infant Emperor Hsuan T'ung who was later brain-washed by Mao Tse-tung's comrades and became a rather good gardener named Pu Yi.

Afterwards we continued our journey to the Western Hills, and at last arrived at a gate leading into the garden of the Lampsons' country mansion. We were a trifle late, so mine host asked me to excuse him as he leapt from his horse and hastened indoors, explaining that his guests would already have arrived, and that he must go to greet them. Gladly agreeing, I urged Mary and Graham to do the same, for I had no wish to reveal to them my awkward incompetence at dismounting. I sat pretending to take a last look from the eminence of my saddle at the surrounding landscape whilst they agilely descended to earth and followed their parent into the house. It was fortunate that I did so, for when my feet eventually touched the ground my plus-four trousers promptly tumbled down, exposing my nether limbs. Apparently during my vigorous gallivantings across the plain every button attaching the breeches to my braces got broken.

The Chinese servants who came to aid us did not betray a flicker of surprise as they observed me pull my trousers up again, displaying the usually faultless, sometimes enigmatic courtesy of their race.

I had no belt, nor even a piece of string, with which to secure my breeches; so I held them in place with my hands as I walked through the garden and up the front steps into the house. Indoors I was horrified to see half a dozen foreign Ambassadors and their wives lined up in a formal diplomatic row to greet me. Quickly gripping my trouser-tops in place by pressing my elbows tightly against my sides, I bowed to each guest in turn and shook them with a hand that seemed suddenly stricken with palsy. I murmured something about feeling dreadfully stiff after my first ride on horseback for more years than I cared to remember; and then I escaped into a bathroom to wash my face, brush my hair—and adjust my dress.

It was a very pleasant luncheon party. I was surprised to find Lady Lampson there, for she had not accompanied us on our expedition, and I assumed that she was not coming. Then I learned that, since she could not ride, she had motored in leisurely comfort from Peking to the Western Hills. Later that afternoon I returned to the city via the Summer Palace with her —by car.

Anti-Nazi

After further journeys in China that year I returned briefly to Japan, and then sailed across the sea to Vladivostock, where I caught a train and travelled for more than a week along the Trans-Siberian railway to Moscow. Staying only three days in the Soviet capital, I afterwards proceeded by quick stages across Europe to London, home—and the House of Commons. I had recently been elected a Member of Parliament, and my presence was urgently required in the division lobbies of the Palace of Westminster.

Less than two years later my father's second Labour Government abandoned office during the 1931 crisis, he felt compelled to create a National Government in its place, and I became an Under-Secretary of State in the new administration. For the next several years I was kept constantly busy at my Parliamentary and Ministerial duties, with little time for occupations outside politics. The history of that period has begun to be written in numerous scholarly and other volumes, as well as being recorded in multitudinous official documents; so I need not burden the pages of this book with a sketch of its mostly rather sombre events. The defects of the Versailles Treaty signed at the close of the First World War were becoming increasingly obvious, Europe's governments were proving themselves incapable of grappling wisely with the consequential problems which arose, the international situation was therefore beginning to deteriorate, and the possibility of a second World War loomed grimly over the horizon. Developments in Germany in particular were being stirred towards disaster by an ex-lance corporal with a feverish genius akin to madness called Adolf Hitler.

II

Early in the year 1932 the then Chancellor of Germany, Dr. Heinrich Bruning, came to visit my father in England. He stayed for a pleasant but busy week-end with our family at Chequers, the lovely country home of Britain's Prime Ministers. As Winston Churchill wrote later in his book *Great Contemporaries*, Bruning had been "leading Germany back to a high and honoured position in Europe". Some crucially important Ministers in other European lands, however, did not sympathise sufficiently with his efforts to remove the sense of frustration which was urging the German people towards desperate courses; and these insensitive men were tardy in making the diplomatic concessions necessary to satisfy reasonable German national pride. The Government in Berlin was therefore coming under ever stronger pressure from the growing Nazi movement, and Hitler was whipping up that vicious force into a state of fanatical patriotic furore which would in due course win it power, cause Bruning's flight from his homeland, and provoke the series of subsequent tragedies which reached their climax in the Second World War.

At the time of Bruning's visit to Chequers Nazi hostility towards him had already reached a pitch where rumour whispered that his life was in such danger from assassination plots that he never slept in the same house two nights running. He was a man of courage as well as wisdom, and the dangers surrounding him did not deter him from continuing his strenuous efforts to reach political agreements with the French, British and other Governments which might check the mad stumblings towards a new Armageddon. He came to England for those days of personal discussions with my father to see whether they could work out together proposals which would be acceptable to other European statesmen, and which would thus ease the situation.

The visit was promptly denounced by the Nazis as the act of a traitor trying to betray his people to their enemies; and throughout the week-end news items from Germany kept reporting a state of anger which boded ill for Bruning on his return to the Fatherland. His critics evidently intended to undo whatever good might come from his peace mission by contriving his death. But no one would have suspected from his calm, charming manner at Chequers that he was aware of this. His benign, ascetic, intellectual face wore the look of a man without a care in the world. Much of the time he spent discussing Europe's difficult problem with the Prime Minister in his study, but in intervals between their conferences he was ever ready to speak light-heartedly about any other topic under the sun. In strolls through the garden, on country walks and at meal-times he was relaxed, smiling and serene.

Yet rumour kept shouting that immediately on his return to Germany he would be assassinated.

The thought of this fate perhaps awaiting him within twenty-four hours filled my mind as a small party of us dined together on the evening of his departure. After the meal he would leave us. drive to the coast, and catch a boat which would land him in Hamburg the next morning. Thence he would hasten to Berlin to resume his duties as head of the German Government—if his opponents allowed him to survive that far.

Our conversation at the table was lively and cheerful. I sat opposite the Chancellor, and kept glancing at his face to observe any signs of concern at the doom which possibly awaited him. He betrayed no hint of such an idea. On the contrary, every feature of his cultured countenance was tranquil as he joined affably in our talk. Now and then his eyes sparkled with humour at some jesting exchange between himself and my father. I felt aware of his immense reserves of courage and strength.

After dinner he took leave of us, and we waved "Good-bye" to him at the front door. For a long time afterwards we stood there thoughtfully watching the lights of his motor-car as they retreated into a dark, starless night.

I went to bed, marvelling—and wondering what news we should hear of our guest on the morrow.

III

For a few hours next morning no tidings arrived. Perhaps Bruning's ship had not yet completed its voyage across the North Sea. I waited anxiously, unable to concentrate my mind on any other matter. Then a flash item of news tapped out on a ticker-tape announced that he had landed in Hamburg, been received there by a vast, silent, inquisitive crowd of his fellow countrymen, and caught a train at the dockside railway station for his onward journey to Berlin. Some hours later we learnt that he had arrived in the capital, and settled back to work at his desk in the Chancellory.

That was all. No screaming headline proclaimed his murder. The next morning's newspapers carried reports of his going about his business as usual. So that was that! The tales of his impending assassination had apparently been false.

Only several days afterwards did I hear what actually happened in Hamburg. The intelligence came by word of mouth from an eye-witness. He told me that as the boat drew alongside the wharf an enormous, expectant multitude of people awaited its arrival. They stood on the quayside staring at the ship, murmuring as a bevy of policemen held them back from a wide open space where the passengers would land, and from a lane cleared through them along which those travellers would walk to a near-by train. Meanwhile on board the vessel an order had been issued that none of the passengers was to leave its decks until further notice.

Gradually the ship was manoeuvred into position, and a gang-plank was stretched from its side to the shore. For a few moments no one stirred. Then a solitary figure appeared at the top of the gangway—Dr. Bruning, the Chancellor. No private secretary or other official stood near him. It was he who had commanded that neither the members of his staff nor any other voyagers or crew-men should emerge until he had descended the stairway alone, walked across the open space amidst the crowded onlookers, and arrived safely in the carriage reserved for him on the train to Berlin.

Amidst a tense hush, with slow, deliberate, almost nonchalant steps he strolled down the gangway, across the open ground, and along the narrow lane. As he went two attempts were made on his life; but both were thwarted by the extremely alert police. Calmly, at the end of his walk, he climbed on to the train—and then the other passengers were allowed to follow him.

IV

Soon afterwards the notorious pro-Nazi Von Papen ousted Bruning as Chancellor, and before long Bruning fled the country. The sad exile went eventually to the United States, where his distinguished qualities as a scholar gained him a Professorship in an important university. That was thirty-four years ago. Twenty-three years ago Hitler died in most humiliating circumstances amidst the ruins of the Berlin to which he brought destruction. Bruning is still teaching wisdom to the young generation in a university—now back in his own homeland, Germany.

Old Kemp

In 1935 my father resigned from the Premiership, and Stanley Baldwin took his place. I became Secretary of State for the Colonies in the reconstructed Cabinet, and my Ministerial responsibilities were thus weightily increased. They forced me to live and work nearly all the time in London. But I needed to escape periodically to fresh air and rustic scenery, and so—now that I was deprived of the pleasure of spending occasional week-ends at Chequers—I bought a country home.

It was a charming, small half-timbered Elizabethan manor house in Essex called Hyde Hall. The dwelling had scarcely changed in appearance since it was built about the year 1600. With it I also acquired a number of associated buildings and amenities, such as an even more ancient tithe-barn that was one of England's recognised historical monuments, an antique coachman's cottage and stables, a Tudor walled garden, the remains of a moat surrounding the pleasance, and other assets. They were all attractive features—but the most pleasing acquisition of them all was Old Kemp.

In spite of the adjective attached to his surname he was the youngest relic about the place. All those other items were several hundred years old, whereas he had not yet quite attained his first century. He could not remember the exact year of his birth, but he had certainly survived nearer ninety than eighty summers. I secured him with the rest of the property as its gardener.

His head had a wonderfully hoary yet gracious look. Except for a few wispish locks of white hair sparsely brushed across his pate, he was bald. In front of each ear, however, long silvery whiskers sprouted, and these stretched continuously in a wide fringe all down his cheeks and round his jaw, leaving his upper lip and chin clean-shaven. They appeared rather like a halo which had slipped from its proper position above his head until it framed instead the lower half of his countenance. His other features were also distinguished—a high wrinkled brow, a hawklike beak of a nose, a well-chiselled, thin-lipped mouth, and sage, gently twinkling eyes.

Out of doors he always wore a dilapidated straw hat, an un-buttoned waistcoat over a collarless shirt, and long baggy trousers. Often he carried a huge scythe for cutting grass in the garden and orchard. He could never be persuaded to use a lawn-mower, for he spurned such new-fangled mechanical contrivances, retaining his confidence in more old-fashioned tools which he had used con-sistently throughout the last seventy years. And when he sheared a stretch of grass with his scythe it became indeed as perfectly close-cropped as any sophisticated mower could achieve.

Armed with that long-handled, scimitar-bladed weapon he looked like Father Time wandering about the grounds. Often as I sat working in my study I could see him through an open window cutting a lawn with great sweeps of his formidable implement. As he approached step by step towards me I pretended that he really was Father Time come to claim me in the summer sunshine, determined to cut short my life in its own summer time. When he arrived just outside the window and—instead of slicing the ground from under my feet—halted, touched his hat respectfully, gave a broad grin, and passed some genial remark about the weather, I heaved a mock sigh of relief. Taking a snuff-box from his pocket, he would inhale some grains of its contents up his nostrils. Then he picked up a smooth stone, sharpened his scythe blade on it, and after a few moments' gossip retreated to resume his labours. I felt like a prisoner in a condemned cell who had just been re-prieved from a sentence of death.

Always he spared my life like that at the last moment—and now (as I write this note thirty years later) he himself has lain buried in his grave for a quarter of a century whilst I still remain alive and kicking. I hope to outlive him by as long again, and so to attain eventually the same august age as he achieved—provided that, like him, I preserve my principal faculties to the end.

His powers of sight, hearing and speech stayed unimpaired until his dying day. So did his sense of good taste, if an endless capacity to enjoy a pint of beer is a proper claim to that virtue. Every evening after work he trudged to the local pub in the nearest village about a mile away to indulge in his favourite refreshment. As he sat there gossiping with younger cronies—mere youths aged three-score years and ten—he interspersed gulps of ale down his throat with pinches of snuff up his nose.

Whenever he came for a chat with me in Hyde Hall he drank a tankard of beer. I wish he were still alive so that I could sit again quaffing stout, taking snuff, and talking with him. I would ask him many questions about his long, almost static and yet far from monotonous life; and then I would write his biography. I am inclined to think its contents would be more significant—and certainly more entertaining—than those of some of the autobiographies of eminent statesmen, diplomats, soldiers and other self-appointed heroes who inflict their memoirs on the reading public.

II

Old Kemp had worked on the farm which was previously attached to Hyde Hall for more than seventy years. He told me that his wage for full-time labour in the 1850s was sixpence a week.

One of his most vivid, haunting memories of those days, which he often recounted at eloquent length, concerned the morning when his master ordered him to drive the first mechanical vehicle which was ever imported into those Essex fields for reaping or binding or performing some other agricultural function. The machine appeared to him like a prehistoric monster, or some awful invention of the Devil. He could manage hoes, rakes, scythes, horses and other similarly tame creatures with expert skill, but he was scared by this new, complicated, wild creation. Commanded to climb on it, sit in its high seat, and propel it by turning some sort of metal handle, he obeyed—but felt terrified of losing his balance as it trundled forwards, of tumbling into its gruesome metal anatomy yawning below him, and of being slashed to pieces by its revolving knives. He never really recovered from that first frightened prejudice against even the simplest modern machinery, and this was the reason why to the end of his days he obstinately used more traditional implements like picks, shovels and scythes. He was a master of such arts as hoeing, planting, harvesting and thatching. Indeed, he was probably the champion thatcher in the whole of Essex. I never enjoyed watching a workman display his ability at a skilled job more than I did when Old Kemp, at the age of over eighty, climbed a ladder on to the vast roof of my historic tithe-barn, balanced precariously there, and proceeded hour after hour and day after day to re-thatch it from end to end. When he finally descended, the building looked like a palace for bucolic royalty.

Throughout his life he only once travelled more than a few miles beyond his birthplace, a village called Great Waltham near Hyde Hall. That unique occasion was when he journeyed about fifty miles to London to join in the celebrations attending Queen Victoria's Golden Jubilee. The experience cured him of any inclination to repeat it. The noise and bustle of the multitudinous city so appalled him that he escaped from it as quickly as possible, swearing that he would never return there—an oath which he faithfully kept. With complete content he stayed amidst the group of small hamlets which were his home in rustic Essex, with no higher ambition than to work from early morning until late afternoon every day cultivating the crops of his native soil—followed each evening by a glass of beer in the local pub.

Nevertheless, he did not confine his creative activities to the production of vegetables, corns and fruits. As a young man he fell in love with a village girl, married her, and by her sired a family of twenty-one children. No doubt exhausted by her share in that effort, she died before I knew him; and he now lived with his eldest, slightly dottled daughter in a tiny cottage a stone's throw from the Hall. His grandchildren were legion, and his great-grandchildren had also begun to sprout. When he and his troupe of descendants strolled along the road to church on a Sunday morning they composed almost an entire congregation by themselves.

III

Countless friends of various types came to stay with me for weekends at Hyde Hall. They included politicians, authors, actors and actresses, workmen, diplomats, and all manner of other exalted or humble beings.

Two of my frequent guests were the artists, Gilbert and Stanley Spencer. Like his more famous brother, Gilbert was a sensitive draughtsman with a genius for pencilling good portraits. And since no nobler head than the one stuck on Old Kemp's shoulders existed anywhere in England, we persuaded its owner to sit for a sketch by Gilbert.

Through two successive mornings from breakfast time until lunch he posed patiently, sitting upright in a Windsor armchair even more antique than himself. Handy on each side of him stood a small table, one of them bearing half a dozen bottles of beer, and the other a silver box full of snuff. These two commodities were to keep him tranquil throughout the long sessions.

He never uttered a word whilst Gilbert painstakingly created a delicate, characterful, magnificent drawing of his glorious head and shoulders. Hour after hour he sat motionless except for slight movements now and then to gulp a mouthful of booze or inhale a pinch of snuff. Sometimes I went to watch the proceedings. Kemp himself could not view what was going on, for Gilbert's drawing-board stood propped between them, and all the model saw was the artist's face periodically peering earnestly at him round its edges.

At last the picture was finished; and the two men rose from their seats. So far Old Kemp had not looked at the sketch at all, content to wait until it was complete. Now he glanced interestedly at it as Gilbert held it up for his inspection.

The grand octogenarian nodded in approval. "I'd like six copies o' that for keeps," he said.

The request was at first mystifying. How could Gilbert be expected to make another half-dozen identical portraits? On enquiry, however, we discovered that the old man did not realise that the picture was devised by the technique of drawing; he thought the artist had spent a few hours of the last two mornings taking a photograph of him! Many years earlier he had heard of a wonderful new invention called a camera by which portraits of people were made. He had never seen any of the results, and so had no notion what they would look like. Therefore he assumed that Gilbert's drawing-board and other gadgets which faced him during those days were a camera taking a snapshot of him by tedious, miraculous processes. And he had been told that such pictures could easily be reproduced by strange devices in a dark room—hence his request for several copies of the portrait.

I hung the drawing in a place of honour on a wall at Hyde Hall, where many people admired it. They liked its vivid representation of Kemp's handsome face, which was rather reminiscent of that of another Grand Old Man—William Ewart Gladstone. Nor were they surprised to see scrawled beneath it the signature of the distinguished draughtsman Gilbert Spencer.

One individual, however, was surprised and perplexed to see that scribble. He was one of Kemp's schoolboy grandsons. Wandering through my rooms one day when he was on holiday, he saw the portrait and stopped to gaze appreciatively at it. After a while the look of pleasure on his face changed to one of disappointment.

He turned dejectedly to me.

"At first I thought that was a picture o' my Grandpa," he said.

"It *is* a picture of your Grandpa," I assured him.

"But it says it's a picture o' Mr. Gilbert Spencer," he remarked, pointing to the signature.

When I explained to him the significance of that scrawl his face beamed with happiness again.

IV

I always introduced my house-guests to Old Kemp, so that he should have the pleasure of meeting them and they would become acquainted with this sample of what was best in still lingering yeoman England. Completely un-shy and natural, he engaged Presidents, Prime Ministers and other illustrious men and women in interesting, racy conversations. His remarks on life and affairs were often shrewd, and sometimes enlightening. For example, during an Imperial Conference in London the leaders of its various delegations from overseas Dominions came in turn to stay with me for successive half-working, half-relaxing week-ends. Each Saturday morning I led a new statesman or group of states-men into the garden to greet my venerable retainer. One day Mr. Joseph Lyons, the Premier of Australia, and Mr. Robert Menzies, who was then his Attorney-General, strolled with their wives into the orchard to be introduced to Old Kemp. He was gathering apples at the time.

"Kemp," I said as Joe Lyons shook his horny hand, "this is another Prime Minister come to see you. He and his friends have come all the way from Australia to visit us."

"Ah!" commented the aged gardener as he nodded his head sagely, "I know where Australia is."

"Do you?" exclaimed Lyons, rather surprised. "Where is it?"

"Well sir," Kemp replied as he raised an arm and pointed across the fields in a certain direction, as if he were guiding an enquiring stranger to a desired near-by destination, "if ye go to Pleshey"—a hamlet two miles from where we stood—"and dig a hole in the ground there, and go on diggin' long enough, ye'll come out in Australia."

I then introduced him to Mrs. Lyons. Knowing the two Lyonses' justifiable pride in the considerable number of their offspring, I said to Old Kemp, "Ask her how many children she's got."

He looked at her interestedly, and enquired, "How many?"

"Fourteen," she answered with obvious satisfaction.

I was horrified to see my gardener shake his head disparagingly, and to hear him observe, "That ain't many. I've got twenty-one."

"Oh, Mr. Kemp, I don't think I've done too badly," retorted Mrs. Lyons genially. "People laugh at me for having so many."

He looked at her more sympathetically, and remarked, "Then ye just laugh back at them—and 'ave number fifteen."

Joe Lyons chuckled, but commented, "No; we're stopping. We won't produce any more."

At that Old Kemp scrutinised Mrs. Lyons's figure appraisingly and said in a tone of authority, "Ah yes, I see. She's finished!"

Everyone laughed, and nobody more heartily than the target for that slightly barbed shaft.

V

Naturally Old Kemp knew I was a member of the Government in London. He comprehended too that I sat in its inner councils as a Cabinet Minister, although he would not have been able to define the exact status or duties of such a functionary. He could neither read nor write, and so was unable to scan the newspapers himself. Snippets of information about me published in them were often read aloud to him by younger members of his family who had received the advantage of an elementary schooling; for the rest he gained his intelligence of what was happening in the wider world beyond Great Waltham, Pleshey and other surrounding villages during gossips with his cronies over mugs of beer in the local public house. Daily they congregated there and discussed every topic of interest to them under the sun, including sometimes the odd activities of us Ministers in London.

Kemp was usually therefore quite well informed on public affairs when I arrived at week-ends for a brief respite from duty in Whitehall. As he and I chatted in the garden he would ask me many questions about current political problems, for the greater enlightenment of himself and his friends; and in return I would seek from him the latest news about various rural events for the improvement of my own knowledge. Although he was illiterate, he possessed much wisdom on matters of elemental importance in the everyday life of the agricultural labourers of Essex, who were just as vital members of the human race as any of us highfalutin politicians in the Palace of Westminster.

I must admit, however, that the information which he received on political matters from his fellow gossips in the pub was not always entirely accurate. A memorable example of that occurred on the occasion of the abdication of His Majesty King Edward the Eighth. I happened to be one of the members of the Cabinet most closely concerned with every stage of that crisis, because I was at the time Secretary of State for Dominion Affairs. For three consecutive week-ends the crisis prevented me from getting to Hyde Hall; but on the first Saturday after its close I motored there. Old Kemp was cutting the long grass round the barn when I arrived; and I went to greet him.

He stopped work, looked up, and grinned with pleasure at my approach.

Touching his hat respectfully he said, "Welcome 'ome, sir! We ain't seen ye for quite a while."

"No; I've been kept very busy in London," I remarked.

He chuckled and observed, "I know what ye've been doin'. My friends 'ave been followin' ye in the newspapers, and kept telling me what ye was up to whilst the King was carryin' on with that there Miss Simpson."

Miss Simpson! My foot!

The old boy—and his cronies too, if he quoted them correctly—had misunderstood the whole reason for His Majesty's abdication.

Abdication

Mention of the Abdication reminds me of an incident which occurred towards the end of the crisis. As I have written, I was continuously concerned in that searing episode throughout its course. I can best explain the nature of my involvement as Secretary of State for Dominion Affairs by recounting an exchange which took place in the first official discussion on the subject among a group of Ministers. One afternoon Stanley Baldwin, the Prime Minister, summoned half a dozen of us to his private room in Parliament to tell us about a conversation he had just held with the King. He reported that he had felt it necessary to raise informally with His Majesty the question of his relations with Mrs. Simpson since this was becoming a matter of increasingly dangerous semi-public speculation. He said that the King responded with friendly candour to his approach, and that an important talk between them took place. After recounting various details of it Baldwin told us that he had advised His Majesty that there were three possible solutions to the problem—and he recited to us those alternative proposals which he had mentioned in the dialogue at Buckingham Palace.

When he finished speaking I remarked, "I'm afraid you're not in a position to offer the King decisive advice on this question."

"Why not?" asked Baldwin. "Surely I must do so as Prime Minister? Of course, I'll consult your colleagues at every stage of the business."

"You're no longer the King's only Prime Minister," I answered. "His Prime Ministers of Canada, Australia and other independent nations in the British Commonwealth are just as much concerned in this problem as you; and each one of them has an equal right and duty to offer His Majesty counsel on it."

Baldwin looked a trifle surprised and shocked; but he accepted my statement as correct. The fact was that the new concept of "a Commonwealth of free and equal Nations" evolving from the old Colonial Empire was still very young in those days; and the Abdication crisis was, indeed, the first supremely important occasion when this Commonwealth's unwritten constitution required that its Monarch should act on the advice not only of one Prime Minister, but of his then group of six.

From that moment onwards throughout the next dozen exacting, uncertain days I was kept almost continuously busy, morning, noon and night, communicating urgently with the overseas Premiers in Canada, Australia, New Zealand, South Africa and Eire on every significant major and minor development touching the King's position and plans. I need not describe here the series of interesting, and sometimes dramatic, situations which arose during those sad, convulsive days when the Crown which commanded the affectionate loyalty of the British people, and which now also united a world-wide Commonwealth of Nations, seemed to be in jeopardy. My efforts as a liaison between the King in Buckingham Palace, his British Prime Minister in Downing Street, and the five other Prime Ministers scattered round the world were of crucial importance because it was vital that all those individuals should reach quickly, spontaneously and unanimously the same conclusion about the constitutional solution to the problem. But here I shall merely mention an event which occurred late one night towards our ultimate achievement of that aim.

By then the crisis had persisted for about ten days. It was occupying so much of the time of Ministers in London, and causing such mental and emotional stress among the British public, that all the rest of the nation's business was in danger of being neglected. Nothing was more desirable than that an early solution should be reached. Nevertheless, all His Majesty's Ministers appreciated that his personal dilemma in having to make a choice between either forgoing his love or abdicating his throne was so heartrending that they did not wish to hasten him unduly into his fateful decision. One afternoon, therefore, when the delay was beginning to cause critical comment, Neville Chamberlain, John Simon and I prepared a draft statement which Baldwin might make in Parliament within the next twenty-four hours, to hold the position for another two or three days whilst King Edward was finally making up his mind. It said that the uncertain situation must not be allowed to continue much longer since this would involve a risk of grave injury to national and Imperial interests, but that His Majesty's delicate position was understood by his subjects throughout the Commonwealth—who all felt affectionate sympathy for him—and that they wished him to have a few more days in which to reach his decision. It added that the King agreed that an early conclusion was desirable.

Baldwin approved of our suggestion, and concurred that I should telegraph the text of the proposed statement to the overseas Prime Ministers for their information. He also, of course, accepted that before I sent it to them I should submit it to His Majesty himself, to ensure that he felt satisfied with its contents.

I took the draft to the able and wise Sir Walter Monckton who, as a close confidant of both parties, was acting as an informal personal contact between the Cabinet and the Monarch. I told him that, provided His Majesty consented, I should like to telegraph it that evening to the Commonwealth Prime Ministers. Monckton answered that he would show the text as soon as possible to the King in Fort Belvedere, the country house where he was staying. He promised to telephone me at my home in Hampstead within a few hours, to give me our Royal Master's reply.

At about ten o'clock that night he phoned to say that His Majesty approved the proposed statement. I thanked him. As it happened, I had in the meantime decided for a minor technical reason not to send the message to the Dominions at once, but to wait until dawn the next day. However, I did not bother Monckton with that detail. We chatted for a short while about the situation, and then rang off.

I was busy dealing with various other Commonwealth problems

which needed urgent attention, and stayed working at these until nearly two o'clock in the morning. Then I went to my bedroom, undressed, and stepped into a bath for a relaxed soak before retiring to sleep. After a succession of full days and half-nights of ceaseless toil I felt so exhausted that I lay lazily unstirring for a long time in the soothing tub.

Suddenly a telephone began to ring. I felt irritated at this interruption breaking the peaceful silence of the night, and tried to ignore it. Everyone else in the house was evidently asleep, for the bell continued tinkling insistently; but I did my best to blot its sound from my consciousness by sinking like a hippopotamus into the bath's depths. Unfortunately, however, the telephone's bell-box happened to be fixed immediately below the floor of my bathroom, so its monotonous summons maintained a damp, subdued clanging noise in my drowned ears. Nevertheless, feeling rebellious, I stayed submerged with only my nose protruding above the water; and after a while the sounds stopped as suddenly as they had begun.

Relieved, I re-surfaced, and resumed my inert lazing. Half a minute later the telephone started to ring again.

Once more I responded by sinking into the deep. Through the water I could hear the obstinate buzzing, but I pretended to be deaf to its yells. Guessing that the persistent caller was some busybody newspaper reporter trying to interview me about this or that aspect of the constitutional crisis, I saw no reason why I should satisfy his curiosity. Indeed, I thought it extremely unreasonable to disturb me in the small hours of the morning; and with a sense of self-righteous propriety I continued to defy the requests.

After a few minutes the tintinnabulation once again ceased, and I resumed my comfortable soaking. I began to think of mobilising my energy to rise from the bath, dry myself, and tumble into bed.

Then the telephone bell began to shriek again.

At last I pulled myself together, saying to myself that I was behaving disgracefully. Was I not a responsible Minister of the Crown holding a particularly important post in the middle of an unprecedented national crisis? The telephone was clearly calling me to perform some compelling duty—and I was behaving like a silly, sulky child in refusing to answer its urgent summons.

I jumped hurriedly out of the bath, wrapped a dressing-gown round my body without making any attempt to dry myself, and ran downstairs two steps at a time to answer the phone.

Picking up the receiver I exclaimed "Hallo!" in as innocent a tone as I could muster.

Walter Monckton's voice answered, "Oh, Malcolm, have you sent that message to the Dominion Prime Ministers yet?"

"No, as a matter of fact I haven't," I remarked. "I decided to wait until the morning."

"Good!" commented Monckton. "His Majesty would like to suggest an amendment."

"Really? What does he want to suggest?" I enquired.

The bath-water dripping from my body made an ever widening pool on the floor as Monckton read me King Edward's proposition. He desired that, after the phrases declaring that the present state of uncertainty must not be allowed to continue much longer since this would involve the risk of grave injury to national and Imperial interests, the sentence about the King's concurrence with that view should be strengthened to say, "No one is more insistent upon this aspect of the situation than His Majesty."

I told Monckton that I thought the amendment a very good one.

"Do you really think so?" he asked.

"Yes," I replied, "because it's an improvement from His Majesty's own point of view. It shows how conscientiously he cares about the public interest in the midst of all his deep private concern."

"Then will you please consult your colleagues, and seek their agreement to it?"

"No," I answered. "I'll accept it for them here and now."

"Hang on," observed Monckton, "while I tell King Edward."

I heard him exchange a few words with someone else in the room at the other end of the line.

Then his voice sounded again on the telephone. "Hold on," it said, "His Majesty would like to speak to you."

I wrapped my now soaking dressing-gown more tightly round me as I awaited the Sovereign—and then I heard King Edward say, "Hallo, Malcolm."

"Hallo, Your Majesty," I replied.

"D'you really think my suggestion's a good one?"

"Yes; it emphasises your own considerate attitude, and shows we're all acting together."

"I'm very glad," commented the King. "And you think Baldwin and your other colleagues will agree?"

"Yes; they'll be pleased."

"Good!" he said. "How are you?"

I did not tell him that I was feeling unusually wet and beginning to shiver with cold, but asserted instead that I felt in the best of health.

He thanked me charmingly for my conduct of all the exchanges with the Commonwealth Prime Ministers, saying that these had been very helpful to him. For a few minutes we chatted genially about nothing in particular, and then he closed the conversation by saying, "Good night!"

"Good night, Sire!" I responded.

I heard him put down the telephone receiver, and I did the same myself.

I relate this incident because I am inclined to think it was the only occasion in Britain's long and glorious history when a King was formally advised on high State affairs by one of his Ministers standing stark-naked except for a dressing-gown thrown loosely round his person whilst his feet splashed in a puddle of bath-water dripping from his sopping-wet body. And I doubt whether that particular scrap of history will ever repeat itself.

Footlights

The reader will have recognised that, through no fault or merit of my own, I became a Cabinet Minister at a rather precocious age. I was thirty-three years old when Stanley Baldwin appointed me Secretary of State for the Colonies in his Government of 1935. The post was offered to me for two reasons: first because I happened to be the son of the retiring Prime Minister whom political leaders in the Administration wished to please by this kindly if rash act, and second because I was one of a small group of National Labour Members in the House of Commons whose representatives in Ministries were all too few, and of whom I was therefore a convenient delegate.

So in my middle thirties—when most young men are otherwise engaged morning, noon and half the night—I found myself working ceaselessly from crack of dawn until eleven p.m. each day at my Ministerial and Parliamentary duties. There was no let-up during those sixteen or seventeen hours, for a constant succession of difficult national and international problems plagued those who occupied responsible Government positions at the time. Indeed, our tasks were so continuous and unavoidable that they overflowed into every week-end, when I had to dispose of five days' arrears of the less important office files before another week's fresh avalanche descended on me. As for holidays, they scarcely existed for us Members of the Cabinet. Throughout Easter, Christmas and similar seasons official telegrams, minutes and other documents kept pouring in on us, demanding our urgent attention. The years from 1935 onwards were filled with hectic, historic events.

I thus had little or no time during the normal waking hours to amuse myself with recreations, divert myself with hobbies, or refresh myself in the company of private friends. I was forced either to deny myself those pleasures altogether, or else to enjoy them between midnight and cock-crow. I chose the latter course.

During the era of the 1920s and 1930s, between the two shattering calamities of the First and the Second World Wars, a spirit of carefree gaiety and even frivolity animated many social circles in Britain, in spite of people's growing concern about some of the formidable events which were reshaping human affairs. Inside Britain Socialism, long conceived, was being born by the Acts of the earliest Labour Governments; in Europe the vicious power of the German Nazi movement was preparing the way first for reactionary and afterwards for revolutionary developments across the Continent; and in Asia, Africa and elsewhere the far-flung British Empire—on which the sun was supposed never to set—was moving inexorably towards its sunset and night, to be followed by the new dawn of a Commonwealth of Nations.

Perhaps partly from an escapist instinct, sober contemplation of these prospects by the then young generation was mixed with a mood of light-hearted fun; and as far as my duties permitted I entered into this spirit of the times.

My last working engagement in the evenings was usually the daily session of the House of Commons. Sometimes it did not actually finish on the same day, but continued as an all-night sitting until breakfast time the next morning. Customarily, however, it closed an hour before midnight, although on occasions when some particularly inquisitive, argumentative or self-assertive M.P. moved a motion on the adjournment it persisted for yet another half-hour. Then at last the debate ended, Mr. Speaker left the chair, and attendants tramped through the precincts of Parliament calling aloud the time-honoured query, "Who goes home?" Most Members promptly took action which responded to that question in the affirmative—but I did not. Instead of going home, as the lights were extinguished on the great national stage where I was a performer I stepped into my car and drove to see actors and actresses still playing on other stages. These were in the theatres on Shaftesbury Avenue, in the Haymarket, along the Strand to

Drury Lane, and at other centres of the professional dramatic art. Their footlights had not yet been switched off, and their final curtains had not rung down. I arrived in time to watch the last scene of the final act in whatever playhouse I had chosen for the night. But I did not slip into a seat in the stalls, the pit or a circle; instead I walked through the stage-door and up the backstairs to the dressing-room of whichever celebrated star I was to visit that evening. All the porters at every entrance knew me when I arrived, and nodded with a welcoming smile as they asked a question or made some comment on the latest political crisis or scandal. They always failed to secure any revealing answer from me; for the time being my mind was closed to politics, although I was ready to discuss any other topic under the sun or moon. They did not mind, for a charmingly tolerant camaraderie inspired all of us associated with the theatre in those days.

I climbed the stairs to the dressing-room which was to be my first port of call. Usually it was Beatrice Lillie's or Dorothy Dickson's or Ivor Novello's. I knocked on the door, and some familiar voice answered, "Come in." Turning the handle, I stepped into that other world where I periodically escaped for a few hours from the important and exciting but too demanding slavery of statescraft.

Often my host or hostess was putting finishing touches to his or her make-up for a final appearance in their current play; and they gossiped spasmodically with me between applications of grease-paint or powder on their faces as they gazed appraisingly at themselves in a mirror. Usually three or four other people were sitting in the room—admirers hoping to secure autographs, devotees expressing their sloppy sentiments towards the room's occupant, or friends awaiting the curtain's ultimate fall, when those of us who were privileged with an invitation would accompany the actor or actress to whatever theatrical supper party was taking place that evening.

Always the stage stars turned half the night into day. They ate dinner not before but after their evening's work in the glare of the footlights, which meant that they dined around midnight. After the meal they sat and chatted for another two or three hours whilst digesting their food and drink before going to bed—and next morning they slept until almost lunch-time. I, on the other hand, had to wake at sunrise, swallow breakfast at eight o'clock, and be in my Whitehall office before Big Ben chimed nine. However, that did not matter; I was young and overflowing with energy in those years.

Sometimes the theatrical celebrities' parties were small and select, consisting of perhaps half a dozen intimate friends; at other times they were large though equally select, numbering a score or two of vivacious individuals. Usually the gathering took place in one of their homes; on other occasions we feasted and frolicked in a night-club. The conversation at those gatherings was always witty and intelligent, and often wise. The drama itself, various other arts, politics, famous personages, love and hate, peace and war, and countless similar intriguing topics were discussed with uninhibited vigour. Many of the participants were experienced and shrewd critics in all those affairs. Among my companions who were frequent attenders, in addition to the group whom I have already mentioned, were Sybil Thorndike and her husband Lewis Casson, Laurence Olivier and Vivien Leigh (then enjoying a perpetual honeymoon together), Noel Coward, Zena Dare, Gwen Ffrangcon-Davies, Emlyn Williams, Edith Evans, John Gielgud, the producer Charles B. Cochran and other leading theatrical personalities. For beauty, brains and character no more sparkling company existed anywhere, and in bestowing sincere friendship they had no superiors. Partly because of their artistically emotional temperaments, and partly perhaps because of the extrovert natures stimulated in them by the glare of the footlights in which they basked, they gave their affection very generously. Many of them were prepared to take any risk, to suffer any sacrifice, and if necessary to lay down their lives for people whom they loved. Their customary form of address to an acquaintance was "Darling," which sometimes represented nothing more than a mere formality, but which often also sprang spontaneously from their hearts.

II

My dearest friend among them was Dorothy Dickson. She was a goddess-like female of gracious personality and breathtaking beauty. It was not surprising that I felt her magnetic charm, for many other men did the same. For instance, at about that time a certain Royal Wedding took place in London with splendid pomp and ceremony, and leading citizens from all over Britain concentrated in the capital to join in the celebrations. Among them came six aristocratic playboys who dined together in a "stag" party on the evening preceding the great event. As they sipped liqueurs and puffed cigars after dinner they decided to play a game. Each one was to act the part of Paris choosing his favourite divine Beauty Queen. Each would scribble on a piece of paper the names, in order of precedence, of the three contemporary members of the fair sex in the British Isles whom he considered the most gorgeously beautiful; and afterwards they would compare their notes. I was told later that when they read their judgements they discovered that the name of Dorothy Dickson headed five out of the six lists. I do not recall who topped her in one of the catalogues, where she was relegated to second place.

Her gifts were many and varied. Among the actresses on the musical comedy stage she was unsurpassed: her appearance was always as lovely as could be, and her singing, dancing and performing were immense box-office attractions. Moreover, her mind was as pleasing as her body. A zealous devotee of the arts, she possessed excellent taste and creditable knowledge of literature, music and painting. She was also endowed with a playful sense of fun. A racy conversationalist, accomplished in both small talk and bigger talk, her commentaries on affairs were invariably graced not only with wit and shrewdness, but also with sincerity. That latter virtue sprang largely from the spiritual side of her nature, for she was a devout member of an earnest Christian sect.

When I first met her she was acting as leading lady in Ivor

Novello's successful musical comedy, *The Crest of the Wave*.
I went to see it no less than fourteen times. Nor were my visits to
the play confined to its run in London; when it went on tour
through the provinces I chased after it and its principal girl in
Brighton, Manchester and Glasgow. Dorothy's popularity with
audiences made me feel proud as well as happy, and this reinforced
my own devotion to her. It was thrilling to watch her sing in her
sweet, slightly husky voice on a glittering stage some sentimental
love song as she threw smiling glances in the direction of the seat
in the auditorium where I sat, or to see her perform some graceful
ballroom dance and to know that an hour or two later my arm
would be round her waist as we stepped the very same capers at a
party in a night-club. She was as lovely a combination of body,
mind and spirit in the form of Woman as has existed in our generation.

III

One of our great friends was the inimitable Beatrice Lillie. In
both Britain and America she was hailed as the most merrily
twinkling star in the whole of the Western theatrical firmament. Her genius was unique. Admittedly it stayed confined
within a narrow sphere—that of gay, naughty, mocking and yet
sometimes heart-stirring comedy—but in this field she attained
perfection.

    In private life she was a charming, unaffected and dazzling
personality, always radiating vivacious friendliness. I first met her
late one evening when Dorothy took me to stay a night with her
in her home on the edge of London. She lived in a dower house
of Osterley Park, the stately mansion surrounded by spacious
grounds which is one of Robert Adam's most famous creations.
The dower house was an idyllic place—a small and gracious
dwelling with something of the air of a "Petit Trianon,"
standing on a wide lawn sloping gently to a lake margined by
weeping willows and smiling flowers. The place was so peaceful

that it might have been situated a thousand miles from London instead of only a stone's throw away.

Dorothy and I arrived there soon after midnight. I had fetched her at the theatre where she was currently playing as soon as I escaped from the House of Commons; and we motored out to Osterley. Bea Lillie was not performing in any show at the time, so she was at home to welcome us. When we rang the front-door bell she opened it herself clad in chic dressing-gown, nightdress and bedroom slippers.

"Come in, you belated revellers," she said.

Dorothy introduced me to her.

"Well, well!" our hostess exclaimed. "This is a great honour and pleasure. I've read all about you in the newspapers."

"Not half the honour and pleasure it is for me. I've read a hundred times more about you than you have about me," I answered.

She led us into an elegant drawing-room where a butler brought us sandwiches and drinks. After we had been chatting frivolously for five minutes Bea suddenly turned to me and exclaimed, "Oh Malcolm, I forgot to tell you; the Prime Minister wants to speak to you on the telephone."

Knowing the delight Bea took in practical jokes, Dorothy treated the remark with sceptical laughter.

However, Bea vowed that it was true: about an hour earlier a secretary of Neville Chamberlain (who had succeeded Baldwin as Premier) had phoned from 10 Downing Street to enquire for me. When Bea—astonished—replied that she was expecting me, but that I had not yet arrived, he answered that the Prime Minister wished to talk with me urgently—so would she please ask me to ring him as soon as possible?

I was not surprised. A serious crisis had arisen in Palestine, then a Mandated Territory for which Britain was responsible to the League of Nations as the administering power, and for which I was responsible to the British Government as Secretary of State for the Colonies.

Bea led me into a study where I could hold a private telephone conversation with my chief in Downing Street. When the Prime

Minister came on the line I learnt that I was correct in supposing he wished to speak to me about Palestine. He asked for my opinion on an important telegram which had arrived from our High Commissioner in Jerusalem that afternoon, and we discussed the question insofar as we discreetly could over the phone. Chamberlain said he was anxious to get my views at once so that he could sleep on the problem and then talk with me further the next morning. In the course of our conversation we agreed that we should send a reply to the High Commissioner before lunch on the morrow. I told him that I planned to be in the Colonial Office by half past eight in the morning preparing a draft for his and our Ministerial colleagues' consideration; but I added that I would come to Whitehall even earlier if this would be more convenient to him. He consulted his list of engagements, and we decided to meet for a preliminary look at my draft on the stroke of nine o'clock.

At the beginning of this rather protracted discussion I sat alone in the room; but after a few minutes I became aware of soft footsteps creeping across the floor behind me. Then, whilst I listened intently with one ear to a long statement of opinion by Chamberlain, I heard Bea whisper into my other ear, "Is the connection working all right?" Without turning round I held out a hand with its thumb stuck upright in a gesture indicating that everything was proceeding satisfactorily. A moment later I felt a pair of arms insinuate themselves across my shoulders, fold themselves round my neck, and hug me tight.

Bea's voice murmured, "I think you're an excellent Secretary of State. Tell the Prime Minister so from me." Her tone was exaggeratedly roguish in a play-acting sort of way.

I could hardly restrain myself from laughing aloud. Chamberlain would have been surprised at such a response to the solemn remarks which he happened to be making at the moment. But I did not move a muscle, having to concentrate my mind on what he was saying. After a few moments Bea observed in a stage whisper, "Oh, you're so calm and sage!"

I turned my head, smiled at her, and held an upraised finger against my lips to enjoin silence.

She chortled mischievously and said, slightly more loudly than before, "Tell the Prime Minister I think you're a poppet."

I covered the mouth of the telephone with one hand so that my leader would not hear what was going on at our end of the line; and I gave a snort of mirth.

Bea feigned astonishment, and asked banteringly, "What joke did Mr. Chamberlain make?"

A moment later he finished his comments, and I removed my fist from the phone's mouthpiece to answer him. As I did so Bea nestled her cheek against mine and remarked in a facetious tone just loud enough not to reach the Premier's ears, but as if she intended him to overhear, "Malcolm darling, you're so wise, wise, wise and so nice, nice, nice."

Whilst continuing to talk to my chief I blew her a silent kiss.

"You shouldn't do that to Neville," she retorted in a teasing voice.

I finished my current comments to the Prime Minister, who promptly took up the conversation again at his end of the line.

Bea pretended to become impatient, and muttered into my unattached ear, "Don't you politicians ever stop talking? Are you going on all night? You're neglecting Dorothy and me." And she gave me another hug as she whispered almost right into the phone, "You're a very charming man, and I'm very fond of you."

My freedom of manoeuvre was restricted, for I had to cling with one hand to the telephone to keep its receiver pressed against one ear so that I should not miss a word of what Chamberlain was saying, and prudence as well as chivalry forbade me to give Bea even the gentlest slap with my other hand lest she should utter a play-acting scream which would echo all the way to the halls of Downing Street. However, I felt confidence in the skill of her theatrical elocution, which was evidently such that she could pitch her voice at just the right strength to alarm her actual audience sitting beside her without its being conveyed along the wires to her potential audience at the other end.

Throughout my discussion on important affairs of State she

continued her flippant charade. It was a brilliant little performance which even the great Beatrice Lillie never surpassed.

Eventually the Prime Minister and I finished our exchanges and bade each other "Good night!" I replaced the receiver on its stand.

Bea clapped her hands, laughed like a happy, naughty child, and escorted me back to the sitting-room. There we found that her son Bobby had joined Dorothy on his return from a dinner party in Town. For a long time afterwards the four of us sat gossiping.

Bea repeated an invitation which she had sent me some days earlier to stay throughout the week-end with her and the others in her Dower House; but I told her that I must return to duty in Whitehall at crack of dawn. Eventually I said that I must snatch forty winks, and went upstairs to my bedroom.

Looking out of its window, I watched a full moon riding amidst a vivid multitude of stars in the dark sky. Its silvery light touched the lawn, the serene lake and the weeping willows with a mysterious, otherworldly beauty; and I wished I could stay for a few days as Bea had suggested in this haven of peace. But I must leave it even before sunrise started to give it a more earthly quality of loveliness. How I cursed the trouble-makers in Palestine!

IV

At that time Dorothy was still playing the heroine in Ivor Novello's musical comedy *The Crest of the Wave*. Ivor himself was acting its leading male role, whilst Zena Dare performed another important part. The rest of the cast numbered almost legion. This latter fact was due to the extraordinary bigness of Ivor's heart. He was more generously affectionate to more people than perhaps any other individual whom I have known. If old actor or actress colleagues came to him with hard-luck stories, and asked whether he could help them to gain employment, he was as likely as not to write a few lines for them to recite in his next play. His list of minor characters therefore sometimes became unduly swollen, and the crowded stage looked as if it were bursting at the seams. He could never refuse any friend practical aid in one way or another. Partly as a consequence of this he was greatly loved by throngs of humble people like stage-hands, performers of walk-on parts, chorus girls and other undistinguished individuals who at one time or another came under his direction.

His popularity with audiences was tumultuous. In his lifetime he was the object of a mob hero-worship in some measure comparable to that of the Beatles in more recent days. Wherever he appeared on or off stage he was besieged by crowds of teenage fans, adult admirers, autograph hunters and other similar types. A stroll down a street with him was an almost crushing, suffocating experience.

One of the reasons for his fame was his genius as a composer of pleasing light music. Those years between the two World Wars were a classic period in the production of such song and dance tunes, for a particularly talented group of writers of them were then in their hey-day. They included such celebrities as Noel Coward, George Gershwin and Irving Berlin; and pre-eminent among them was Ivor. Week after week their latest melodies were sung and played by vivacious crooners and orchestras in the theatres, ballrooms and night-clubs, making the world seem a joyous, carefree place. Some of that gay, sentimental music will never die.

Twice I broke sufficiently free from political preoccupations to go with Dorothy to spend summer week-ends with Ivor and parties of our friends at his country house called Redroofs near Maidenhead. The atmosphere there was delightfully relaxed. Ivor was a most genial host to the always refreshing company. Usually a troupe of additional acquaintances joined us on the Sundays, when we all sat gossiping in the garden, swimming in a plutocratic bathing-pool, and enjoying a sumptuous picnic lunch with champagne to wash down other rich delicacies.

What I liked best of all on those occasions was lolling on a sofa in the drawing-room whilst Ivor sat at a grand piano composing new songs for his next musical play. He would hum experimental catches of a tentative tune, strum them inventively on the key-board, scribble notes on sheets of paper, launch into longer passages of harmony on the piano, contrive little modifications in this or that promising refrain, seek comments from two or three people who were a critical audience in the room, resume more confidently his provisional performance, and so gradually construct whole sequences of fresh enchanting music. Thus one would be a witness of the birth-pangs of popular triumphs like "We'll gather Lilacs," "I can give you the Starlight" and "Waltz of my Heart."

Probably Ivor's best known song-hit was the very first that brought him fame. He wrote it as a youngster during the first World War and called it "Keep the Home Fires Burning." Within weeks it was being sung on every stage in Britain, hummed along every trench on the battlefields in France, and proclaimed from every gramophone throughout the Allied lands. At that time another prodigious figure in English life, called Winston Churchill, became one of Ivor's good friends and admirers; and so he remained ever afterwards. I remember an incident on the historic day a quarter of a century later when Churchill became Prime Minister during the Second World War. That morning Ivor sent him a telegram of enthusiastic congratulations, and a few hours later a reply arrived from Churchill saying, "Thank you, dear Ivor. Now write another 'Keep the Home Fires Burning'."

V

As I have said, on countless evenings during the years before the outbreak of that second war my friends and I gathered for dinner as soon as the curtains rang down on my show in the Palace of Westminster and on theirs in the Gaiety, the Savoy, the Haymarket and other playhouses. Sometimes after the meal eminent members of the company would perform impromptu acts. Ivor would strum some new, unpublished dance tune on a piano, Emlyn Williams would recite a grand speech from one of Shakespeare's tragedies, or Bea Lillie would sing a ditty so outrageously naughty that even she would not dare to mouth it on a public stage. The room was full of chatter and laughter; and frequently the party continued until three or four o'clock in the morning.

As often as not the conversation would turn to serious topics. One of the most stimulating talkers on these occasions was Noel Coward. He would hold forth like a particularly gifted orator on a soap-box in Hyde Park, silencing all other speech for a while by his insistent eloquence, and provoking hotly sustained intellectual and witty arguments. Frequently the discussion drifted into national and international politics. I would then be cast to play the principal role; and if I did not recite my lines convincingly —which was often the case—all the expert dramatic critics in the assembly would tear my performance to pieces. During those years the Government's "appeasement" policy in foreign affairs was a subject of violent controversy in Parliament, in the Press and among the populace; and the protagonists on both sides argued passionately. Their conflicting views were represented by different individuals in our nightly gatherings.

By the autumn of 1938 the European situation had arrived at the crisis immediately preceding Neville Chamberlain's meeting with Adolf Hitler at Berchtesgarten. As it happened, the first night of an ambitious production of Shakespeare's *Henry V* by Ivor Novello was being staged in Drury Lane that very week. Ivor played the part of the King of England whilst Dorothy acted as the Princess of France. Their two or three opening performances were box-office failures, for the auditorium was almost empty. London's citizens were too worried by the dangerous international prospect to feel like relaxing of an evening in a theatre. One night at supper Ivor complained jestingly to me that the actions of us politicians and our counterparts on the Continent were ruining his business. In responsive mood I promised to try to make up a little for this by advertising his show at the meeting of the Cabinet which was due to take place next morning. That gathering was to be the first of two earnest conferences among Ministers to discuss the war threat immediately before Chamberlain's departure to Munich.

I kept my promise. The Cabinet discussion opened with two or three bellicose speeches by some of the younger Ministers like Duff Cooper, who advocated a tough line with Germany which would probably result in a prompt outbreak of war. At that point I thought I should intervene with a rather more cautious expression of views, partly in order to show the senior statesmen present that not all the members of the rising generation favoured resort to hostilities on the issue of that moment. I was in fact the "baby" of the Cabinet, a few twelve-months junior to anyone else sitting round our council table.

I had a particularly powerful reason for advising caution. As Secretary of State for Dominion Affairs (as well as Secretary of State for the Colonies) I was responsible for co-operation with the overseas Dominions, and for striving to maintain unity within the British Commonwealth. And I felt almost certain that if we were to declare war at that time, our Commonwealth would be grievously split from top to bottom. If it is fatal for a democracy to go to war whilst its people are insufficiently united to give solid support for that extreme enterprise, it is six times more fatal for a fraternity of half a dozen democracies to attempt to do battle when they are hopelessly disunited about the cause for which they are supposed to fight. And that was the situation facing us just before the Munich talks in 1938. In Great Britain itself at least half the population were opposed to declaring war on the European issue of the day, and a similar division afflicted our allies in Canada, Australia and South Africa as well as Eire. Only in New Zealand did a strong sentiment exist in favour of supporting the Mother Country "right or wrong" if she got involved in a new Armageddon.

As Secretary of State I was in daily touch with the Governments of those partner nations, both by exchanges of telegrams with the Prime Ministers in their various capitals, and by hours of discussion with their High Commissioners in London. I therefore knew that if Britain declared war, not only Eire but probably also South Africa would remain out of the conflict, and that even if Canada and Australia did join in, they would be crippled by a great deal of opposition among their own peoples. Such a situation could not only break the Commonwealth; it would also possibly open the way to a great victory for Hitler in the struggle in Europe.

I therefore warned my colleagues in the Cabinet room in 10 Downing Street of that gloomy prospect; and I urged that if we were forced to go to war—which I thought possible at a later date—we should wait until the situation developed in a way which ensured our Government the support of both a united British people and a virtually united British Commonwealth.

In the course of my remarks I mentioned incidentally that we must remember that if and when we went to war the battle would not be a small, romantic affair such as could be seen any evening in Ivor Novello's impressive stage production of Shakespeare's *Henry V* at Drury Lane: it would be instead the most violent, cruel and devastating holocaust of all time. Some of my fellow Ministers took note of my remarks not only about the contemporary political situation in the Commonwealth, but also about current dramatic affairs in London. They told me later that as a result they bought seats for the performance of *Henry V*, and found it a refreshing relaxation from our sad official preoccupations.

VI

Chamberlain flew to Munich, and the whole world waited with bated breath to hear the result of his talks with Hitler. The outcome was by no means certain. Would their discussion promote peace, or unleash war? Among the capitals which awaited the news with most intense nervousness were those of the overseas Dominions, and their Prime Ministers were anxious for me to send them information at the earliest possible moment. Chamberlain and I therefore arranged that he should telephone me personally from Germany as soon as his final talk with the Fuehrer ended, when he would know whether he was bringing home an olive branch or an ultimatum. I would then immediately see the High Commissioners in my office in Whitehall, to give them the good or bad tidings for telegraphing to their Governments.

The decisive talk between the statesman and the tyrant at Berchtesgarten was more protracted than had been anticipated earlier in the day. It continued all through the evening and far into the night. Hour after hour I sat solitary in my vast room in the Colonial Office expecting the telephone call from Germany, whilst all the High Commissioners stayed impatiently in their homes awaiting a summons by me. As it happened, at the same time another company was gathered in Bea Lillie's flat in Park Lane (where she then resided) hoping for my arrival there with the latest news. Bea was giving an after-theatre party to a group of friends, and several days previously I had promised to attend. When I phoned her about midnight to say that I might be very late because I was still in my office expecting a call from Munich, she answered that she and her guests were so anxious to hear the crucial information that they would stay up all night if necessary to greet me as soon as I could get free.

At last my telephone tinkled; and when I picked up the receiver the voice of Sir Horace Wilson, the Prime Minister's chief adviser at Berchtesgarten, said that if I would hold on a few moments Mr. Chamberlain would speak to me. Almost immediately afterwards the Premier came on the line. In a few crisp sentences he told me all I needed to know about his historic talk with Hitler which had ended some minutes earlier.

My private secretary had meantime telephoned the High Commissioners; and soon afterwards they began to arrive posthaste in his ante-room. They were a distinguished team including Vincent Massey, Stanley Bruce and John Dulanty; and I had told the secretary to usher them into my chamber as soon as they were all assembled. When they came through the doorway I welcomed them by turning several cartwheels across the floor and clapping my heels in the air at every convolution. They somehow gathered that this meant Chamberlain had succeeded in achieving an agreement in Munich which averted war; for I heard them laughing in a gleeful, explosive way indicating suddenly relaxed nervous tension. Afterwards we sat round a table and I told them such details as my chief had reported to me. They expressed the unanimous support of all their Prime Ministers for what he had done.

Whilst they hastened away to send messages to their Governments I hurried off to Bea's party. When I arrived I found it crowded not only with her invited guests, but also with a lot of gate-crashing acquaintances who had learned that I would appear in due course to play the part of either an Angel of Peace or a Harbinger of War. As I entered the apartment a dozen people were arguing loudly; but at my appearance a tense hush fell on them all.

I told the company the gist of the news, and a sigh of relief went round the room. Then a few voices were raised in protest. Other voices at once retorted vehemently, and the debate which had evidently been proceeding before my arrival was hotly resumed. Soon some authoritative fellow called for silence, and when the throng were quiet he asked me to tell them everything I felt I could about the situation, and to express my own opinion on it.

The gate-crashers drifted away, having gained the information they came to glean, and feeling that they were now *de trop*. The rest of us entered into an earnest discussion which continued for two or three hours. The great majority of those present agreed with our Prime Minister's policy; but a few begged to differ.

The most eloquent critic of Neville Chamberlain in those friendly but heated nightly arguments was Noel Coward. He was a passionate advocate of the rival views of Winston Churchill, and at the time of Munich he thought the British Government should have made a stand which would compel the Nazis either to retreat or to fight us forthwith. He accepted that the result would probably have been war within twenty-four hours; but this did not deter him. He reckoned that we should have to join battle with Germany sooner or later, and I remember a vigorous speech illumined by all his intellectual force in which he argued that, if we fought the enemy now, we could crush them and be victorious, whereas if we waited longer, the Huns' military power would grow more rapidly than ours, and we should be vanquished. He ended his plea with the emphatic declaration, "Chamberlain's wrong to postpone the issue. It's now or never!"

In the momentary, stunned silence that followed Dorothy Dickson remarked, "You don't mean it's now or never; you mean it's Noel or Neville!" A burst of laughter through the room relieved the tension.

VII

In September 1939 war broke out, and life for everyone suddenly changed in many ways. I remained Secretary of State for the Colonies until Churchill succeeded Chamberlain as Prime Minister in the early summer of the following year. Churchill then appointed me his Minister of Health, with responsibility for many of the Home Defence arrangements in preparation for the Battle of Britain; and so I was urgently busy throughout every day and much of every night. I saw less of my theatrical friends. In any case they too were more intensely occupied than ever before, not only acting in London but also playing for the troops all over the country and sometimes on other war fronts. We lunched together now and then and kept in touch by periodic telephone calls; but otherwise we met much less frequently.

In 1941 Churchill developed his policy of sending Ministers of Cabinet rank as his Government's Representatives in important Allied capitals overseas, and he appointed me High Commissioner in Canada. Very reluctantly I prepared to wave "Good-bye" to all my war comrades in the battered but unbowed island of Britain.

I had a few free days between ceasing to be Minister of Health and sailing to take up my new duties in Ottawa. On my last evening in London I invited a group of friends to dinner in the Café de Paris off Leicester Square, which had been our favourite place for dining and dancing in earlier, more carefree times. Bea, Zena, Ivor and several others were able to come. We sat at the table in the centre of a gallery of the ballroom which was always reserved for me when I gave supper parties in that famous night spot. The fat, genial manager, Mr. Poulson, gave us a warm welcome, as did other members of the staff who had not seen us for quite a while. The smiling Negro band leader, a talented conductor of dance music whose lithe movements as he waved his baton earned him the nickname "Snakey-hips," expressed his delight by making the orchestra break into a succession of what he knew to be our best-liked tunes. Nostalgia was in the air as we glided round and round the ballroom floor; and for a while we forgot whatever air raid was occurring out-of-doors.

The next day I flew to Greenock to start my voyage across the Atlantic Ocean. I sailed in H.M.S. *Revenge,* whose captain was under orders to do battle with the notorious enemy warship *Bismarck*—loose in those waters at that time—if we should come within hailing distance of her. Unfortunately she never appeared; so I missed the only opportunity of my life to take part in a naval engagement. A few days later we landed in Canada.

In an air raid on London soon afterwards the Café de Paris received a direct hit from a bomb which shattered the building and killed many of its occupants. Among the dead were Poulson, "Snakey-hips," several of his jazz bandsmen—and every member of a party who happened to be dining at the gallery table which my friends and I had invariably occupied.

VIII

Except for quite frequent flights across the Atlantic to join in wartime consultations in Whitehall about Anglo-Canadian co-operation against the enemy, I did not return to London until the spring of 1946. Then I stayed there only a few days before departing again to assume new duties as Governor-General in Malaya and Singapore.

On my last afternoon in England Bea Lillie lunched with me at Claridge's Hotel. She was as sparklingly gay as ever, and we enjoyed a cheerful, gossiping meal in the crowded dining-room. As we had not met for nearly a year, there was much for us to discuss. We reminisced about the past, exchanged opinions concerning the present, and speculated on the future. In the course of our talk I broke a piece of news to her.

"The day before I left Canada last week," I announced, "I got engaged to be married."

She glanced at me in surprise, and asked rather incredulously whether I was telling the truth.

I assured her that I was.

She opened her eyes wide in exaggerated astonishment, and fell off her chair to the floor. People at neighbouring tables looked concerned, and one or two gentlemen rose in readiness to assist, in case first-aid were needed. However, with complete sang-froid Bea picked herself up and settled on her seat again.

"Tell me more," she said as she sniffed at a bottle of smelling salts.

When I told her more she congratulated me warmly, and we continued our conversation about the world, the flesh and the devil. Afterwards I drove her in my car to her flat. I was to leave London early the following day on the first stage of my flight to Singapore; and we did not know when we should meet again.

"Our friendship's wonderfully deep and true," Bea remarked as we said good-bye. "There's only one thing I regret about it."

"What's that?" I asked.

"That we've never had an affair."

We both laughed.

"What are you doing to-night?" I enquired jocularly.

"That's top secret," she replied.

Then she added also in jest, "What are you doing this afternoon, darling?"

"I've got to go to the Colonial Office," I said, "to finish a lot of a different kind of top secret business there."

We kissed and parted.

An hour later as I sat in my room in Whitehall, busily completing all the work I must do before leaving England, a private secretary brought me a telegram that had just arrived.

Tearing open its envelope, I read, "If you don't break off your engagement, I'll sue you for breach of promise. Love, Fifi."

At first I felt bewildered by the message, especially as I did not know any girl named Fifi. Then I had a slight suspicion who its sender might be.

Five minutes later the secretary entered my room carrying another telegram for me. It said, "You can't do this to me, you unfaithful dog. Love and kisses from Lulu."

My suspicion grew stronger.

Not long afterwards a third telegram arrived. This time it declared, "If you don't come back to me, honey, I'll take an overdose of sleeping-pills. Fondest love, Gloriana."

A little while later two other similarly desperate, pleading missives came from a couple of unheard-of suicidal females. I telephoned Bea, and thanked her for all her messages—and to this day I can hear her delicious laughter over the phone.

Blitz

As I have mentioned, when Winston Churchill became Prime Minister in May 1940 he asked me to be a member of his Government. Like all the others whom he invited to fill such posts, on the morning of his assumption of the supreme office I was summoned to meet him in his room in the Admiralty, where he had hitherto been working as First Lord. I arrived there a minute before the appointed hour and was ushered into his private secretary's anteroom. The official told me that Mr. Leo Amery was with the Prime Minister at the moment.

Not long afterwards the door into Churchill's room opened, and through it came a smiling Amery, seeming rather pleased with himself.

I entered the presence. The great man was striding up and down the chamber with his head thrust forward on his massive shoulders and his hands gripping the lapels of his jacket, as if he were making a speech in Parliament.

He looked round, caught sight of me, and said rather oratorically without halting his pacings, "My dear Malcolm, I'm glad to see you. I've nothing to offer you except . . ." He hesitated deliberately for a moment in his utterance.

I felt disappointed, thinking he could have no more senior office to give me than that of Postmaster-General or some similar minor job.

Then he continued, ". . . blood and toil, tears and sweat."

I was taken aback, wondering whether he had created a new war-time Ministry, and was asking me to become the Secretary of State for Blood, Toil, Tears and Sweat.

He glanced at me to observe my reaction, stood still, and in a voice suddenly changed to friendly informality remarked, "I want you to be Minister of Health in my Government." He added that this would be an important task because Hitler and the Nazis might later start an all-out assault on Britain, and the Ministry of Health would be responsible for many of the services protecting and sustaining the assaulted islanders through the crisis.

I naturally accepted the proposal without hesitation. The Prime Minister and I then exchanged a few pleasantries, and afterwards I left the room whilst he recommenced his pacings to and fro, again with his fists gripping the lapels of his coat.

Amery was waiting for me in the private secretary's office. He looked at me enquiringly, and I told him that I was to be the Minister of Health.

He expressed satisfaction, and then asked, "Did he also offer you blood and sweat and toil and tears?"

I answered in the affirmative; and Amery remarked that he had received the same proposition.

"He must be rehearsing his speech for Parliament this afternoon," he commented.

Miss Ellen Wilkinson arrived in the room, and was shown into the Premier's study whilst Amery and I hastened away to start our new jobs without delay.

That afternoon we all sat in a crowded House of Commons listening to Churchill making his first speech as Prime Minister. In the middle of it we suddenly heard him utter the well-rehearsed and now immortal phrase, "I would say to the House, as I said to those who have joined this Government, I have nothing to offer but blood, toil, tears and sweat."

II

One Saturday afternoon about four months later I paid a visit to my great friends Thelma Cazalet Keir and David Keir in their country house in Kent. It was a bright summer's day, and I proposed to relax for a few hours, resting from more or less cease-less war-time Ministerial toil. As we sat in the sunlit garden the peaceful hush of Nature was suddenly disturbed by a loud droning of aeroplanes overhead. Looking up into a clear blue sky, we saw several bomber aircraft flying in precise military formation to-wards us from the direction of the coast, escorted by a number of smaller fighter planes circling round them like a flock of butterflies. After a startled moment we realised that they were a group of German Junkers arriving to make their first bombing raid on London—the large craft to launch the assault, and the small ones to defend them.

I abandoned my plan to relax and forget about the war for a while, sent for my motor-car, and drove as quickly as possible to my office in Whitehall. As I passed along the southern bank of the Thames I saw some buildings on the opposite side of the river being consumed by flames, with columns of dark smoke belching from their burning roofs.

The date was the 7th September. The Battle of Britain had begun.

III

From then onwards England was blasted by air raids almost every night, usually in various parts of London. As Minister of Health I was responsible not only for the emergency medical and hospital services, but also for the efficient working of the public air-raid shelters, the food-and-rest centres for people bombed out of their homes, the evacuation of children and old people from threatened areas, and various other vital schemes for protecting the civilian population. During the actual "blitzes" I wished to observe with my own eyes the practical implementation of our policies, so that I could detect promptly any mistakes we were making and correct them before the next enemy onslaught started twenty-four hours later. Every evening I therefore worked in my office until the night-ly attack commenced, and then I sallied forth to this or that

London borough, often to one where a raid was taking place. First I would sit for a while with the local officers in their underground operational headquarters, observing them on the job; then I issued into the streets to see our ambulance teams, first-aid parties and other civil defence staffs performing their duties. I stayed out-of-doors until the raid ended, usually in the small hours of the morning, and then motored home to snatch a few hours of sleep in my house in Hampstead.

I was one of millions of Londoners engaged in waging the Battle of Britain against the enemy. It was a perpetually enthralling experience, sometimes made more exciting by fire-bombs or high explosives tumbling unpleasantly near my little group of companions and me. The sound of angry responsive barkings from our anti-aircraft guns was like music to our ears.

One of the new friends whom I made on the battlefield of London was Edwina Mountbatten, the wife of His famous Lordship. Her pre-war reputation was not endearing, for she was somewhat notorious as a spoilt plutocratic playgirl of the smart Mayfair set, more interested in the gay, selfish life of high society than in doing any serious work. I therefore felt annoyed when one morning, as I sat hectically busy at my office desk during the first few critical days of the bombings, my private secretary announced that Lady Louis Mountbatten had telephoned to request an early interview with me. I saw no reason why I should be diverted from my urgent tasks to speak with one of the idle, irresponsible rich. However, a principle which has always guided my official conduct is that every high Officer of State is a servant of the people, and that anyone—however humble or exalted—who wishes to see him has a right of direct personal access. I therefore asked my secretary to let Lady Louis know that I would talk with her at twelve noon that day.

When she entered my room she was very smartly dressed in the uniform of a Commandant in the St. John's Ambulance Brigade. I was not impressed, for she seemed too much like a fashion model aware of her physical attraction on parade. Then she started speaking, and for a few moments I listened in a mood of bored tolerance—which quickly changed to intense interest. She wasted no time and minced no words. Saying she knew I was very pre-occupied and that she would not keep me for more than five minutes, she told me that she had spent the previous night working among the poor people in a certain gigantic air-raid shelter in Stepney where she thought my Ministry were making several serious mistakes in administration.

I asked her what the errors were, and she described them.

"What are you doing to-night?" I enquired.

"I'm going to the Stepney air-raid shelter again," she answered.

I told her I would meet her there at ten o'clock in the evening so that I could consider on the spot whether I agreed with her strictures.

We kept our rendezvous in a vast, semi-underground tunnel in Stepney which was occupied every night by many hundreds of working people and their children, who never went to their own homes in the neighbourhood after dark, but brought their suppers, bedding and other necessities to this huge cavern where they re-sided through the next twelve hours like cave-men of our barbaric twentieth century.

Her Ladyship showed me what she thought our Civil Defence personnel there were doing wrong; and I found myself in agree-ment with every one of her criticisms. At once I authorised all the necessary changes. As I left the place, to continue on my round of other similar subterranean haunts where the common men and women of London were protecting themselves in the battle, I told her that she need never come to see me when she thought my Ministry were doing things correctly, but that I would always be ready to meet her at a moment's notice whenever she considered we were making mistakes. I had learned to my astonishment that evening, that this rather celebrated good-for-nothing playgirl had become a woman unselfishly dedicated to the national service, and also that her abilities, judgment and humanity were of a supremely high order.

She accepted my proposal, and on several later occasions telephoned me to seek my aid in this or that problem touching Government policies. That episode in Stepney saw the birth of one of the most worth-while, pleasing friendships of my life.

IV

Thus was night life in London suddenly transformed for us all. Each evening I went, as before the war, to my favourite night spots and stayed in them until the small hours of the morning—but the nature of those haunts had changed. Instead of the Café de Paris, the Four Hundred Club, Chez Henri and other such delectable, light-hearted places, they were the Civil Defence operations rooms, first-aid posts, air-raid shelters and other front-line positions in the embattled capital. My activities were still accompanied by music, but in place of the gay strains of popular dance tunes played by jazz orchestras, the more thrillingly syncopated bangs of exploding bombs, whining crescendoes of tumbling fire-crackers, and responsive refrain of anti-aircraft guns filled the air. This noisy symphony continued without cease until its final movement of wailing air-raid sirens announced that the concert was ending for the night.

Sometimes during the daytime I visited other stricken towns like Bristol, Manchester and Coventry; but always I returned before nightfall to be with my war comrades in London. Only once did I stay away overnight, when I inspected some hospitals in Oxford through an afternoon, and went afterwards to dine with friends in their house on the edge of the city, and to sleep in their quiet home. I had been advised to take twelve hours off duty, and to indulge in one good night's rest. But as darkness fell, and the moment for the start of air raids approached, the silence out-of-doors became incongruous to me. I began to feel miserable. I kept wondering what was happening in London, and how my friends there were faring, and which borough was taking the worst beating that evening. As I lay restless and almost sleepless in bed I felt like a deserter who should be court-martialled and shot at dawn. I could hardly wait for daylight to reappear, for breakfast to be served, and for my car to arrive to carry me as swiftly as possible back to London.

V

Probably the worst, most perilous raid was that launched on the night of the 27th December in 1940, when the City of London went up in flames. The attacking German aircraft rained a hurricane of fire-bombs from the skies, and these fell pell-mell on the close-packed buildings in the capital's heart. Quite a strong breeze was blowing, which aggravated the situation by wafting showers of sparks from already burning structures to others not yet alight, so fanning a formidable conflagration. This was the sad occasion when many of Christopher Wren's churches were destroyed.

Nevertheless the great master's grandest creation, St. Paul's Cathedral, survived the storm. That merciful deliverance was achieved by strenuous efforts on the part of its special troop of guardians. A team of architects, builders and similar professional men had volunteered to protect the noble church every night for the duration of the Battle of Britain. My brother Alister was one of them. Twice each week he did duty from dusk until dawn, and he was on the job on the eve of the 27th December. Sitting on the roof of the huge nave beneath a starry sky, he had a supply of defensive weapons like fire-extinguishers, piles of sand and pails of water standing handy in case of need.

Of a sudden the assault on the City began, and before long a hail of fire-bombs was tumbling on St. Paul's. For the next few hours its protectors were kept continuously busy extinguishing them before they could set the place ablaze. Three or four colleagues were distributed along the roof with Alister, and between them they held things under control. However, a similar fiery tornado was hurtling down on other buildings close around, and these were not so adequately served by defenders. Before long some of them were violently alight, and their flames often leaped from one side of a narrow street to the other and then travelled onwards, spreading havoc wherever they went. Even after the enemy aeroplanes had departed, this chaotic burning all around the cathedral posed a great danger to it. Showers of glowing embers kept flying from the encircling bonfires, and Alister was ceaselessly occupied coping with them wherever they alighted. His most effective weapons were some prayer hassocks heaped beside him for this very purpose. He kept raising a cushion above his head and bringing it down with a suffocating thud on kindled fragments of wood and other threatening stuffs which landed on the roof. So vigorously and persistently did he have to perform this act that after a while all his hassocks were battered or burned to bits. Before the last one finally broke in pieces he telephoned to the operations headquarters situated in the cathedral's crypt, and asked the supplies officer to send up another consignment of prayer-cushions.

The fellow in the church's bowels laughed through the phone and remarked, "Alister, it's time you stopped kneeling so hard and praying so fervently that you're wearing all the hassocks out. However, another lot will arrive in a minute. Good luck!"

An ample quantity of tough cushions did appear soon afterwards, and Alister and his colleagues continued to bash out the sparks. So St. Paul's stayed one of the few undamaged survivors of that second Great Fire of London.

VI

On another, later night the cathedral was again exposed to grave peril. An unexploded bomb fell into the ground close beside it and lay there, threatening at any moment to blow the place to smithereens. As soon as its presence became known all the great church's guardians were evacuated, an area round the missile was roped-off for safety of human life and limb, and the building was abandoned to its fate. Devotees in the vicinity got down on their knees and prayed that the bomb would not burst, so that the pride of London could be spared. But their hopes were dim. They expected that by daylight little of St. Paul's would remain except a broken skeleton standing amidst heaps of rubble.

Earlier that evening I had gone on a tour in West Ham. My companion was Admiral "Teddy" Evans, the gallant, genial sailor who was a survivor of Scott's Antarctic expedition in 1912, the commander of H.M.S. *Broke* in a classic sea battle during the First World War, and now Regional Commissioner for Civil Defence in London. We spent several energetic hours in the East End, and some time after midnight left that area to motor back to our homes. In the meantime we had received news of the bomb lying alongside St. Paul's, and we decided to visit the sacred precincts on our way to sleep, to see whether the glorious building still precariously survived. We wished to catch a last death-bed glimpse of it, and to pay it our final respects before it gave up the ghost.

As we drove along Commercial Road towards the City we saw evidence of much destruction wrought during the night's raid. Flames flickered obstinately in buildings where fire brigades were still at work, craters yawned here and there along the pavements, and occasionally a street was flooded with water gushing from broken pipes or hydrants. The air was filled with the noises and odours of those various catastrophes.

Teddy Evans's wife was a Norse lady, and he often accompanied her on visits to her parents in Scandinavia. As we sped along the road he closed his eyes and murmured dreamily, "I love the smell of burning wood and the sound of rushing waters. They make me think I'm picnicking beside a mountain stream in a Norwegian fiord."

Eventually we came to the neighbourhood of St. Paul's. When we stepped from our car the Civil Defence guards told us that the bomb had not yet exploded, and they guided us to the nearest vantage point where we could gain a safe view of the doomed cathedral. Its stately bulk loomed dimly against a dark sky, un-illumed by any lights because the black-out of war-time London was in full operation. Yet we could see Wren's beautiful dome silhouetted serenely against a cloudless, starlit heaven. We felt sad and sentimental, presuming that we were bidding the historic masterpiece "Good-bye" for ever. For half an hour we lingered there, and then reluctantly tore ourselves away.

Next morning I visited the cathedral again and saw it still standing intact. And so it remained. The bomb never did explode. At dawn that day a heroic expert descended into the pit where the monster lurked, tinkered with its mechanism, extracted its fatal gadgets, and rendered it impotent. For this very risky deed he received the high award of the George Cross. The nation uttered up prayers of profound thanksgiving—and St. Paul's has lived happily ever afterwards.

VII

I survived those nightly jaunts without a bodily scratch. The nearest I came to being hurt was one evening when I stood beneath the protection of my tin helmet in a street suffering a high ex-plosive bomb attack. Suddenly the blast from a bomb swept my spectacles off my face and hurled them to the ground, where they lay shattered at my feet.

Those were days and nights when the British people revealed the greatest qualities they possessed. As their grand warrior chief, Winston Churchill, said in one of the deathless phrases which he spoke at the time, it was "Their finest hour." A marvellous spirit of defiant, unyielding heroism infected the whole population. The dangers which everyone shared abolished distinctions of class, creed and character among them, creating a true national, human unity such as had rarely existed before, and—alas!—has dis-appeared again since. In those bombed, broken and burning streets we were all comrades together, equally exposed to the same risks, somehow displaying a similar cool and often laughing calm, and determined to suffer whatever sacrifices were necessary to sustain our British liberties.

I remember one of the many occasions when the imperturbable and frequently gay mood in which the multitude of ordinary people played their parts was displayed. King George VI and Queen Elizabeth were touring a London borough which had suffered a very destructive raid during the previous night. They were viewing the ruins of a street where twenty-four hours earlier numerous families had lived, but where nothing was now left except heaps of rubble in which not only their houses but also all their possessions lay smashed. The local residents of a sudden owned nothing but the clothes they stood up in.

The Queen was commiserating with a group of cockney house-wives who crowded enthusiastically round her. In answer to her questions they described their experiences through the night, and told her of their losses. One said she had searched for a precious set of crockery, but found only a broken cup-handle and a frag-ment of saucer among the debris; another cursed Hitler in scorch-ing terms for having smashed her husband's pipe, which was the only means of keeping him good-tempered; a third explained with a grin that her arm was in a sling not because of a bomb splinter, but because she had sprained her wrist climbing out of her air-raid shelter after the raid ended.

Their talk was not in the least mournful; on the contrary, al-though the women regretted their losses, they spoke cheerfully, and their primary feeling at the moment was pride at being visited by Her Majesty the Queen. Only she was sad, so affected by the terrible hurt which she saw they had suffered that at one moment she almost burst into tears. In tremblingly sorrowful words she expressed her sympathy for them.

At that one smiling old girl patted her affectionately on the arm and remarked, "Oh, don't you worry about us, Mum. Look after yourself. You're important, but we don't matter much. We'll always be all right so long as we can 'ave a cup o' tea."

Often as I drove home in the small hours of the mornings, with the guns of anti-aircraft batteries in Hyde Park, Hampstead Heath and elsewhere barking their final shots against the retreating foe, I felt a sense of elation and thanked God that I was privileged to be a citizen of London during the supreme adventure of the great capital's history.

Up in the Air

I have always been fond of flying, and am frequently up in the clouds both physically and (many people would say) mentally. My first bodily flight was taken in the early 1920s when I was holidaying on my native heath in Scotland. An ex-Royal Flying Corps pilot asked me whether I would like to go for a jaunt through the skies in his small two-seater aeroplane. I readily accepted the invitation, and settled into the open cockpit behind him. The machine rushed along the ground and climbed into the air, and before long we were careering around the heavens. I looked with wondrous appreciation at the world below, recognising various spots with which I was familiar at ground level, such as the harbour of the little fishing-town of Lossiemouth, the River Lossie winding through the surrounding countryside, and the southern shore of the Moray Firth stretching away towards the North Sea.

After a while the pilot shouted to me through the earphones which were our only means of communication, "Would you like to loop-the-loop?"

"Yes," I answered with rather dubious enthusiasm.

"Okay; get ready!" he remarked.

I was not sure how to obey that command. Sitting unprotected in a cockpit open to the sky, I felt no wish to fall out and crash to the earth a few thousand feet below when the aircraft turned topsy-turvy. Yet how could I avoid that fate? I searched for lap-straps with which to fasten myself on to my seat; but no such contrivances existed. For a moment I considered asking my companion whether they had been removed by mistake; but then I thought he might suppose I felt frightened, and so from a different sort of cowardice I held my tongue. Clasping the arms of my chair very firmly in my fists, I determined to hold on for dear life, riveting myself more or less in position whilst the plane performed its somersault. .... A moment later I sensed the first convulsive, somewhat stomach-churning movement of the craft starting to tilt sharply upwards; so it was now in any case too late to tell my leader that I had changed my mind, that I was so fascinated by the wide landscapes and seascapes below us that I would prefer to stay erect surveying the scene, and that he need not bother to make the flying-machine turn head-over-heels.

Then I felt a very unexpected, inexplicable, contrary physical sensation to what I had anticipated. As the aircraft circled round, instead of tumbling upwards towards the open air above I seemed to be literally glued to my seat below. Even if I had wanted to jump, dive or just slip out of the aeroplane into space, I could not have done so. Indeed, had my purpose in making the flight been to commit suicide, I would have been frustrated in that desire—for my backside was jammed so firmly against the cushion beneath me that I seemed more in danger of being thrust through the vehicle's substantial bottom than of falling out of its roofless top. Even when I tried experimentally to lift my hands off the seat-arms I found difficulty in doing so. I began to adjust my mind to the situation, and realised that as the plane circled upwards and over in a complete somersault a centrifugal force drove my body towards its floor. Only if we stayed upside-down for quite a long time would that force relax, and release me to tumble out.

A few moments later the pressure on my hindquarters eased, and glancing over the cockpit's side I saw the land, sea and sky all swiftly reverting to their customary positions. I understood that our loop-the-loop had ended.

"How did you like that?" the pilot's voice called through my earphones.

"It was wonderful!" I exclaimed.

Then I realised that I had missed the chief novelty of the experience, for I had been so perplexed at the strange physical sensation accosting me that I forgot to gaze at the earth above my head and the firmament below my feet whilst I was poised the wrong way up.

"Can we loop-the-loop again?" I yelled to the pilot.

"Certainly," he replied.

At once we repeated the contortion; and this time I sat as relaxed as if I were reclining right-side-up on a comfortable sofa, whilst I was in fact turning turtle in space. And as I revolved I watched the Earth enact a much more colossal somersault all round me. It was an enthralling sight.

II

During the last three decades I have probably flown more millions of miles than any other passenger. My duties in various successive posts in the vast regions of North America, South East Asia, India, Europe and Africa have kept me winging across immense continental and inter-continental distances. For example, when I was High Commissioner in Canada in the early 1940s I held the record for trans-Atlantic flights by a civilian, crossing the ocean twenty-eight times.

Our vehicles of transport for that journey in those years were the Liberator bomber aircraft being flown in large numbers by ferry pilots from America for use in Britain's war against the enemy. Being bombers, they were not furnished with any comforts. Sometimes a few hard metal seats were ranged along a cabin wall, but as often as not we squatted instead on the empty floor of the bomb-bay. No heating apparatus existed, and the temperature was especially low in the Far Northern winter months. At that season we wore not only thickly-padded flying suits, but also quilted sleeping-bags throughout the voyage. If our gloves fell off our hands or our helmets off our heads as we slumbered, we were apt to wake up with frost-bitten fingers or ears. And when we ascended higher than 14,000 feet we had to wear oxygen masks all the time, which made even the lightest dozing impossible.

It was all good, adventurous fun—although occasionally the

element of adventure became a little excessive. For instance, on one westwards flight from Scotland to Canada through a stormy night in the dead of winter we lost our way. Headwinds seriously delayed our progress across the sea, and we arrived several hours late in the skies above Newfoundland's coast. The amount of oil in our petrol tanks was steadily diminishing; but we flew onwards without seeking to land, since the crew reckoned we had enough fuel to carry us to our destination, Montreal.

Then we took a wrong turning. Instead of proceeding in a rather southerly direction towards that city we started to go northwards towards the Arctic Ocean. Our captain was an experienced civilian pilot of pre-war days named Stewart who now worked for the R.A.F. Transport Command on those trans-Atlantic journeys; and he had made more such flights than almost any of his colleagues. His navigating officer, however, must have been less capable. Misreading a code message which came aloft to him from some airfield nearly 20,000 feet below, he thought we had arrived over the American coast a long way south of Newfoundland instead of immediately above it, and so he advised Stewart to turn our machine north-west. Having confidence in his team-mate, the skipper acted accordingly, and we began to make our way towards the North Pole.

For a while we proceeded without anyone questioning this decision. The heavens outside our aircraft were pitch-black, for the time was the early hours of the morning and the sky was covered with clouds. We could therefore get no hint from any appearance of land below us or of stars above whither we were going. Fortunately my fellow travellers in the bomb-bay happened to be three young Air Force ferry-pilots who, a day or two previously, had flown other aircraft across the ocean to England and were now returning to take the next lot of those reinforcements there. After some time their instinct told them that we were heading in a wrong direction.

They went to Stewart sitting in the pilot's seat, and expressed their concern. He told them to go to hell; they were mere passengers with no right to try to teach the crew their business. The youths endeavoured to argue with him; but he quoted the message which his navigator had received. They then went to talk to this navigation officer (who in those Liberators sat with his wireless equipment in a separate compartment), contesting the accuracy of his reading of that message, and putting to him their reasons for believing we were travelling along a mistaken route. He resented their uncalled-for intervention and told them so in unmistakable terms. They disputed with him for a while, but in vain. All this controversy occupied a considerable time, and meanwhile we continued to speed towards the inhospitable Frozen North.

Feeling frustrated, the trio of officers returned to their seats in the bomb-bay to hold a council of war. By now the first light of earliest dawn began to peer over a distant horizon on the Earth far below us, and we could see dimly some of the features of that world. These looked forbidding. Deep snow covered the ground, an occasional ice-bound lake appeared amidst wild forest, and there was no sign whatever of human habitation. It seemed unlikely that we were advancing in the direction of the great St. Lawrence River flanked by Quebec's farmlands.

My travelling companions went again to the captain's cockpit to present him with this latest evidence of our erroneous ways. Earnestly they urged him to alter course. At first he was obstinate and resisted their pleas. However, they were now so convinced he was wrong that they answered toughly, declaring that if he would not immediately change course, they would stage a mutiny, eject him from his pilot's seat, and themselves take control of the aircraft. At that he conceded with good grace, especially as the proofs they produced of his navigator's misguidance were so persuasive that he felt he could no longer abide loyally by his colleague's advice. The aeroplane thereupon made a wide-angled turn through the skies, and we headed in a new direction.

By now we had lost a lot of time, distance—and petrol. It seemed doubtful whether enough fuel remained in the craft's tanks to carry us all the way to Montreal. Stewart thought it likely we would run out of gas prior to arrival there, and that we should have to choose a convenient spot short of our destination where we could jump from the aircraft before it crashed. We therefore donned our parachutes, and one of the flying officers instructed me how to leap clear of the plane, unfasten my umbrella-like apparatus in mid-air, and float down to earth.

For the next hour we sat awaiting further orders. My companions maintained a great deal of merry chatter. Through parts of the journey I had been reading some books; but I now lost interest in them, and tucked them into pockets on the thighs of my flying-suit. A member of the party noticed them, and remarked, "I see you're going to do a lot of reading whilst you glide slowly down to the ground."

As things turned out our petrol just lasted until we arrived over Dorval airport on the edge of Montreal. Stewart had meanwhile sent a wireless communication to the authorities there, explaining that we might have to do a forced landing. As a consequence when we peered down at Dorval's air-strip and buildings we noticed ambulances with stretcher parties waiting to receive us. I expressed the opinion that another group of people standing near-by looked like a troupe of clergymen ready to read the burial service over whatever bits and pieces of us eventually alighted.

Nevertheless, all seemed to be going well. Stewart sent us a verbal message saying that the last drops of petrol were now making their exit from the tank and that they would suffice for him to circle the airport once before landing so that he could make a correct entry on a runway. We sat tight, feeling rather pleased.

A few moments later he sent us a revised message. It announced that although the pair of landing-wheels below the main body of the aircraft had descended into the right positions for our touch-down, the single wheel below the cockpit refused to follow suit, and that if we were to alight on the two other wheels alone, the machine would tilt forwards with such a violent bump that all the delicate control equipment in the pilot's cabin would be smashed to pieces, the crew would perhaps be killed, and we sitting slightly farther in the rear might also be hurt. Therefore Stewart proposed to do a crash landing on the aircraft's tail so that the sudden meeting of its hindquarters with the runway would put a brake on its speed, and (he hoped) prevent such disastrous consequences.

His message ended with an intimation that, since our petrol was now exhausted, he must descend at once—so would we please get ready to play our parts in this difficult operation.

One of his officers instructed us in those parts. We passengers were to shift to the hind-end of the bomb-bay so that our collective weights would help the tail to act as a drag on the machine when it struck the ground, thus preventing the plane from tipping forwards. Two members of the crew were given a less enviable task. They hurried into the rearmost compartment itself, and squatted at its farthest extremity just above the actual tail, to keep it slanting at a fairly sharp angle where it would be sure to contact the runway before any other portion of the plane. They were to stay there until a fraction of a second before the contact, when they must rise quickly and rush the few paces into the bomb-bay in the hope of avoiding bodily damage to themselves. The door between them and us was left open so that they could make this hasty escape, and the doors to Stewart's cockpit were also open to enable him to signal to them at the right moment. He would raise his hands as a warning an instant before the tail was to hit the runway.

We took up our allotted positions. As the plane gradually descended towards the earth I kept turning my eyes from the pilot in his cockpit to the couple crouching above the tail, watching for their fateful instant of communication.

Suddenly Stewart raised a hand, and at the same moment the two men rose and dashed towards us. Half a second later we were all violently jerked in our places, a crashing noise sounded—and the aircraft's tail broke off. We saw the snow-powdered runway receding through a gaping hole where it used to be. But the pair of crewmen stood safely gripping the sides of the doorway between us and that glimpse of fast rushing ground. For a while the aeroplane continued to slither and bump forwards, but at a lumbering, slowing rate; and eventually it dragged to a halt—still upright.

Stewart raised his fingers in the famous Churchillian "V" sign of victory, and we all laughed with relief.

As we emerged from the aircraft, ambulances drove alongside and doctors and nurses stepped out. But none of us had received so much as a scratch. We strolled to the airport buildings, very happy to find ourselves still alive and kicking.

For many weeks afterwards, on all the maps in operations rooms of the Royal Air Force Transport Command throughout Canada, the words "North Pole" were scratched from the Arctic regions, and the new geographical name "Stewartland" substituted. Stewart was demoted from his captaincy and for a while served in a more junior rank. However, the error made on our flight was not his fault; and he was so eminently capable that soon afterwards he became elevated to his post as captain again. Before the end of the war his score for flights across the Atlantic Ocean topped a century.

Those were indeed somewhat dangerous years for fliers of the Atlantic. The scientific equipment of aircraft was much less sophisticated than it has since become, and there were ever-present risks of losing direction or suffering other mishaps. Although most of us who made those journeys on duty managed to survive, a few of my friends disappeared without trace in the ocean waves.

III

Perhaps I should add here an account of another flying adventure which I experienced several years later on the opposite side of the Earth. It occurred during one of my visits to Indonesia when I lived in South East Asia. I had gone to view the glorious Borobadour Temple and other ancient ruins in East Java, to hold talks with the wise Sultan of Djokjakarta in his near-by capital, and to enjoy glimpses of the beautiful indigenous arts and crafts practised there. I inspected the making of lovely, flamboyant batiks in artisans' workshops, sat on the floor beside silversmiths hammering out their gracious, richly decorated wares, and watched magnificent performances of traditional dancing and music.

After three days I flew back to Djakarta. I travelled in a small R.A.F. aircraft piloted by a Wing Commander. Taking off from an airstrip outside Djokjakarta, we rose into the sky, and soon all the beautiful landscapes of that corner of Java were spread like a living map below us. The most dramatic feature of the scene was the tall, conical, active volcano called Mirapi. Its handsome summit, rearing some 14,000 feet above sea level, belched forth a great plume of smoke which rose fluttering into the sky like a vast black ostrich feather. Arranged up the mountain's sides were terraced padi fields, and all around its foot spread other tropical vegetation, both cultivated and wild. No scenery could be more beautifully, more extravagantly luscious.

According to ancient tradition, Mirapi was a home of the gods. The golden flames leaping within its crater and the dark smoke rising from its peak were signals of their presence; and the current mood of the deities could be divined from the appearance of those natural phenomena. If the fires were moderately subdued and the smoke coiled calmly from its highland chimney, they were in a genial temper; but if the flames protruded boisterously above the volcano's summit, and the smoke vomited with filthy vivacity above them, the gods must be angry. That would be a sign to all the mere mortals living around to beware of their wrath.

That afternoon the lordly ones' mood seemed to be somewhere between those two extremes. A lofty column of smoke rose ceaselessly from the crater, so sootily dark that, although no actual flames emerged from the furnace below, its fires were evidently tumultuously active not far beneath the surface. The sight was noble, and I wished to take photographs of it. I asked my pilot whether we could fly round the mountain-top where I could secure dramatic snapshots. He agreed to the proposal.

As we approached the volcano our aircraft gradually ascended higher into the atmosphere until we attained the 14,000 feet elevation of the smoke-puffing summit itself. First we circled round

Mirapi from some distance away, and then drew nearer so that I could secure some real close-ups of the eruption. It was exciting photography.

When I had satisfied my desire for pictures I asked, "Can we fly through the belching smoke? I'd like to look down into the crater and catch sight of the gods within."

The Wing Commander silently nodded his head, and flipped whatever switch was required to make the aeroplane mount higher. Slowly we climbed another few hundred feet, and then the plane turned its nose towards the voluminous tower of smoke—and flew into it. Until that moment our passage had been steady and smooth, but as soon as we entered the murky cloud our craft tossed and rolled violently this way and that, continuing to do so until we emerged once more into clear air on its farther side. I clung to a hand-grip to hold myself steady as I gazed down into the mountain's nether regions, where I saw several leaping flames licking the smoke, but no supernatural beings. I was too fascinated by the wild sight to try to take a photograph.

"Can we do that again?" I asked after we issued into the clear blue sky.

The pilot nodded his head once more, saying not a word.

We repeated our performance; and again the flying-machine pitched vehemently up and down and this way and that as we penetrated the viciously agitated smoke. The view that I saw in the crater below was like a premature, preparatory glimpse of hell-fire. I attempted to take a picture of it, but the angle was too sharp for success; and I felt I could not ask my airman guide to tilt the aeroplane sideways so that the camera could get a straight view of the cauldron's awful conflagration.

When we emerged from the plume of smoke our vehicle at once resumed its steady, calm flight.

I thanked the Wing Commander for being so confidently daring as to fly us through the volcano's spouting excretions.

He smiled and remarked, "I'm glad you don't want to do it again."

"Why?" I asked.

"Because this aeroplane's not supposed to fly above 12,000 feet," he answered.

I felt very impressed by his cool courage, and I remarked that on my return to my headquarters in Singapore I would recommend him for immediate promotion to the rank of Air Chief-Marshal.

He laughed and begged me not to say a word to any Air Force authorities about our escapade, otherwise he might be deprived of his present commission and demoted to the ranks!

As he said this I noticed that he was making the aeroplane drop as rapidly as possible to an altitude comfortably below 12,000 feet.

Lopokova

One of my enthusiasms when I was an undergraduate at Oxford
was the Russian Ballet. I had gained my first glimpse of it when,
as a young boy, I saw the supreme dancer Anna Pavlova perform
one evening in London. That was an unforgettably beautiful,
almost magical sight. Through the next several years I went to
boarding-school in Hampshire, and during my holidays I usually
departed to Scotland, the Norfolk Broads or somewhere else
away from Town; so I had little opportunity then to be dazzled
by other theatrical stars in the capital.

Later I spent more of my vacations in London. As it happened,
those years from 1918 to 1921 coincided with the renowned
Diaghilev Ballet Company's earliest seasons there. They were
glorious times for audiences who revelled in the grand art of ballet.
In Diaghilev's team a remarkable group of geniuses were gathered
together under the leadership of the temperamental but brilliant
director himself. The principal musical composer was Stravinsky,
the chief choreographer Leonide Massine, and among the designers
of costumes, décor and scenery were Picasso, Matisse and Derain.
As for the dancers, the ballerinas included Lopokova, Tcherni-
cheya, Sokolova, Danilova and Karsavina, whilst the most prom-
inent male performers were Massine, Idzikovski and Woizikovski.

Whenever the Diaghilev Company came to London I was one of
their zealous devotees. I had little spare cash to spend on enter-
tainments—or anything else—in those days; and I could not afford
to sit in a box, among the stalls, or even amidst a circle of the
theatre. Instead I first stood for two or three hours in the queue of
other impecunious enthusiasts on the pavement outside the gallery

doors, and so qualified in due course to watch the show from "the gods" within.

From the gallery's Olympian heights I became familiar with *The Sleeping Princess, The Three-Cornered Hat, La Boutique Fantasque* and other enthralling ballets. Their music enchanted me, but what made me truly ecstatic was the dancing. I felt as if I could watch until Kingdom Come its every step, glide, leap, pirouette and other graceful movements enacted with such perfect skill. All my fanatical companions in the gallery evidently felt likewise, for we stayed tensely hushed and motionless—completely spellbound—throughout each scene; but when it ended no other part of the audience burst into such prolonged, thunderous applause.

The dancers appeared like some kind of divinities to me, even though I knew them to be mere mortals. They were artistes who achieved superlatively one of the most lovely of the arts. Among them my favourite masculine performer was Gorgi Idzikovski, and my favourite female Lydia Lopokova.

At that time I was not acquainted with anyone who moved in distinguished theatrical circles; and so I had no opportunity to meet either my hero or my heroine. I never got nearer to them than the vast distance stretching between "the gods" and the stage. From that remote, impassable point of separation I watched them night after night, and for me they remained dream figures in a gorgeous hallucination occurring in the glare of the footlights.

II

Nor did I know in those days another celebrated personality who happened to be present every evening in the same playhouse. To me he was just a name printed now and then in the newspapers—and I was completely unaware of his existence in the theatre. He was John Maynard Keynes, the great, world-famous and indeed world-shaking authority on economics. He did not appear in the gleam of the footlights during the ballets; nor was he one of the shadowy figures sitting near me in the gallery. He was lost to my view in the darkness of the auditorium yawning like a chasm below me. Every night (I learned later) he occupied a seat in the stalls.

Keynes was a man of various distinguished attainments. The most potent economist of his generation, and perhaps of the century, he exerted an influence in national and international affairs more profound than that of almost any contemporary statesman. He also had several other claims to fame; and among them was his scholarly interest in the arts. His special passion was music, and he became an eminent patron of both the opera and the ballet.

Yet his affection for the ballet was not the prime reason for his nightly attendance in the stalls during the Diaghilev Company's season in London. He had fallen in love with more than the music and dancing; he had given his heart to Lydia Lopokova. And that was little wonder! Her small, slim, lithe figure poised on tiptoe in an elegant white ballet dress, with her face lit by the inspiration of dance, seemed angelic.

In fact Maynard Keynes was courting her. If I had known this at the time, I would perhaps have dropped something rather crushing on his head from my lofty seat in the gallery. But I was ignorant of the wooing, and so it continued without disturbance. Before long the attraction became mutual on both sides of the orchestra. Lydia fell in love with Maynard; and soon afterwards they became betrothed. Then she retired from the stage and the happy pair got married.

III

I met them in the flesh for the first time more than twenty years later, when I was the British High Commissioner in Canada. One day in 1944 Lord Keynes (as he had become) arrived in Ottawa to conduct some important financial negotiations with the Canadian Government; and his wife came with him.

I went to meet the distinguished visitors at the airport. On an early summer's morning I waited beside a runway to welcome

them. Beside me stood a somewhat formal Canadian Minister of
Finance, whilst at our backs were marshalled two rows of his
and my officials. They were a parade of solemn-faced financial
experts wearing neat black jackets and pin-striped trousers. The
Keyneses' aeroplane alighted, and we watched it as it taxied slowly
towards us. At last it came to a halt twenty yards away, its pro-
pellers flipped round a few more times and then stayed still, and
its noisy engines suddenly fell silent. An expectant hush enveloped
the scene.

A ground-crew wheeled a high stairway to the aircraft's door
so that the passengers could alight. As the entrance opened I
advanced to greet Lord Keynes—but instead of him a female
figure emerged on the platform at the head of the stairs. She
looked at me, and smiled. How well I remembered that charming
and characterful, if rather peasant-like Slavonic face! For a few
seconds she hesitated on her high perch—just as I had often seen
her stand motionless until the audience's applause died down at
her first entry on the stage in Diaghilev's programmes—and then
she began to trip down the steps towards me. She no longer wore
her neat white ballet dress and tights, but was sumptuously
wrapped in a brown fur coat and hat. I thought I detected that her
body was somewhat plumper than it had been when I last set
eyes on it many years ago; but this did not matter. At once I knew
that her personality possessed all its old magic, and that she was
not so much Lady Keynes as Lydia Lopokova.

Since she and I had never met, I stepped forward to introduce
myself politely to her. But she ran with out-stretched hands towards me, flung her arms round me in a warm embrace when we
came together, and before I could say a word exclaimed aloud
with a slightly Russian accent, "Oh, my dear High Commissar,
how are you? Last night I dreamed zat I was lying in bed, and
zat you were lying in my arms."

No doubt the Canadian Minister of Finance and our teams of
advisers were rather startled by this unorthodox meeting; but with
impeccable official decorum they betrayed no hint that they had
noticed it. They pretended to be deaf and blind. So far as I was

concerned, I hoped that in the hush of the early morning the whole population of Ottawa had overheard my greeting from the great ballerina.

Lord Keynes followed several paces behind her, and his and my exchange of welcomes was also cordial, if rather more conventional. I introduced the two visitors to the waiting Minister and our array of officials. We all chatted together for a while, and then jumped into motor-cars to drive into the city.

IV

An hour later I went with my advisers to call on Keynes in the suite of rooms where he was staying in the Château Laurier Hotel. We were to hold a preliminary talk about the financial negotiations which he would start with the Canadian authorities that afternoon.

We sipped cups of coffee and chatted for a while prior to commencing serious business. The reason for this delay was that Keynes had misplaced the key to the official red box containing his secret documents and so could not get at the papers which he needed for our discussion. He thought he had given the key to his wife to keep with other precious objects in her handbag; but she declared that he had not done so, and that, in any case, it was not there. Whilst the rest of us conversed about the local weather, the latest war news and other items of topical interest she busied herself in their bedroom searching through the pockets of his trousers, her trinket boxes, various recesses in their suitcases and other likely places—but in vain. She kept passing in and out of the sitting-room where we talked, reporting to him one failure after another. She felt very concerned, and uttered little exclamations like, "Oh, dear Maynard, someone must have stolen ze key" or "Perhaps you dropped it, Maynard, in ze aeroplane, and it's now on its way back to London." He remained exceedingly calm in the face of what appeared to be a dangerous disappearance of a top-secret object, expressing the opinion that it would turn up somewhere in due course.

At length he decided to wait for the key no longer, remarking that he could probably remember everything that was written in the documents. We therefore repaired to a private study to start our conference. As he, my officials and I settled round a table, Lydia waved *au-revoir* to us and told Keynes she would go to have a bath and change of dress before a lunch party which the Prime Minister, Mr. MacKenzie King, was to give later in their honour. She still wore her fur coat, for the crisis about the missing key had preoccupied her completely ever since their arrival.

We shut the door and started our discussion. Keynes told us the views of the British Government on the matter for negotiation, presenting the case with that brilliance of argument for which he was famous. I explained to him the likely opinions of the Canadian Ministers; and we began to analyse the problems to which we must find solutions.

Whilst we were in the midst of considering a difficult point a knock sounded on the door.

Keynes called, "Come in."

The door opened, and into the room slipped Lydia Lopokova. She was no longer wrapped in furs; nor did she wear even a dress. For a moment I thought some whim had made her put on a ballet costume, for her long, shapely legs were as exposed as if she wore tights. Then I realised that they were naked, and also that the dramatic skirt of a ballerina's outfit was missing. In fact she wore nothing but a short white chemise (presumably with a pair of brief drawers below) which hung flimsily round her otherwise bare body. In that state of near nudity she stood in apologetic manner casting a half-guilty, half-mischievous look at Keynes as she said, "Oh Maynard darling, I am so sorry. You did give me ze key; and I forgot zat I hid it for safety between my little bosoms." At that she clutched in her hands a ribbon hanging round her neck, and as she lifted it over her head raised from between her breasts—which so far as we could detect were not quite so small as she suggested—the lost article.

Keynes chuckled with laughter, remarked that he had said the treasure would turn up somewhere, and accepted the key from her.

She blew him a kiss, turned in a ballerina's pirouette on her toes, glided through the door, and closed it behind her.

V

During the Keyneses' visit the summer temperature in Ottawa rose very high, reaching a few points above 100°F. The atmosphere was almost intolerably hot not only through the daylight hours, but also in the middle of the nights.

One afternoon when I was drinking tea with Lydia and Maynard he described to me a sight which he alleged he had seen in the small, dark hours of that morning. Owing to the breathless heat in their bedroom he could not sleep, and lay uncomfortably conscious on his mattress. He heard Lydia tossing on her near-by bed, evidently also wide awake. Then the sounds of her restless movements ceased, and he became aware of her rising from her couch, quietly opening the door, and stepping into the corridor, where she switched on a light. He rose to see what she was doing, and to enquire whether he could help her. Looking into the passageway, he observed her perspiring, stark-naked figure hastening purposefully along it and then disappearing round a corner leading to their kitchen. Curious, he followed her, and reached the turning in time to see her slip into the kitchen and close its door behind her. He continued his inquisitive pursuit. When he pushed the kitchen door ajar and poked his head into the room he spied her opening the lid of a large ice-box, squeezing her body into the freezing interior, and shutting the lid "like Alice in Wonderland disappearing down the White Rabbit's tunnel."

Lydia laughed at his tale; but she did not either confirm or deny its veracity.

VI

After that I often saw Maynard and Lydia, and we became great
friends. Sometimes the three of us reminisced together about
the earlier days when we were all so near and yet so far in a theatre
in London—Lydia dancing on the stage, Maynard sitting in the
stalls, and me perched in the gallery. Now and then we went to
the ballet together; but we did not part at the theatre door and
distribute ourselves in those separate places. We all sat side by side
exchanging comments on the music, the dancing and the décor.
Lydia's memories were particularly vivid on those occasions, and
she often told fascinating stories about her own theatrical experiences, triumphs and sorrows.

She gave us, for instance, her version of the reason why the
name of Tchaikovsky's ballet which should be called *The Sleeping
Beauty* got changed to *The Sleeping Princess*. In the Diaghilev
Company's performance of that classic she was cast to play the
heroine's part; but Diaghilev felt bothered on a certain point,
and mentioned it to her.

"Lydia," he said, "we mustn't do anything that might arouse
criticism of our production. We must maintain our standards of
perfection. The critics might make derogatory remarks about my
casting when you play the Sleeping Beauty, because your face is so
plain that no one could say you're beautiful. So I think I'll change
the title to *The Sleeping Princess*.

VII

She and Maynard were perfect partners in life. They shared
many cultural interests, and yet they were in some ways remarkably
contrasting personalities. One part of him was the cool, superbly
educated intellectual genius, whereas intellectually she was in
some ways nearer to an untutored though intuitively wise little

"gamine." Another part of him was the warm artistic enthusiast, and there she came nearer to being his equal in knowledge whilst being also his superior in practice. Each was superlatively distinguished in his and her own main field of endeavour. At the same time they were both charming human beings—friendly, unassuming, intelligent, and unspoilt by their respective fames. Lydia was an entirely natural, uninhibited person who always said exactly what she thought—and her chief thought was that Maynard was the ideal man for whom she would give up everyone and everything else in life. On his side, he loved her very dearly.

In his latter years his health deteriorated; he suffered from a heart weakness which made it essential for him to be careful in all that he did. He never allowed this circumstance to interfere with his important work, prudently taking no unnecessary risks yet generously taking all other chances. She was constantly at his side to help him. Thus, whenever he had to discuss highly confidential matters with guests at a meal which required that no servants should be present, she herself waited hand and foot on him and them.

I remember one such occasion in Washington when Lord Halifax (then our Ambassador in America), Maynard and I were conferring upon an important secret problem over lunch in the Keyneses' hotel rooms. A waiter and butler had brought our foods and wines, put them on a sideboard, and then withdrawn. For the next two hours we sat engrossed in our conversation at the table whilst the great ballerina, Lopokova, played the part of our waitress, periodically flitting silently round us as she served our soup, entrée and sweets and kept our glasses filled with drinks. She never spoke a word until we were about to sip cups of coffee. Our talk was then nearly finished, and as she handed round a tray with milk and sugar Maynard suggested that she should join us for this refreshment.

She put a hand affectionately on his shoulder and said with mock sorrow, "No, my darling! I used to be ze première ballerina but now I'm just ze second fiddle."

The Gouzenko Affair

On 6th August, 1945 an atomic bomb was dropped on Hiroshima. Soon afterwards the Japanese sued for peace, and the World War came to an end.

As British High Commissioner in Canada I held a garden party to celebrate the cessation of hostilities. To it came all the Ministers in the Canadian Government, the Foreign Ambassadors and Commonwealth High Commissioners, numerous Members of Parliament and other leading citizens in the capital with their wives—many hundreds of people sipping tea, munching cakes and expressing joy on my sunlit lawns on a high bluff overlooking the Ottawa River.

I stood in the garden receiving the guests as they processed past me in single file. My friend the Soviet Ambassador clicked his heels, held out a hand to greet me, and grinned. He could not speak a word of English, and I talked no Russian; but one of his second secretaries called Vitali Pavlov always acted as his interpreter. As usual this clever young man stood faithfully beside him. His Excellency muttered something in his native tongue, and Pavlov translated the sentence. It was the usual joke about my hobby of bird-watching. "Has any little bird whispered any important secret to you lately?" he enquired.

"No," I answered. "Have you caught any big fish in the last few days?"

This was a reference to the Ambassador's own favourite recreation—angling. Our conversations were invariably opened by an exchange of diplomatic pleasantries on those topics.

Pavlov interpreted my enquiry into Russian. The Ambassador smiled and shook his head.

I noticed a rather weary look in his eyes, and ventured another light-hearted remark.

"Too bad!" I said. "You look as if you'd been out fishing all night. The fish can't have been biting."

Pavlov looked startled; but before he had time to translate my observation to his chief the next guests pressed forward to shake my hand and the Soviet pair moved onward to join the crowd gossiping on the lawns.

II

A few minutes later I received a telephone message from Mr. Norman Robertson, the Permanent Under-Secretary in the Canadian Department of External Affairs. He sent his apologies for being unable to attend my party and explained that he was detained in his office by urgent business which had suddenly arisen. Indeed, he added that he wished for my help and asked whether I would go and see him as soon as my party ended.

I promised to do so.

When my last guest disappeared I therefore stepped into a car and drove to the department. I was ushered into Robertson's room, where I found him in conference with two high officers of the Royal Canadian Mounted Police.

"Come in, Malcolm," he said, "I've got something interesting that the Prime Minister wants me to tell you. He'd be grateful if you'd report it by top-secret telegram immediately to your P.M., Mr. Attlee."

He then told me the news. On the previous day a member of the Russian Embassy called Igor Gouzenko had come surreptitiously to the Canadian authorities, given himself up, and presented them with many official documents containing important Soviet secrets. Gouzenko had now been transported hundreds of miles away from the capital for safety from his recent Communist masters, and the papers which he had brought with him were being translated by expert linguists in Ottawa. Robertson asked me to tell Attlee that the Canadians would let him have further information as quickly as it became available.

He then said that one valuable document surrendered by Gouzenko had already been translated. It contained a list of spies working in Canada for Stalin and his comrades. Among a total of seventeen names was that of a woman on my staff in the British High Commission—a certain Miss Kathleen Wilsher. Robertson told me that the authorities had not yet decided what they would do about these apparently treacherous individuals, some of whom held important posts in Canadian Government Departments, in the Bank of Canada and in other similar institutions. Ministers would reach a decision shortly, after due consultation with their allies in London and Washington. In the meantime they would be grateful if I could keep a discreet eye on Miss Wilsher to ensure that, without arousing her suspicion, she had no access to fresh confidential official information which we did not wish the Russians to possess.

Robertson then said that Mr. MacKenzie King, his Prime Minister, would be grateful if I could serve on a small informal committee consisting of Robertson himself, his deputy in the Ministry of External Affairs, two top Intelligence Officers in the Royal Canadian Mounted Police, myself and my deputy to advise him on each stage of the handling of this surprising affair. As the Russian documents were translated they would no doubt reveal many unexpected and perhaps dangerous circumstances. In addition to other assistance which I could give, my membership of the group would enable me to report promptly to Attlee every aspect of developments, since MacKenzie King wished to share all the secrets with his colleague in London.

I of course accepted the invitation.

III

Igor Gouzenko's story is soon told. He had arrived from Moscow two years earlier to work as a cipher clerk for the Military

Attaché in the Russian Embassy in Ottawa. A young man of twenty-six, he was accompanied by his wife Svetlana and their infant son. At the time of his defection she was expecting their second child.

Life in Ottawa gave him many pleasant shocks. He had been led to suppose from propaganda fed to him and his fellow countrymen that existence in the capitalist world was miserable, with a tyranny that imposed abject poverty on the workers and withheld liberty from all citizens. He discovered a very different state of affairs in Canada. The system of Parliamentary Government prevented tyranny by anyone; infinitely more freedom for the individual prevailed than was the case in contemporary Russia; and the Canadian workers' standard of living was much higher than that enjoyed by the proletariat in the Union of Soviet Socialist Republics. Indeed, Canada was obviously a land of grand promise and spacious opportunity. Soon after they settled in Ottawa, Igor and Svetlana began to think they might prefer their young children to grow up in this free society instead of in the confined one of Russia.

From that moment onwards Gouzenko had it in mind to leave his post in the Embassy at an appropriate opportunity, in order to seek asylum, secure a job and make his home in Canada. To prove his sincerity to the Canadian authorities when the time came for his defection he would bring them a valuable gift. With this in view he started to select certain files in the safe of the Military Attaché's office, marking them with a private sign of his own which would enable him to steal them quickly when that became necessary.

According to the story I heard, he felt that the moment for his change of loyalty had arrived when an error which he made in the Embassy was discovered and reported to the powers-that-be in the Kremlin. By mistake one evening he left a secret document lying among various unimportant papers on his desk. He found it there the next morning—and at first felt upset. Apparently, however, no one had noticed it, for it remained untouched. As a precaution he reported the slip-up to his boss, the Military Attaché, a certain Colonel Zabotin. The Colonel was a capable and genial man who

recognised that, if he informed higher authority about it, young
Gouzenko might be punished to an unfairly severe extent. So—
assuming that nobody else was aware of the error—he read Gouzenko a little lecture about efficiency in safeguarding security, but
otherwise held his tongue.

Unfortunately his assumption was incorrect. The document on
the office desk had in fact been noticed by a certain significant
female. She was the charlady who cleaned the place every morning
—and who was an agent of Moscow's Secret Police (the N.K.V.D.)
appointed to keep a privy eye on Colonel Zabotin and his assistants. She came under the orders of one of the Embassy's second
secretaries, the same Vitali Pavlov whom I have already mentioned
as the Ambassador's interpreter. His prime, unrevealed function
in Ottawa was to act as the chief representative of the N.K.V.D.,
with the duty of spying on the Ambassador and all his staff.

When Pavlov received information from the charlady about
Gouzenko's carelessness he did not mention the matter to Colonel
Zabotin. Nor did he refer it to the Ambassador. Instead he reported the gaffe direct by telegram through his own private network to his masters in the Kremlin; and a few days later a message
arrived in the Embassy asking why Colonel Zabotin had not reported the incident. It ordered Gouzenko's recall to Russia.

Very disturbed, the thoughtful Colonel warned his cipher clerk
of what had happened; and Gouzenko promptly decided that the
time had come to transfer his allegiance from Russia to Canada.
When he left the Embassy after work on his last evening there he
extracted the files which he had already marked in the safe, hid
them on his person, and carried them away with him.

I should mention at this point that, as a result of subsequent
developments, a few months later Colonel Zabotin himself was
recalled to Moscow. He left the shores of North America on a ship
bound for the Soviet Union; but I am not sure that he ever arrived
there. Rumour whispered soon afterwards that he had jumped
overboard when the vessel was at sea, preferring death among the
ocean waves to the fate which was likely to greet him on dis-
embarking in his native land. I felt very sorry at the news, for I

knew the Colonel well, and respected him not only as a charming man and a competent soldier but also a devoted servant of his country.

IV

On leaving the Embassy Gouzenko went first to the office of an Ottawa newspaper, where he endeavoured to reveal to a member of its staff his identity and wish to transfer his allegiance to Canada. The journalist, however, could scarcely understand his broken English, felt sceptical, refused to assist him, and politely advised the young Russian to go and tell his story to someone in a Government department.

Frustrated, Gouzenko returned to his home, where he told his wife that the time had come for their flitting. She had long expected this, and early next morning the pair set out with their small son to surrender themselves to the Canadian authorities, taking nothing except the clothes they wore—and a brief-case containing the precious secret files which Igor had stolen from the Embassy.

The trio spent a fruitless day visiting office after office. Even a few officials who partly comprehended Gouzenko's tale did not appear to take it seriously. One of the places where they called was the headquarters of the Royal Canadian Mounted Police. I was told that Gouzenko had explained to a constable whom he encountered at its door that he was a member of the Russian Embassy who had grown tired of Soviet rule and desired to declare his loyalty to Canada. Unfortunately the policeman did not happen to be one of the most intelligent of Mounties. He replied that Gouzenko was trying to play a silly practical joke, that the Royal Canadian Mounted Police had more important things to do than talk to lunatic impostors like him, and that he should go away. When the alarmed Russian asked earnestly to see a senior officer in order to explain his case fully the other fellow became more cautious, wrote down Gouzenko's name, and told him to leave now, but to return on the morrow. The young cipher clerk did not dare mention to such an irresponsible individual the secret documents which he carried; and he had no choice but to depart.

He and his family emerged into the streets like stray waifs with no home to go to. They wandered helpless through the city. If at any time in their desperation Igor and Svetlana contemplated throwing themselves into the Ottawa River to drown there, the thought that they would first have to hurl in their little boy prevented them from committing that heart-rending deed. They sat on a bench in a public park and tried to devise some new plan; but none suggested itself to their baffled minds. Eventually they decided they had no alternative but to return to their flat for another night, hoping that the clerk's stealing of secret files from his office had not yet become known to his late masters, and trusting that some means of salvation would turn up.

They re-entered their apartment in the early evening. Soon afterwards someone knocked on its door and called Igor's name. He recognised the voice of a chauffeur in the Russian Embassy and made no answer. Very nervous now about his and his family's personal safety, he got in private touch with the occupant of a neighbouring flat who was a sergeant in the Canadian Air Force, and told him of their plight. Explaining his friendly intentions towards the Canadian Government, and disclosing his wish to give himself up with certain important Soviet documents, he sought the good man's aid. The two considered the problem together, and arranged for the Gouzenkos to quit their own apartment and spend the night in that of another helpful neighbour on the same floor of the building. Then the airman bicycled to the city police station to seek discreet protection for the hapless family.

In the meantime the incident at the R.C.M.P. headquarters had been reported to higher authority, and came to Norman Robertson's knowledge. He discussed it with an eminent officer in the British Secret Service who happened to be visiting Ottawa at the time, and they agreed that Gouzenko should be clandestinely received by Canadian officials in case he had valuable information to impart. At once the R.C.M.P. were instructed to act according to their motto—and "Get Their Man."

The police were therefore prepared to play their parts when the airman told them of Gouzenko's departure from his own flat to another. The stage was set for the next scene in the drama. Shortly before midnight the sergeant heard a tramp of feet on the landing outside his apartment, followed by a knock on the Gouzenkos' door opposite. After a brief silence he became aware that intruders were breaking into the locked and deserted flat, and he promptly telephoned the police. Soon afterwards two constables arrived and since the door of the flat was not tight shut, they walked in. A diplomatic skirmish followed. The Mounties found in the rooms, not their rightful occupants but four Soviet officials led by Vitali Pavlov. This quartet appeared somewhat embarrassed—as well they might, for the place was now a shambles. It looked as if a typhoon had blown through it, with armchairs tumbled upside-down, loose covers torn off sofas, beds stripped of blankets and mattresses, and cupboards flung wide open with their contents spilt on the floor.

One of the constables asked politely what the search party were doing. Pavlov answered that Gouzenko had left some official papers in the apartment, and that they had his permission to fetch them. When the policemen enquired where the Gouzenkos were, the Russian replied that they had gone to Toronto. At this one constable remarked that it seemed strange, if they really had got Gouzenko's agreement to their visit, that they should come without a key and be forced to break into the premises. Pavlov commented that the flat was Russian property, with which they were free to do as they liked. The argument continued for some time, until eventually both parties departed separately from the place.

V

Early next morning Gouzenko was taken to the R.C.M.P. headquarters, where he could at last tell his story coherently to a select audience of eager listeners. After a preliminary recital of its main facts an intelligence officer present expressed the view that this development was too important, and too pregnant with valuable possibilities, for them to risk destroying its potential results by keeping the Gouzenkos in Ottawa. By now Pavlov and his minions must be anxiously searching for every possible clue to their whereabouts, and the longer they stayed in the city, the greater would be the danger of discovery. He suggested that the present interview should therefore be broken off, and that the Gouzenko family with one or two experts should be motored to some more remote place where the talk with Igor could be resumed. Their discussion would obviously continue profitably for several days; and in the meantime his collection of Russian documents could remain in safe keeping in Ottawa, where a team of interpreters would start translating them.

This plan was promptly agreed. Gouzenko heaved a sigh of relief, and the meeting adjourned.

Shortly afterwards two cars began a journey which carried the defecting family, a couple of intelligence officers, a guard and a cook hundreds of miles across country to lodgings where they would stay undetected and undisturbed through the next week or more. For hours each day Gouzenko would tell the officers everything he knew about Russia's policies on various matters.

VI

That tense succession of events occurred on the day prior to my garden party.

Naturally Gouzenko's disappearance caused alarm and despondency in the Russian Embassy. Pavlov learned during the day following the cipher clerk's departure that he had extracted some files from a safe. He reported the loss to the Ambassador, and went that night with aides to Gouzenko's flat to arrest him and recover them. When they found that the young man and his wife had fled, one of their first guesses was that he had surrendered himself to the Canadian authorities; but this impression was shaken when mounted policemen suddenly turned up at his flat, apparently themselves ignorant of his whereabouts. The element of doubt in the Russians' minds was encouraged by a deliberate leakage from the Canadians—through discreet channels which they knew would reach the Soviet Embassy—that Gouzenko had attempted to secure an interview in the police headquarters and had been summarily ejected from the place. Canadian officials also learned quickly about Gouzenko's vain effort to be received in a newspaper office, and they likewise arranged that this incident should come to the knowledge of the Russians. So the Soviet representatives were given an accurate impression of Gouzenko's frame of mind in the early evening when his efforts to give himself up had failed. Knowing his youthful inexperience, the intelligence sleuths in the Embassy felt that this series of rebuffs might have produced in him a suicidal mood. They realised that he must be terrified lest he should be recaptured; and they wondered whether in helpless despair he had thrown himself with the secret documents into the Ottawa River.

They certainly considered this possibility, for I learned that members of the Russian Embassy spent the small hours of that morning searching the river banks for any relics of the missing clerk and papers. No wonder Pavlov betrayed startlement at my party when I remarked casually to the Ambassador that he looked as if he had been out fishing all night, without success!

VII

For the next few days the Canadian authorities kept a watchful eye on the agents whose names appeared in the first of Gouzenko's documents to be translated; but partly in order to keep the Russians guessing as to whether Gouzenko himself was alive or dead, in touch with the Canadian Government or wandering somewhere in apprehensive loneliness, none of them were arrested. We also hoped that one or more of these individuals might take some step which would reveal additional facts about their clandestine activities. But none of them did.

They were a mixed bunch of characters ranging from quite important to much humbler beings, all of whom in one way or another had access to Canadian official secrets.

The case of Miss Wilsher threw an interesting light on methods used by the Russians in recruiting their agents. She was a respectable and quite brainy spinster nearer forty than thirty years old. A pleasant if rather plain, spectacled woman, she perhaps suffered from a double sense of frustration. First, being a single female with no apparent prospect of marriage, and also with no boy-friend, she never received any satisfaction for her romantic instincts. Second, although she was a quite capable graduate of the London School of Economics, she had not achieved the promotion in Government service which she felt was her due. In both the emotional and the intellectual spheres, therefore, she probably nursed grievances; and some Communist acquaintance may have recognised these feelings in her, and played on them to secure her agreement to certain improper actions which no doubt inflated her sense of self-importance.

She had been for several years a zealous member of the Canadian Communist Party; and at periodic meetings of one of its study groups she gave to another, male member bits of information which she gleaned from official records in the British High Commission. In that commission she was the assistant keeper of the Registry, where stacks of important papers were stored—although fortunately the most confidential documents of all (such as those describing work then being done in the United States, Britain and Canada towards the production of the first atomic bomb) were not among these.

Later, by a clandestine arrangement, she used to be picked up every now and then after dark in an Ottawa side-street by another man. He would take her for a drive in a car, during which she gave him interesting intelligence which she unravelled during her work in the High Commission. Afterwards he dropped her at some convenient place out of doors. That was all. Nevertheless, she no doubt got a little thrill of pleasure out of the intrigue; and in some degree it flattered her 'ego'.

In all this she was perhaps innocent of any conscious treachery to her country. The men who were her contacts were not Russians, but Canadians. Possibly all she knew was that they were fellow-members of the local Communist Party, and she remained unaware that they served also as spies for the Soviet Embassy. Therefore she may not have realised that every bit of intelligence which she gave them was passed to the Russians; she thought it was merely given to her Canadian comrades for furthering the Marxist-Leninist cause in Canada.

VIII

Perhaps the most dangerous agent from the point of view of the information he might be able to leak to the Russians was a certain Dr. Alan Nunn May. He was a member of a British team of nuclear physicists working in a laboratory in Montreal on experiments which—unknown to all of them except their chief, Professor (later Sir) John Cockcroft—were connected with the prospective making of the first atomic bomb. No one knew about that supreme secret except President Roosevelt and a small number of high officers in the United States, Winston Churchill and a similar group in Britain, and MacKenzie King with another select handful of men in Canada. The Canadians came into the picture because a uranium mine beside Great Bear Lake in their Far North was the principal place within Western Allied control where the rare raw material required for the potential weapon could be found.

For this reason I had been told confidentially a considerable time earlier of the shattering revolutionary prospect of the bomb. One day without warning a "Top Secret" telegram from Downing Street arrived in my office, to be deciphered by nobody but myself. Fortunately it contained only a few sentences; and so I was able to translate it without too much difficulty. It announced that a certain nameless individual would arrive by a special aircraft at a precisely specified hour at Ottawa airport on the following morning; and it instructed me to meet him in person, since he had information of the highest importance to impart to me alone. The message added that his name would be divulged to me in a further cable which would come into my hands that evening. Sure enough, the second missive arrived several hours later containing nothing but the solitary surname.

I met the fellow next day. For a while we discussed the weather, and then he asked me where we could go to talk alone. Since my house happened to be full of guests, I invited him to lunch with me at the Rideau Club, explaining that after the meal we could withdraw to the card-room on its top story, which no one ever entered until the nightly bridge games started several hours later. He agreed to this proposition—and after a hearty luncheon we ascended to the lofty, empty room.

He looked carefully behind its curtains, and found no one lurking there. Then he closed all the windows. Glancing beneath the card-tables in the otherwise unfurnished chamber, he recrossed the floor, opened the door to see whether anyone was standing outside, and then shut it again and locked it. Afterwards, with a surreptitious gesture, he motioned me into a chair, drawing another seat for himself alongside me. I wondered whether he might be a sadistic murderer planning to put me painfully to death; so I sat down cautiously, ready to leap up and defend myself at the slightest suspicious movement. He smiled affably, however, and peaceably settled at my side.

Then in a hushed, almost inaudible voice he delivered his message. He announced that scientists working in unheard-of laboratories at unmentionable places had just discovered the means of making a secret weapon which would defeat our enemies and end the World War "in five minutes." It was an atomic bomb. He explained that Winston Churchill had sent him to see me because the only place in Western Allied territory where an essential raw material for its manufacture could be mined was at Port Radium on Great Bear Lake in Canada. Our Prime Minister therefore wished for my advice as to the minimum number of people in the Canadian Government whom we should tell about this discovery, so that we could gain their secret co-operation.

I gave him my counsel; and that afternoon we went to break the news to MacKenzie King.

One result of that unforgettable day was the establishment in Montreal of a team of scientists who would toil on research projects associated with the production of the bomb. As I have already mentioned, John Cockcroft was the leader of the group, and Nunn May was one of his assistants. Cockcroft himself knew exactly what was the principal purpose of their labours; but the doctor knew only a fragment, and not the decisive fragment, of that aim. Nevertheless his individual contribution was significant, and from its nature he might possibly be making some guesses. Those of us in the know were therefore appalled when we saw his name on Gouzenko's list of Russian agents, for we realised that he must have been passing to his foreign masters at least some scraps of information which they should not be allowed to know.

We decided that I must summon Cockcroft immediately to Ottawa, and warn him confidentially that we had just learned that Nunn May was a spy for Russia. In order to reduce the chance of his sudden visit to me becoming known to May and his Soviet bosses, my message said that he must tell no one of his journey, that he should make it by driving himself in his own car the whole distance each way, and that he must start from Montreal around the time at night when everyone else in the city had gone to bed, and return there before other people awoke in the early hours of the morning.

He reached my house at about two a.m. I poured him an extra strong whisky-and-soda as we sat down to talk. After apologising for summoning him at such an unconscionable hour, I emphasised that his visit must remain unknown to anyone else in his Montreal team.

He was a calm, almost phlegmatic man, ready—as a brilliant scientist should be—for any unexpected situation; and he nodded his head sagely.

Then I told him that we had just received secret intelligence that Nunn May was a spy for the Russians.

To this day I can see the jump of astonishment which he gave.

For a moment he stared at me incredulously; but then he accepted the statement as one of fact. In reply to my questions he informed me exactly how much and how little the doctor knew about the scope of their work in Montreal, so that I could report this to our chiefs in Ottawa, London and Washington.

I told him that we did not propose to arrest his colleague for a while. In the meantime we wished Cockcroft to keep a very cautious eye on him. The fellow should be allowed to continue his work as before, so as not to arouse in him any suspicion; but care must be taken to ensure that he received no new significant knowledge.

Cockcroft then mentioned that Nunn May was due to fly to England in the following week to take up some work in London; and he asked whether any change might be necessary in this plan.

Surprised, I answered that for the time being it should stand, and that I would let him know after consultations with our masters whether or not the English visit could be allowed to take place.

For a day or two the top authorities considered whether it should be permitted, or whether the doctor (and therefore all the other agents) should be picked up before he was due to depart. The balance of argument seemed in favour of the latter course because, unlike Miss Wilsher, Nunn May was a direct, conscious informer for the Russians; and examination of the legal position showed that, whereas under Canadian law it would be simple to arrest and detain him in Canada, under British law it would be impossible to do so in England for such an offence committed in another country. We therefore decided that he and all the rest of the Soviet agents should be picked up before the date for his flight across the Atlantic Ocean.

Then a development occurred which made us reverse this decision. The new factor arose from the translation of one of Gouzenko's surrendered documents. It turned out to be a telegram sent from Moscow to the Soviet Embassy in Ottawa containing instructions to Nunn May about an appointment which he should keep after his arrival in England. From it we learned that he was to meet a certain other Russian spy in London; and, although the message of instructions was careful not to divulge any hint of that other person's identity, it contained exact details about how the doctor would contact him.

Nunn May's orders were that they should meet at eight o'clock in the evening on either the 7th October, the 17th October or the 27th October—all dates within about a month of his arrival in Britain. The rendezvous was to be at a specified point outside the British Museum. He himself should arrive there promptly at the appointed hour with a copy of *The Times* held under his left arm. A few moments later the accomplice would appear holding a copy of *Picture Post* in his left hand. The newcomer would step up to him and enquire, "What is the shortest way to the Strand?" The Doctor was then to answer, "Well, come along. I am going that way." The two would stroll off side by side, and as they went the English agent would remark, "Best regards from Mikel." If Nunn May showed no surprise at this greeting, his companion would know that he was the correct contact, and would proceed to tell him of another place where they should meet at an agreed time on a later day. Afterwards they were to part promptly, for it was only at the second meeting that exchanges of important information between them would take place.

As a consequence of this our Intelligence experts were extremely keen for Nunn May to proceed to London, so that they might learn from the tryst outside the British Museum the identity of the other individual. If they could do that, it would enable them to keep a close watch on him afterwards, and perhaps to make a vital break into a Russian spy ring in Britain. For this reason it was important for the doctor to be free to fly to London. So we decided to cancel his detention before he left Canada, and to risk being unable to lay legal hands on him after he landed in England. This meant postponing the arrests of all the other agents in Canada, since action against any one of them would immediately indicate to the Russians that the Canadian Government were definitely in touch with Gouzenko, and that they possessed all his secrets. We still hoped the Soviet authorities felt uncertain about Gouzenko's fate.

IX

An amusing incident occurred in connection with Nunn May's departure from Montreal airport on his transatlantic flight. We were anxious to keep an eye on him throughout his journey; so we arranged for two plain-clothes police officers to make the crossing as fellow travellers on the same plane.

An English group-captain was in command of an R.A.F. unit operating from the airfield. He happened to be a charming fool. He was also a personal friend of one of the detectives who would make the trip; and we feared that, if he were around the place when the passengers gathered for their embarkation, he might catch sight of the fellow and blurt out jocularly, "Hallo Charles, what on earth are you doing here out of uniform?" That could give Nunn May, standing near-by, a tip-off.

It therefore became necessary to ensure that the group-captain was nowhere near the airfield at the time of the aeroplane's departure. I sent him an invitation to come to tea with me in Ottawa that afternoon; and I received an effusive letter of acceptance in which he wrote that my proposal was extraordinarily kind, that he felt very flattered by the honour I did him, and that he always admired my informal friendliness. As I read it I blushed with shame.

When he arrived at my home we sat eating, drinking and discussing all sorts of trifling matters. He was very pleasant; but he gushed without stopping, telling me his views about the latest football games, Wild West films and war scares. One of my ears was cocked all the time to hear my telephone bell ring, for I had arranged that someone at Montreal airport should call me as soon as the plane carrying Nunn May and his police escorts took off. I would then know that it was safe for my guest to return to his normal duties.

In due course the bell tinkled. When I picked up the receiver I heard a voice say that the aircraft had just departed—and I told the group-captain that it was a great pleasure to meet him, but that I should not keep him away from his work any longer.

X

Nunn May's aeroplane landed safe and sound in London the next morning.

On each of the evenings of October the 7th, the 17th and the 27th an Intelligence Officer sat behind curtains in a near-by window watching the fateful spot along a street outside the British Museum. Neither Nunn May nor any other person carrying either *The Times* or *Picture Post* put in an appearance on any of those dates.

Obviously the spies' instructions had been cancelled.

By then other reasons had arisen why we should postpone for a further period the arrests of the members of the spy network in Canada; but eventually they were all detained. Although Nunn May was still in England, means were devised a few days later for achieving his arrest also; so the whole company of people on Gouzenko's list were safely locked up.

XI

Once or twice every day throughout the first few weeks of the Gouzenko affair Norman Robertson and I met secretly with our other colleagues to consider the latest problems it presented. The progressive translation of the documents which the defector brought from his Embassy kept providing us with fresh material for examination, all of it dramatic and some of it astonishing. During that period we lived like participants in a fabulous detective novel, the unfolding of which required quick decisions every few hours.

In the meantime Gouzenko and his family were enjoying themselves in their well guarded hideout. At our meetings we sometimes got amusing scraps of news about their activities. For example, they originally gave themselves up with no wardrobe except the clothes they stood up in; and one of the first duties of the detectives who accompanied them was to measure them all for new underwear, suits, dresses, stockings and footgear. The attendant mounties spent a hectic morning with improvised tape-measures making records of Igor's, Svetlana's and their child's vital statistics, and also drawing tracings on sheets of paper of the exact sizes of the trio's feet. Moreover, since Svetlana was steadily advancing in pregnancy, they had to plan ahead and to send us judicious orders for her maternity costumes.

When the time came for her confinement she was taken to a local hospital, where she pretended to be the wife of an immigrant Polish farmer. One of the policemen disguised himself as that imaginary settler, and several times visited the maternity ward to sit at his alleged spouse's bedside through her crisis. After the baby was born he showered paternal admiration on his supposed progeny, always speaking in carefully rehearsed broken English. The infant was a girl who weighed seven pounds, twelve ounces at birth; and in a gesture of cordial welcome the Royal Canadian Mounted Police in Ottawa sent a complete set of nappies, blankets and other requirements as a gift for this newest little Canadian.

Igor Gouzenko and his growing family have all survived; and so his and his wife's great ambition that their children should grow up as citizens of spacious, free and happy Canada has been realised.

Concubine Street

When I left Canada in 1946 I went to live on the opposite side of the world. For the next two years I was Governor-General of Malaya, Singapore and British Borneo, and afterwards I became Commissioner-General in South East Asia with responsibilities covering the whole of that vast, attractive and somewhat tumultuous region. During those years I came in touch with a different sort of international Communist activity from that revealed by the Gouzenko affair. The Reds employed other means to stir up trouble for the Western Powers and their friends in the Orient. For example, in 1950, the jungle war initiated by Chinese guerrilla fighters broke out in Malaya.

Soon after it started I began travelling widely through the country, visiting not only local administrative authorities in dangerously exposed areas, but also rubber planters on remote estates in order to discuss their problems with them on the spot, encourage them to stay calmly in their jobs, and make them feel that we top Government Officers living in safer urban centres shared their troubles. This involved many journeys through forest regions where the foe might (or might not) be lurking in ambush among thick-growing trees beside the road.

The High Commissioner in Kuala Lumpur and the Governor in Singapore, supported by their police and military advisers, tried to insist that I should be accompanied by an armed escort wherever I went; but they could not issue orders to me. My superior official status enabled me to resist their opinions, which were compelling on everyone else. I argued that it would spoil the helpful effects of my excursions to people living in perilous districts if I arrived with a gun-bristling troop of defenders: I should show the same disregard for danger as we expected them to demonstrate. When my colleagues retorted that some of the rubber barons hired a bodyguard to sit with a rifle on the front seat of their cars, and that all of them at least armed themselves with pistols, I answered that the poorer ones had to do without the former protection and that I personally was such an erratic shot with a pistol —which was true—that the latter resort would involve undue risk to innocent lives. I added that I was a very small man, that my chauffeur was a very fast driver, and that I was therefore about the tiniest and swiftest-moving target in all Malaya.

The authorities had no choice but to shrug their shoulders and accept what they regarded as my obstinate stupidity. They urged that, in any case, I should not advertise my presence to the foe by flying the Union Jack on my car as I sped through the countryside; but this counsel I also rejected because part of my purpose was precisely to "show the flag" in defiance of the enemy. Only some years later, when that forceful character General Sir Gerald Templer became High Commissioner in Malaya, did he firmly insist that I should either travel up-country with a bodyguard or else not at all—and I decided on the latter. I could not bring myself to visit fellow participants in the struggle who were in danger whilst enjoying absolute security myself. In any case Gerald's great abilities were by then getting the situation well in hand.

As it turned out, throughout that period my excellent Chinese chauffeur, named Kiat, and I both escaped without a scratch. Only once did a bullet whizz through our windscreen and pass safely out of a side window. On another occasion I did think that perhaps I faced instantaneous death. I was travelling with a District Officer for dozens of miles through the thick jungle of Pahang which we knew to be occupied by Communist rebel gangs. Suddenly, on rounding a sharp bend, we spied a fallen tree lying across the road twenty yards ahead of us. Presumably it was an ambush. We brought the car to an abrupt halt and waited breathlessly. Moments passed without a sound or movement. We gazed with tense, apprehensive concentration into the forest all round us, with its myriad trees staring unco-operatively back at us. Nothing happened. For two or three minutes we sat motionless except for our eyes searching this way and that into every visible nook and cranny of the nearby undergrowth. Then slowly and deliberately we opened the doors of the car, stepped out, and approached the tumbled tree to remove it from our path. We thought that as we stooped to drag it away—thus momentarily immobilising ourselves for protective action—shots might ring out. Yet the dumb quietude continued unbroken throughout the exercise. The tree must have fallen by accident across the road. Afterwards we drove safely onwards.

A few miles later we received a second shock. Rounding another corner in the road, we suddenly caught sight of a rather formidable-looking object obstructing our path. It appeared like a camouflaged striped sack, perhaps filled with sinister explosive materials. As our vehicle once more slowed down the heap stirred itself into action, rose on to its four legs and strolled with leisurely dignity into the forest alongside the road. It was a magnificent tiger.

II

Even in Singapore city itself the Government authorities feared that an eminent official like myself might not be wholly safe. Knowing my habit of taking friends to eat tasty Chinese food at informal dinner parties in back-street restaurants where some of the best Cantonese chefs practised their art, they advised me that I should either abandon this practice or else permit armed police to guard the spot during my presence there. I refused both suggestions, urging that it would be a psychological error to change in any respect my way of life in apparent concession to the enemy. In any case (I said) if our foes intended to kill me, they would presumably find means of succeeding regardless of protective measures. No doubt this attitude on my part was a piece of foolhardy and pompous bravado—but I felt strongly that I should show contempt not only for the Communist bandits' cleverness, but also for our own security advisers' nervousness.

A few days later I was annoyed to discover that those officials had ignored my instructions and appointed a bodyguard to watch over me on all my outings in Singapore. One evening I gave a dinner party in my favourite Chinese restaurant. The place consisted of a small, rather dirty room filled with tables and chairs open to a public roadway. It was typical of many such gourmet establishments in the city's populous areas; and if its furnishings were untidy and its waiters rather shabbily dressed in only singlets, shorts and sandals, its crockery was nevertheless spotlessly clean, and its food delicious—unsurpassed anywhere in the world outside Peking, Shanghai and Canton in China itself. I often took V.I.P. house-guests there, to give them a glimpse of that aspect of Singapore's character as well as to enjoy a sumptuous banquet eaten with chopsticks.

Incidentally the place was situated in a locality where certain other pastimes were pursued. The lane's official name was Keong Sek Road, but it was generally known as "Concubine Street." The area did not constitute part of the city's red-light district, but certain ladies of perhaps somewhat easy virtue occupied rooms in an upper story along its quiet way. They were not prostitutes, but the recognised mistresses of quite respectable Oriental gentlemen who paid periodic visits to them there. Whether they entertained other occasional customers was anybody's guess, and nobody's business.

On the morning after my dinner party I was irritated to hear that a police squad had clandestinely followed me to the restaurant and taken up positions along its street to protect me from any would-be assassin's gun. I learned this when I was told that the ladies in question had been considerably alarmed, since they feared the officers of the law had come to raid their premises. I protested strongly, complaining that the police had disobeyed my orders, and remarking that, quite apart from this act of insubordination, it was inconsiderate of them to disturb unnecessarily the profitable occupation of some of Singapore's most peaceful citizens. They apologised, abandoned their efforts to guard me, returned to more useful duties, and (so far as I know) left me ever afterwards to my fate.

I continued to patronise periodically the excellent restaurant in Concubine Street. My guests were always delighted with its fare. One evening I entertained in it the world-famous 'cellist Pablo Casals. He had come to give a concert in Singapore on his way towards a tour of Australia and New Zealand. When he finished playing his 'cello gloriously to a crowded, enthusiastic audience in the local theatre, and had performed his final "encore," he came with me and a few other friends for supper in Concubine Street. We ate a delectable feast of about a dozen courses all washed down with cupfuls of *mao-tai*.

"They tell me, Your Excellency," the great musician remarked at one point in our conversation, "that you can walk on your hands. Surely that's not true; it must be a legend."

I confessed that the rumour was correct.

He looked astonished. "I don't believe it," he said.

"All right; I'll prove it," I answered.

The hour was about one o'clock in the morning, and the night was quiet, with most of Singapore's citizens already in bed. Concubine Street was a narrow thoroughfare with comparatively little traffic even at the busiest times of the day; and now it was empty except for our cars parked alongside a pavement. Only a few belated pedestrians now and then wandered through it.

I invited Casals to step out-of-doors, where my other guests joined him. In the middle of the road I stood on my hands and proceeded to walk upside-down along the street. At its farther end I turned round and strolled back, still topsy-turvy on my hands. Casals was very pleased, and kept crying loud exclamations of surprise. When I restored myself to my feet in front of him he was good enough to shout "Encore" with a similar sincerity to that of his own audience at the concert two hours earlier. I therefore repeated the act.

When I righted myself once more someone drew my attention to the windows of the rooms of the ladies living on the upper story along the street. Usually those windows were discreetly covered by curtains which obscured everything except a glow of light within; but now all the curtains were drawn partly aside, and through a chink in each one I could see a pretty female face peering down at me. Some of them were accompanied by a masculine countenance.

Remembering my strictures on the police, I felt ashamed at having disturbed them. However, I noticed looks not of fright but of amusement in their eyes; and I felt glad that I had contributed to the entertainment of them and their visitors as well as of my own guests.

Bullfight in Borneo

During my years in South East Asia I often visited the so-called "wild men of Borneo" in their homes in the jungly interior of Sarawak. Generally known as Dayaks, they are in fact divided into several different tribes, the principal among them being the Kenyahs, the Kayans and the Ibans. The greatest of these—though not in every way the most gifted—are the Ibans.

I have described in my book *Borneo People* my experiences among those capable, dynamic, likeable characters, and the friendships which I made with many of them. The noblest of those friends was the Paramount Chief, Temonggong Koh. In earlier days he had been the most accomplished and renowned headhunter of his generation, but now, in his seventies, he had reluctantly become a reformed character in that field of his activities. Universally revered, he was an elder graced with mellow wisdom who gave kindly leadership to his people. I shall write more about him in the next chapter.

Another close friend of mine was his principal lieutenant in tribal affairs, Penghulu Jugah. A much younger but also talented man, after Koh's death several years later he became his successor as Paramount Chief. In some ways he was a more suitable leader than the old man for the Ibans during the crisis in their history which they now faced. Vast changes were occurring everywhere round the world in the hectic mid-twentieth century, and even the natives living in Borneo's remote interior could not completely avoid them. And whereas the veteran Koh was so wedded to the traditional customs of his race, which had persisted virtually unaltered throughout his lifetime, that he did not comprehend the inevitable changes confronting Sarawak, Jugah's habits were less rigidly formed and his mind was more ready to understand novel ideas. Gradually he adjusted his thoughts and actions to some fresh notions. His shrewd intelligence was fortunate for his people at a period when they needed sagacious leadership.

They were in fact beginning to pass through the unforeseen, challenging experience of an unnaturally rapid transition from a rather primitive form of society to a more sophisticated modern one—a transformation which in recent times had upset the well-being of many hitherto simple, unspoilt tribes in various parts of the world. Some of the revolutionary changes taking place touched the economic basis of the Ibans' lives. Dependence on a wholly jungle economy was being steadily modified. Methods of agricultural production, means of communication, and habits of trade were all in process of alteration. Among other developments, the hitherto commercially unenterprising natives had started to be shopkeepers, partially ousting the immigrant Chinese from their monopoly as merchants in remote up-river bazaars.

Jugah himself had become the owner of two shops. One of these did business in a tiny market town called Kapit, whilst his other store stood solitary in a small forest clearing on the bank of a river in Borneo's distant interior. There a little timber shack owned by him was furnished with a couple of show-cases displaying women's sarongs, men's shirts and shorts, cheap jewellery, hurricane-lamps, frying-pans and other household utensils coveted by the Dayaks, who paddled their slim boats called prahus for dozens of miles up- or down-stream to make purchases over cups of coffee, glasses of rice-beer or bottles of a strange, newly imported liquid called Coca-Cola. Close beside the shop a bungalow accommodated whichever members of the Jugah family happened to be in charge of the business at the moment. In a rough paddock around it the chief grew an orchard of banana trees and fed a few hens, pigs and cattle. It was a modest yet radical trading-cum-agricultural Iban enterprise.

II

I often travelled with Jugah up the rivers into Sarawak's heartland discussing contemporary problems with him as we went, and observing their practical effects among the Ibans. I stayed with him and his family in their long-house on a bank of the Mereirei River deep in wild tropical jungle. His handsome wife Bini Jugah was a charming hostess, and their attractive daughters Siah, Sani and Anchang and intelligent sons Linggi and Alo treated me as an elder brother. In the evenings in their private room—in the centre of a row of other such family apartments stretching along the vast house—we sat on the floor eating and drinking, chattering and laughing. As we sipped native rice-wine after dinner the girls sang *pantuns* or songs of welcome to me, and we all exchanged news and told stories.

Sani was a vivacious young woman in her early twenties married to an Iban youth. Her face looked scarcely more than childlike, with innocently pretty features. Her black hair was straight and shining, her slanting Mongolian eyes and quick-smiling lips were comely and her limbs were lithe and smooth. Only her ripe breasts indicated her maturity. As was the case with all Iban females in those times, she usually wore nothing except a knee-length native skirt, although on gala occasions she donned also silver ear-rings, necklaces, bangles, belts and anklets. For the rest her adornment was simply the lovely honey-coloured skin of her race.

One evening she related an episode which had recently occurred to her. She and her husband usually lived in the crowded communal long-house, where they were busy from morning until night with the labours of running a vast household, as well as planting, cultivating and harvesting hillside padi, catching fish, hunting game and gathering jungle fruits. Every now and then, however, the pair left that sociable home to go and stay in lonely state many miles away in the bungalow connected with Jugah's shop. This was an isolated existence for people accustomed to waking and sleeping, working and playing, gossiping and laughing amidst a perpetual multitude of other human beings residing under the same extensive roof. In their solitary dwelling they might almost have been exiled to the barren lands of the Arctic—except for the dense forest filled with birds and beasts all around them. Their neighbours were the monkeys, wild boars, mouse-deers, hornbills and other inmates of the woodland encircling their tiny patch of cleared ground. Human visitors came only in small boat-loads spilling out of their prahus to visit the shop—such parties arriving perhaps two or three times a day on particularly busy days.

The empty hours passed slowly in the hot, humid, alternately sun-soaked and rain-drenched atmosphere. There was little work to occupy the couple. Besides an occasional brief spell of selling goods and serving drinks to customers in the shop, they had only a few hens and pigs to feed. They also tended a herd of one bull and three cows cropping the unkempt grass in the paddock.

That quartet of cattle had immense significance. They represented one of enterprising Jugah's boldest experiments, for they were to be the progenitors—the single Adam and a trio of Eves—of a large dairy herd-to-be which would provide a ceaseless, bounteous flow of milk for the local Iban population. Jugah was proud of the beasts, and very solicitous for their welfare. They had been brought from pastures in another tropical land; but it was still uncertain whether they would acclimatise themselves to Borneo's particularly hot and damp interior. One vital, and as yet unanswered, question was whether they would succeed in producing healthy calves. Would the bull continue to be potent? Would the cows remain fruitful? Jugah felt rather worried about the prospect, for although they had already lived on his property and guzzled his fodder for a considerable time, no sign yet appeared of any impending offspring.

He wondered uneasily whether his bull was qualified for the virile pioneering task assigned to it. He had bought it as a veteran which had proved its prowess in many other farmyards; but was it now too much of a veteran? Were its ageing powers too feeble, its potency too exhausted, to succeed in siring calves on the enervating Equator? Pondering earnestly on the problem, he decided that he should not stake everything on one animal of dubious merit, and he therefore bought a second, possibly more likely, founder-father for his dairy herd. This time he did not acquire an old, trusted and tried—perhaps over-tried—beast, but a youthful, lusty bull which would surely play havoc among the little harem of cows.

This new male was shipped up-river from the distant capital of Kuching. Jugah himself met it when it landed several days later at Kapit many miles down-river from his home, for he wished to escort it personally on the last lap of the journey. At first the suspicious brute refused to go aboard his prahu driven by an outboard motor; but eventually it was induced to settle amidships in a berth prepared for its comfort on a mattress of hay beneath an awning. Nevertheless it was not a docile passenger, trying more than once to jump overboard when the vessel tossed through rough waters. However, a mixture of cajolery and strong-arm methods preserved it from these attempts at suicide; and at last the boat arrived alongside the high bank climbing to Jugah's shop. Proudly the chief led the animal ashore.

Sani and her husband were looking after the shop at the time; and Jugah's wife had travelled from their long-house to join in giving the newcomer a cordial welcome. That evening they caught their first view of it only by lantern-light, for the troublesome voyage had taken so long that darkness was already falling. Jugah locked the beast into a shed for the night lest in nervous ignorance of its surroundings it should wander into the near-by jungle and never be seen again. He then gave his wife and Sani instructions how to care for it during its first few days, because he himself, with Sani's husband, must depart before sunrise the next morning to attend to some urgent tribal business farther up river.

At crack of dawn the two men departed, leaving the pair of women in charge of the homestead and its residents.

III

Whilst her mother was cooking breakfast that morning Sani let the young bull out of its shed so that it could begin to make itself at home browsing in their paddock. It ambled out nervously, sniffed the air, and apparently felt reassured, for it strolled a few more steps and started to graze with hungry satisfaction.

A minute later Sani was climbing the shop's steps to open the premises for the day when she heard a vicious snorting near the forest's edge. Looking round, she saw the old, long-resident bull standing there staring at the young bull with surprised disapproval. Its eyes bulged with rage, its muscles were taut like the string of a bow about to let fly an arrow, and its tail flicked slowly from side to side with displeasure.

Sani glanced at the younger creature, and saw that it had raised its head from feeding. It gazed at the other brute with an air of uncertainty about the proper protocol for their introduction.

The old beast pawed the ground testily for a few moments, and then started to advance purposefully towards the new arrival. The latter backed cautiously away, assuming a defensive posture. Suddenly the veteran gave a loud bellow, lowered its head and charged full tilt at the other. The youngster tried to side-step the attack, but was not quick enough to avoid a severe butting by the aggressor's flank as it careered past. The newcomer now also lowered its head to join in a duel; and when the other beast checked its onrush they glowered at each other with mutual antipathy.

Sani stood rooted to the ground, her eyes wide and her lips parted in shock. With no man around to help, she wondered what she could do to prevent their evident dislike for each other from breaking into violent hostilities.

But even if she could have thought of any appropriate action, it was now too late. With horror she saw the old bull advance again towards its rival, this time with more self-control, until their horns clashed as in the preliminary sword-play of a pair of fencers.

Their initial skirmish was brief. The senior animal was inspired by furious anger, but the junior was moved by no such powerful emotion, being still somewhat bewildered about the cause of this enforced contest. If the first's attack was passionate, the second's retaliatory action was therefore comparatively feeble. It gave way step by step, showing every sign of wishing to arrange a truce.

However, the elder's ire was uncompromisingly aroused, and would not permit any thought of peaceful co-existence. Instinctively it recognised the youngster as a challenger to the lordship over the herd which by established custom belonged to itself. The impertinent intruder must therefore either retreat completely from the scene, or be done to death. So the old bull persisted in harassing its adversary, periodically butting the youngster in efforts to gore it. Forced to defend itself, the other retaliated to the best of its perplexed ability; and a grim battle ensued. Yet it was a sad, unequal contest. Whatever the comparative prowess of the two might be in love, in war the veteran was the undoubted master.

When the protagonists were in the thick of their fray Sani ran past them from the shop to the house, shouting to her mother in the kitchen. The two women then watched the tourney from a window, feeling none of the enthusiasm of Spanish signoras observing a bullfight from seats in a theatrical arena. Their one desire was to stop the engagement—but they possessed no means of doing so.

The younger beast was so clearly defeated and so apparently condemned to destruction, that Sani's heart bled for it. She wished to put it out of its agony quickly. The thought filled her mind with apprehension, for she knew with what important hopes her father had introduced it into their family circle—but she could see no alternative. So she grabbed Jugah's hunting-gun from a nail where it hung on the kitchen wall, and asked her mother for a cartridge with which to shoot the poor animal.

The ammunition was kept in a locked box beneath Jugah's bed; and his wife refused to give Sani the key. The girl begged for a bullet, but her mama maintained firm opposition to the notion.

In view of her husband's interest in the new bull she did not wish to assume any personal responsibility for its death. If the evil spirits who haunt the Iban world had decreed that it should die, that was another matter, and the old bull would then no doubt kill it. Let that creature, not herself, be the agent of the sprites in executing their will.

Sani felt every blow delivered at the victim of the assault almost as if it were being inflicted on her own body. Then of a sudden she observed something which made her heart leap with joy. The younger animal backed away from its opponent, turned tail, galloped down a path descending steeply to the river, and plunged panic-stricken into the water. When the leaping foam of a gigantic splash subsided she saw its head floating on the stream's surface, with only its horns and face protruding from the depths. For some moments she feared that these too would sink from sight; but the animal's mask kept afloat and, turning towards the river's opposite shore a hundred yards away, began to advance gradually across the channel. By some strong instinct for survival the four-footed land-lubber managed to swim, keeping its puffing snout just above the water. Its legs, however, were poor substitutes for a fish's fins, and as it progressed slowly towards mid-stream the wild current grew stronger and swifter. So the struggling amateur swimmer was washed farther and farther down-river, almost disappearing from sight round a distant bend.

Nevertheless it persevered and eventually arrived safely on the other side. Sani clapped her hands when she saw first its whole head, and then its body rise from the deep a few yards from the bank. Planting its feet firmly on the ground of the shallows, it hesitated for a few moments, then wrenched its hooves free from mud, and half-stumbled, half-slithered ashore. Arriving on the dry, grassy bank, it turned and gazed back towards the house. Opening its mouth, it bellowed loudly in triumph, or humiliation, or challenge, or whatever other emotion a young bull feels in such a situation.

The old bull uttered a mild, contented retort, almost as if it were cocking a snook of contemptuous dismissal at its vanquished adversary. Then it ambled away to rejoin its cows feeding along the jungle's edge.

IV

Sani felt relieved but baffled. What should she do now? Fearful that if the new bull was left to wander alone on the opposite shore until Jugah returned two days later and decided on a right policy, the evil spirits would step in and take a wrong decision in the meantime, she considered what she could contrive to protect the situation. She consulted her mother, holding with her a council of war.

As they talked, a plan of action formed in Sani's mind; but she did not confide it to the cautious older woman lest she should forbid it. At the end of their discussion she slipped from the house and visited the old bull with his trinity of cows. The beast was accustomed to her periodic attentions, and did not suspect that on this occasion she harboured an ulterior motive. Whilst she talked to it in her usual ingratiating manner it permitted her to grasp it by a horn and lead it to a shed where it always sheltered during stormy weather. Still taking her friendliness at its face value, at her prompting the animal obediently entered the shed. Nor did it register any protest when she shut the door and bolted it.

Sani hurried to the river's edge and jumped into a prahu moored there. Untying the boat from its stake, she sat in its stern and started its motor. When her mother—with curiosity aroused by the sudden sound of an engine—arrived on top of the bank to see what was afoot Sani had already steered the craft into mid-stream. The girl waved nonchalantly to her parent as she turned the prahu down-river in the direction that the escaping bull had taken.

The journey covered a considerable distance, for the current carrying the swimmer along the channel had been strong. However, the animal still stood where it had landed on the opposite bank, looking disconsolate and forlorn. It did not move when Sani dropped anchor at a spot several yards away. She shut off the engine, stepped overboard waist-deep into the water, and turned the craft round so that its prow pointed back towards the house. Then she waded ashore.

The bull appeared quite glad to see her, making no motion beyond tossing its head when she approached, as if in some sort of non-committal greeting. Yet it eyed her doubtfully. She walked to it with feigned casualness. It readjusted its balance slightly on its legs, evidently ready to dash away if she made any hostile movement. Otherwise it stayed motionless, seeming lonesome and lost, and in need of a friend.

When Sani patted its neck, it relaxed its tension, accepting the gesture in the companionable spirit in which it was offered. The girl then spoke a few sympathetic words in the Iban tongue. Her companion could not have understood them, being a stranger in the land; but their tone did have a soothing effect on its hurt feelings, for it raised its eyes at her in a lugubriously mournful, gratefully sentimental gaze. She continued her ingratiating monologue, and the beast stayed unstirring, like a domestic cat or dog accepting a fondling.

Sani did not hasten to force the issue. From considerable experience she had a tactful manner with animals. Ibans are kind to all their dumb neighbours, making pets of monkeys and hornbills caught in the jungle, sharing their rooms with cocks and hens, and maintaining civilised relations even with the pigs which invariably live beneath the floors of their high-stilted homes. So Sani continued patting the bull, and addressing an occasional remark to it. Gradually its pride—which had been so grievously offended by the other animal's vicious behaviour—was appeased; and it turned its head and nuzzled its snout against her body.

She knew then that she had partially won its confidence. Slowly she raised a hand to clasp one of its horns. The beast registered no objection. However, when she tried to pull it gently forwards it resisted. She resorted once more to the magic of coaxing speech, and after a minute that worked. The animal took a step towards her, and then halted. She advanced another pace nearer the river, tugging with ever so gentle persuasion at its head to indicate that it should follow suit. The bull seemed sceptical, but after a brief hesitation obliged with cautious docility. In a few strides they reached the water's edge.

Sani waded ankle-deep into the shallows, attempting to draw her charge after her. At that point the beast again resisted. She pulled a little more strongly at its horn; but the bull stayed obstinate. Yet it did not toss its head, nor seek in any other way to free itself from her grasp, as it could easily have done. Instead, it raised its eyes to her and gazed into her face with a look of curious, pleading enquiry so comical—yet at the same time so trustful— that she would have burst into laughter if she had not feared lest the animal should misunderstand such an explosive response.

She looked back reassuringly at it and, greatly daring, placed her second hand round its second horn. At first she pulled with tender enticement rather than commanding force; but when the bull still resisted she increased the pressure of her otherwise polite invitation.

Again the situation became uncertain, and the result hung in the balance. One false move by Sani, and she would have lost control. The beast might at any moment resent her impertinence in seeking to persuade it to join her in a bath in the river, shake its head in abrupt, vigorous annoyance, and escape her grasp. She divined that it felt undecided, whereas she knew exactly what she wished to happen. Once more she murmured phrases in reassuring, seductive tones whilst at the same time increasing her tug on its horns.

She was nevertheless rather astonished, as well as relieved, when her resolution decided their difference of opinion, and the bull took a succession of slow steps into the water after her. Cleverly she did not make straight for the boat, but waded ever deeper into the stream until she was submerged almost to her armpits. She kept a tight hold on both the creature's horns as it paddled after her, sinking gradually up to its flanks.

She knew well the nature of the river-bed along its edges, for it was her regular bath-tub. From their earliest childhood the local Ibans splashed and washed and swam several times each day in its depths; and so they were almost as much at home in it as a shoal of fish. Sani therefore stayed sure-footed. Perhaps because the bull was less accustomed to this form of exercise—feeling in water almost as strange as a fish out of water—it followed her with surprising obedience. Apparently the farther she led it into the deep, and the more it felt out of its element there, the more consciously it relied on her experience to sustain it. She had won the dumb creature's trust to a point where it permitted her to drag it into a situation in which it had nothing to rely on but her protective goodwill.

Whatever the explanation, her companion made no protest when she turned, led it alongside the boat, and lifted herself into the stern without loosening her grip on one horn. It even waited patiently whilst she picked up a paddle with her free hand and started guiding the vessel towards mid-channel. At one moment it did try to make a stand, having half a mind to refuse to proceed any farther; but Sani maintained a tight grasp on its head and, for some reason, it could not reach a quick decision to force a parting from her. Probably it regarded her as its only friend in a very strange world and disliked the notion of breaking contact with her. In any case it altered its resolution once again, and followed the prahu step by step, sinking ever lower into the river.

She did not start up the engine until the animal was immersed shoulder-deep; otherwise the sudden noise might have given it such a fright that it would have turned tail and run helter-skelter for land. Instead she waited until it was so submerged that in its terror at the initial splutterings of the motor it would raise its hooves for flight, lose foothold, flounder helplessly in the torrent, and be forced to submit entirely to her will. Sure enough, at the engine's noisy awakening into life that sequence of events occurred exactly as she had foreseen; and an instant later the bull found itself struggling vainly in mid-stream whilst being dragged quickly forwards beside the accelerating boat. It sank almost completely, with only its face protruding above the water's surface whilst one of Sani's fists firmly clasped its horn to pull it safely along. Helpless, the animal resigned itself to whatever fate she decreed for it.

Thus, with one hand grasping the tiller and the other gripping the bull, she piloted the boat and the beast together across the long stretch of river back to her home. The operation was a delicate one requiring nice judgement to strike the right speed. She must make their progress sufficiently slow for the bull to manage to keep itself upright as well as afloat, and at the same time sufficiently fast for the prahu to make progress against the strong down-rushing current. But Sani was a typical Iban, with an intelligence, enterprise and boldness capable of coping with all sorts of difficult situations.

Eventually she brought the craft to shore below the house. As it came to rest she shut off its engine, and lifted her hand from the tiller. But she did not remove her other hand from the quadruped's horn. Instead, when she stepped overboard, she once more clasped its second horn in her second fist—for she feared lest a memory of the old bull resident on that point of land would make the youngster lose courage, turn tail impulsively, and navigate its way back to the opposite landing stage.

However, its recent odd adventure with her, the boat and the river had apparently so bewildered the poor brute that for the moment all other recollections were blotted from its mind. Stumbling to its feet in the shallows, it stood awaiting her next command. When she pulled at its head to induce it to march up the bank, it unhesitatingly did so. At the top her mother joined them, and together the women led the dazed animal to a chicken-run strongly fenced to protect the hens at night from marauding jungle predators. The old bull was still imprisoned in a nearby shed. They locked the new captive in the poultry's spacious cage, where it sank exhausted to the ground. Sani heaved a sigh of relief.

The other bull glimpsed its rival through a window in its stall, and at once became enraged. Bellowing and stamping, it heaved itself about like a miniature typhoon—but it could do nothing more. The women went indoors to perform their day's housework, leaving the antagonists to glower and swear at each other, if they were so disposed, at a harmless distance from one another. Gradu-

ally the old beast's anger subsided as it realised its frustrated help-
lessness.

Silence descended on the lush, sunlit scene, broken only by the
occasional shriek of a hornbill or chatter of a monkey in the forest.
For the next two days the quietude continued undisturbed.

V

When Jugah and Sani's husband returned on the following evening
their wives told them the story of the bullfight. The four promptly
formed themselves into a court of justice to try the case, and to
determine what they should do with the prisoners locked respectively in the shed and the chicken run. After long cogitation they
decided that, although the older animal might still be the more
powerful in war, the younger was probably more potent in love.
They therefore passed judgment that the former should be condemned to death, whilst the latter was preserved to fulfil its
destiny as the Creator of a great dairy-herd for the Iban people
in Borneo's interior.

Next morning the old bull was led from its cell, and shot at
dawn.

Death of a Titan

When I first met Temonggong Koh he had already passed man's allotted span of three score years and ten. As I have already written, in the prime of his manhood he was the greatest head-hunter of his generation. This proud fact was still displayed on his hands. It had been an Iban custom that, when a warrior chopped off somebody's head, he could advertise this success by tattooing with blue dye one joint of one finger on one hand. If he later bagged an additional top-knot, he could similarly adorn a second joint. For a third such trophy he could extend the decoration by the same extent . . . and so on. On Koh's two hands every joint of every finger, both thumbs, and much other space was covered with those enviable, bloodthirsty patterns.

However, under the rule of the famous White Rajahs of Sarawak, during recent times this favourite national sport had been gradually suppressed. The law decreed that all perpetrators of such acts should be treated as criminals; and the last recorded case of slicing off a head had occurred in the early 1930s. The Government authorities insisted on getting the somewhat reluctant help of powerful Temonggong Koh in enforcing the law; and they believed that the ancient, hallowed custom had finally fallen into desuetude.

Then the Second World War broke out. Its start was soon followed by the retreat of the White Rajah and his administration from Sarawak and by the occupation of the country by the Japanese. The Ibans and other tribes living in Borneo's interior were sorry at the change, and decided that it was their duty to take revenge for the Rajah's defeat. Rightly or wrongly—and they did not care which it was—they felt that he would have no objection to their capturing as many as possible of the intruders' heads; so they revived with gusto their old recreation. Woe betide any Japanese soldier in the Army of Occupation who strayed from camp for a short distance into the jungle! Some native hidden behind a tree would first shoot a poisoned arrow at him from a blow-pipe, and then (when the victim collapsed fainting on the ground) step forward and cut off his top-knot with one professional stroke of a parang or sword. It was said that during the war some 400 Japanese heads were acquired in this way and hung as trophies in the captors' long-houses.

I was told that one of the victims of these assaults was the Director of Education in the Japanese army. He was an intellectual type of fellow, with a refined, cultured face but short-sighted eyes. He therefore wore a pair of gold-rimmed spectacles. The Iban who cut off his pate bagged the spectacles as well; and when he dangled the head from a ceiling in his house he balanced the spectacles on its countenance exactly where they had always been during the deceased's lifetime. And each morning the chief of the house respectfully took the glasses off the head, cleaned them, and replaced them on what remained of the Jap nose.

II

My initial meeting with Temonggong Koh took place in 1946 at Kapit, nearly 200 miles up-river in Sarawak's untamed interior. The place was not only a bazaar township but also the administrative centre for a wide Iban area, and the Paramount Chief assembled his lesser chiefs and numerous other followers to greet me ceremonially on my first arrival there. When I landed from my motor-launch an immense throng of natives in gala dress waited to salute me. They stood expectantly beyond a grand Archway of Welcome which they had raised in my honour. It was a magnificent piece of temporary architecture constructed of bamboo and richly decorated with posies of beautiful wild orchids amidst luscious jungle vegetation. But its principal adornments were two sliced-off Japanese heads hanging among the flowers on each column of the arch. I glanced curiously at them, and they stared vacantly (yet I thought rather reproachfully) back at me. Their black hair was close-cropped in military style, their yellow-skinned flesh still clung on their faces, and their eyes were half closed by lids on which eyelashes protruded as neatly as they must have done when their owners were still alive and kicking.

The first man to greet me when I walked through the arch was the veteran Koh. I already knew his grand reputation as the most revered chieftain whom the Ibans had possessed in living memory. At that first glimpse of him I learned more about his character from his wrinkled, expressive old face—his physical robustness, his mental serenity, his natural, unassuming self-confidence, and his genial personality.

I stayed with him and his followers at Kapit for the better part of twenty-four hours. We performed various pagan ceremonies, enjoyed traditional dancing and singing, and discussed together many local problems. By the end of the visit the Temonggong and I had laid the foundations of a great friendship.

I have described in my book *Borneo People* how that friendship grew into one of deep affection on both sides. I have also written there how Koh did me the honour of making me an adopted member of his family. On one occasion when he, his wife, his daughters, son and I had just finished playing our various parts in some traditional rites alleged to appease the good and evil spirits who haunt the pagan world, he suddenly called for silence. Addressing me through an interpreter (for he could talk no English) he spoke the following words:

"Master, you are the mightiest man in these parts, for your power stretches over many countries and numerous peoples. I am but the paramount chief of the Ibans on the Rejang River in Sarawak. Beside you I am like a mouse-deer beside an elephant. But I am an old man and you are young. In age I am to you like a father to a son. If you will allow me, I would like to call you my son. It is fitting because I and all my family feel bound to you by ties of deep affection."

He used the Iban word *anak* for son, which denotes the closest fellowship that can exist between an older and a younger man.

In spontaneous exclamations his wife and youngsters expressed their delight at this proposition. I felt touched and proud, and accepted the chief's suggestion in impromptu sentences with deep pleasure sounding in my voice. I addressed him as *Api*, which was the name by which his children and most intimate friends always spoke of him. And *Api* I continued to call him throughout the remainder of our years together.

III

By the time I knew him Koh had become a reformed character so far as head-hunting was concerned. This circumstance did not spring from his own free will. After the period of enthusiastic relapse into that earlier pastime during the war, the Ibans were once more compelled to deny themselves the pleasure of collecting human heads. Rajah Brooke had ceded his country and its peoples to His Majesty the King of Great Britain and the law was being even more rigorously applied under British Colonial rule than it had been before.

As a loyal subject of the Crown—and indeed one of its most important servants in his office as Temonggong—Koh asserted his influence to achieve obedience to the Government's orders. Nevertheless an element of reluctance persisted in him. An inclination to cut off other folk's heads lay deep in his and his followers' blood: the sport was a most honourable part of their ancestral heritage and they could not fully comprehend why they should be denied the right to demonstrate their manly virtues by indulging in it. They itched to resume their exercise of the ancient art.

I remember an occasion when this desire expressed itself. I had many critics among the more old-fashioned white settlers in Malaya, Singapore and the British Territories in Borneo because of certain policies which I pursued as their Governor-General. My opponents thought me too radical in my aim of preparing the local peoples for eventual self-government, too "pro-native" in my social mixing with Malays, Chinese, Dayaks and others as equal members with us British of the human race, and too informal in some of my flouting of long established Gubernatorial protocol. Every now and then they wrote angry letters to the local newspapers complaining that I was selling the British Empire down the drain, undermining the dignity of the God-sent white man in the East, and committing various other heinous offences. Often the epistles closed with a demand for my dismissal.

One day I arrived in Kapit for consultations with Koh and his subordinate chiefs. We sat Iban style on the floor in the district officer's house and discussed our official business. Then Koh extracted from a fold in his loin-cloth a few bits and pieces of paper and handed them to me. As I perused them I saw that they were half a dozen of those letters.

I smiled, and asked Koh what he wanted me to do about the correspondence.

He looked at me earnestly, as did all his fellows squatting at his side, and enquired, "Can we go and take the writers' heads?"

I laughed as if this were a good joke.

The Temonggong looked serious, and declared that it was no jesting matter. He remarked that he and his Iban people felt angry at the letters, for they loved and trusted me and wished to support me. They would therefore like to go and liquidate my enemies; but they could not do so without my permission.

With remarkable magnanimity (it seemed to me) I firmly forbade them to do anything of the sort. The chiefs expressed heartfelt disappointment. Apparently they thought they had hit on a clever means of gaining my consent to a head-hunting spree, for surely I could not resist the temptation to get rid so effectively of my critics.

I refrained from suggesting that they should write a letter to the newspapers announcing that the Ibans disapproved of those other scribblers' strictures on me, and that the heads of any future such authors would soon be hanging in the long-houses in Sarawak.

I sometimes wondered whether my critics would have changed in any measure their disapproval of me if they knew that I had saved them from unpleasant deaths. Probably it would have made no difference to their views. They were sincere, dedicated, out-of-date fanatics with all the courage of their convictions; and many of them would readily have suffered martyrdom for their lost cause.

IV

Koh was very conservative in his ripe old age. He cherished the customs, traditions and beliefs which for centuries had ordered the lives of the Iban people, and which had persisted virtually unaltered throughout the first seventy years of his own existence. When numerous new ideas began to penetrate up-river after the World War he could not really adjust his mind to understand them. Other, less aged Ibans started to accept fresh notions about proper "civilised" behaviour. For example, many men cast off the slim loin-cloth which hitherto had been their sole article of clothing, and donned shirts and shorts instead, whilst some young women adopted the fashion of covering their previously bare breasts with brassieres, if not with blouses as well. Again, numerous youths got the long hair which until then they had worn dangling pony-tail style down their backs so shorn that they looked like English college students.

In more fundamental ways fresh, mostly Western notions began to invade the Bornean jungles, altering not only personal tastes in dress but also social customs, political ideas and even spiritual faith. In the sphere of religion, for example, Christian missions made significant headway in undermining the Iban's animist belief in the existence of countless good and evil spirits inhabiting the rivers, forests and hills all around them, and in place of this ancient, hallowed, hitherto unquestioned mythology introduced the notion of one Christian God. Several of the younger Iban chiefs, including Penghulu Jugah, became converts to this new religion. They got baptised, and joined Methodist, Roman Catholic or other chapels or churches. In the same way they cast off other antiquated concepts and practices, adopting novel ones in their place. Their acceptance of these fresh ideas was genuine. They did not always comprehend fully what they were doing, but they felt they were guiding their followers wisely in directions which would enable them to play creditable parts in the changeful modern world. Just occasionally they preferred some old habit to a new one and sought to preserve it; but usually they felt that the traditional customs must at least be modified, if not completely altered, to meet the requirements of up-to-date progress.

The attitude of the septuagenarian Temonggong Koh was quite different. He was an unapologetic exponent of the old way of life. When compelled by some irresistible force to abandon this or that aspect of it—like head-hunting—he bowed to the inevitable with good grace. In a few other instances, too, if he considered it expedient to make a concession to new-fangled notions, he did so without undue hesitation. Thus he sent his youngest daughter Segura—my enchanting little sister by adoption—to learn how to become a modern young lady in a down-river boarding-school, with the dramatic consequences which I have described in *Borneo People*.

Another attitude which, for some reason, Koh thought it politic to assume was a nominal profession of Christianity. No news that I have ever received surprised me more than the tidings I heard one day that he had been baptised a Methodist. I could scarcely believe my ears. It seemed impossible that he should abandon his profoundly felt faith in the whole multitudinous, variegated hierarchy of pagan deities, sprites, hobgoblins and other invisible yet ever-present creatures who—according to him—presided over our human destinies.

When next I went to stay with him and his family in their home I realised that, although the fact of his baptism was true, I was not mistaken about the event's utter insignificance. The most distinguished Christian convert in Sarawak had not the foggiest notion what Christianity meant! He listened to its preachings with one ear, nodded his head sagely, and promptly let them slip unheeded out of the other ear. They were never for an instant permitted to approach, let alone linger, anywhere near his soul. I observed much evidence of this during the visit. Throughout it— and during my every subsequent stay with him—we engaged in the hallowed, fervent succession of pagan ceremonies which had been practised from time immemorial among his people. All of us in the crowded long-house took endless trouble to flatter the good and appease the evil spirits who might otherwise take umbrage at our acts; and there was never a whisper of Christian worship.

I suppose the old man thought it diplomatic to acquiesce in some missionary's suggestion that he should become a member of an apparently harmless sect. After all, his favourite lieutenant Jugah and other of his counsellors were being baptised—so he might as well follow the prevailing fashion. Possibly he performed a special private act of appeasement of the pagan divinities to ensure that they would not misunderstand his odd action; but more likely he realised they would know it made no difference whatever to his devout relationship with them.

He often told me that those invisible sprites had been wonderfully benevolent to him; and great good fortune had indeed attended him during his life. He was convinced that this resulted from the respect he always paid them in his worship of them, from the efforts he invariably made to seek and obey their will, and from the cordial personal communion which had gradually grown between them and him through the years. He felt deeply grateful to them; and these feelings were so profoundly rooted in his inmost being that they could not be dislodged. A man of high integrity, he would have considered it an act of despicable, unpardonable betrayal to desert them in favour of any other God.

V

In due course he became four score years old. For some time afterwards he remained remarkably hale and hearty. It was always a joy to go and see the noble elder, to look upon his characterful face, gaze into his shrewd eyes, hear his gentle laughter, and listen to his mellow opinions about the world and human affairs.

At eighty-two years old he still survived, an antique chieftain supremely loved by all his people in their homes up Sarawak's rivers. But gradually his strength declined, until he could do little more than sit around quietly on the veranda of his vast, tumultuously populated long-house. He retained all his mental faculties, but his physical energies were sapped; and in his own private thoughts he was preparing to depart from this world.

One day he fell into a coma and news spread quickly through his wide principality that he was at death's door. He lay peacefully unconscious on a mat on the floor of his room. The small chamber had the primitive simplicity of such apartments in a typical Iban dwelling; yet it was also distinguished by attractive native weaving hanging like tapestries on its walls, and by a score of large antique Chinese jars standing along its edges like show-pieces in a museum. These were specimens of the ancient pots in which traders from Cathay during the Ming dynasty imported various types of merchandise into Borneo—and which the unschooled, illiterate and supposedly "wild" old Temonggong had collected over many years with the discriminating eye of a cultured connoisseur.

Now he lay dying. Round him knelt his wife, children and grandchildren, all weeping. Other women crouching respectfully at their backs also kept wiping their eyes, and even some of the men standing around made no attempt to restrain their tears.

The hush was momentarily disturbed by the soft footsteps of a new arrival. All but the closest members of the family made way for him, for this was Jugah, the most important chieftain after Koh himself. A few hours earlier he had heard by "jungle telegraph" of his leader's collapse into unconsciousness; and he hastened up-river to pay his last respects to the great Temonggong. Himself a devout Christian, he knelt at the old man's side and uttered up a prayer.

At that Koh opened his eyes. Glancing towards the group assembled round him, those eyes flashed in momentary protest as he said, "What are you all doing kneeling here? Why all this blubbering? I'm not ill. I never felt better in my life. But it's time for me to go and join the spirits in the other world. They're asking me to come to them. Get up, Jugah, and hurry down-river to Kapit to make the preparations for my departure. I'll leave you all later to-day."

He closed his eyes again. His final command to his earthly friends had been spoken—the last words he ever uttered. A few minutes later he drew his last breath.

Jugah promptly went to do his master's bidding. Hastening from the house and descending the high tree-trunk staircase to the river bank, he stepped into his boat and sped to Kapit, where the headquarters of the local Methodist mission were located.

On the following day Koh's corpse was conveyed there, and after a Christian funeral service the unrepentant old pagan—who left strict orders that he must not be interred in any cemetery—was brought back for burial in a traditional tomb amidst thick forest on the opposite side of the river from his home.

Several times since then I have gone there with other members of the family to pay affectionate homage to the illustrious dead. Always his daughters weep and wail aloud as we pour rice-wine on the ground above his coffin, set a plate of food in the sanctuary, and place beside it a packet of cigarettes, so that our father can enjoy eating, drinking and smoking with the spirits in the other world where he now resides.

Hail and Farewell

I met Pandit Jawaharlal Nehru for the first time in January 1948, a few months after he triumphantly assumed office as Prime Minister of independent India. I was staying for two days with my friends Dickie and Edwina Mountbatten, the former of whom had recently ceased to be the last Viceroy and become the first Governor-General in Delhi. On the evening of my arrival Nehru came to dinner with us. As he left the stately ex-Viceregal Lodge he invited the Mountbattens and me to lunch next day. Dickie, however, was already committed to entertaining numerous Maharajahs, so Edwina and I went by ourselves to the Prime Minister's house.

No one else was invited. Our host and we sat on the grass of a spacious lawn shaded by flowering bougainvillæa bushes, enjoying a picnic meal in the glorious sunshine of a Delhi's winter's day. Nehru was at his most charming; and although our conversation roamed over many serious topics, it was informal and relaxed.

At one interval during the talk Edwina turned to the Prime Minister and remarked, "Malcolm can do something you can't do, Jawaharlal."

"What's that?" asked Nehru, with a slight frown at such an impertinent suggestion.

"He can walk on his hands," she answered.

Nehru looked surprised. "I'd like to see him do it," he said in a tone of scepticism.

We were eating excellent curry, and I begged to be permitted to finish my share of it before I demonstrated the truth of Edwina's statement. The others agreed to this temporary postponement of the antic.

When we had all swallowed our fills I rose and strolled on my hind-legs thirty or forty yards away, then turned round, raised myself upside-down on my hands, and walked topsy-turvy back across the lawn to Nehru's side. I halted within a few inches of him, and restored myself to an upright position there.

He laughed and looked quite impressed. In retort he wagered me that he could stand on his head for a longer time than I could stand on mine. I did not dispute the claim, for I knew that he stayed in that posture for considerable periods every morning before breakfast as part of his regular Yoga-style exercises. But I commented that I should like to see him in reverse. He promptly took off his Gandhi cap, put his head on the ground, and with the agility of a schoolboy turned his neat figure the wrong way up. I stood on my hands, and walked round him half a dozen times. At that we called our acrobatic contest a dead-heat.

He asked me whether I practised Yoga. I replied in the negative; to which he answered that the exercise would help me to keep physically fit, mentally alert and spiritually serene. When I en-quired what precisely I should do, he at once sat cross-legged—Buddha-like—on the grass and demonstrated a few examples of the physical jerks he recommended.

Perhaps at first glance he seemed surprisingly small for a man of his colossal political stature, for his trim, always neatly costumed figure stood only about five and a half feet tall. But any im-pression of insignificance was immediately dispelled by the arresting splendour of his face. Nehru's features had the aristocratic refinement of a Kashmiri Brahmin, with a softness of skin that to his dying day left it smoothly unmarred by any wrinkles. Some elements in the face betrayed delicate sensuous-ness—his full, sometimes pouting lips, his classically modelled nose with sensitive nostrils, and his contemplative, often sad and yet penetrating eyes.

Now, however, that grace became warped. His visage assumed various grotesque aspects as he displayed to Edwina and me his disciplined control of this and that set of muscles which Yogi exercises encouraged. He quivered his eyebrows, rolled his eye-balls, trembled his cheeks and twisted his mouth into violent grimaces, in between periods of static facial calm whilst he transferred his physical contortions to other parts of his body, such as alternate contractions and bulgings of his stomach in a succession of vigorous in-and-out motions. His appearance then was sometimes sublime, and at other moments diabolical.

That was the start of my friendship with the mighty—and for many years in India the virtually almighty—Pandit Nehru.

II

Later that afternoon I went to call on the other supreme historic leader of free India, Mahatma Gandhi. I knew him from an acquaintance which had grown up between us at a pregnant moment in the past, when in 1931 his country's future was being debated at the second Indian Round Table Conference in London. My father was its chairman; and I was able to act as a go-between—unnoticed by watchful, inquisitive newspapermen—taking secret messages from him to Gandhi and back from Gandhi to him.

Seventeen years later the Mahatma still remembered this, and when he learned that I was in Delhi he asked me to come and see him. For a couple of hours we talked alone together in a sunny garden surrounding the millionaire G. D. Birla's house, where Gandhiji was staying at the time. He reclined like a sun-bather on a couch in the balmy open air, wearing nothing except a white loin-cloth on his wizened brown body. Unlike Nehru's, his face was wrinkled and rather ugly. Whilst we chatted he sipped a glassful of orange-juice. This was to be his last meal for several days—if not for ever—because, he told me, on the morrow he would start a fast unto death.

The date was the 12th January, 1948. India had gained her national Independence five months earlier, having first been partitioned from her now equally sovereign neighbour, Pakistan. As a result of those joyful but disruptive events awful trouble had broken out between the Hindu and Muslim populations in various parts of the sub-continent where they lived side by side. Riots, massacres and panic-stricken migrations were occurring on a large scale. The happy future of both the new states seemed to be in jeopardy.

Gandhi was almost heart-broken by this tragic turn of events. In protest, the great, universally beloved Mahatma was about to employ against his fellow countrymen the same weapon as he had often used in his non-violent struggle against "the Imperial oppressors" of those people—a fast unto death. He hoped they would all—Hindus and Muslims alike—be so appalled at the prospect of becoming responsible for his disappearance from this world that they would cease their mutual slaughtering, make peace with one another, and live in neighbourly harmony ever afterwards.

As we sat in the sunshine that afternoon he spoke of many things. First he referred to the past, reminiscing about our earlier meetings during the Indian Round Table Conference. He expressed warm appreciation of the part my father had played over many years in assisting the Nationalist movement of the Indians, and declared that the recent hostility between the Indian and British peoples would now be replaced by the strongest of friendships. With characteristic broad-mindedness he said that the Indians' opposition to the British had never amounted to enmity; on the contrary, he and his scores of millions of followers remembered with gratitude the remarkable contribution their British rulers had made to India's reawakening and progress during the last two hundred years. As he spoke his old eyes gleamed with affectionate sentiment and his thin lips often curved into a broad smile.

Then his thoughts returned to the present, his look became sorrowful, and he spoke heart-rendingly about the Hindu/Muslim blood-bath. He was impartial between the two sides, understanding both, finding fault with both, and loving both. He explained to me the causes of the trouble, criticising the attitudes of some of the communal leaders, and making no self-righteous attempt to excuse his compatriots and throw the blame on others.

On the contrary, he talked objectively about some of the Indians'
weaknesses of character and said their main problems were
now being created by themselves, and must be resolved by themselves.

He repeated that, in an attempt to induce the leaders and masses
to stop their violent fratricidal strife, he would commence his fast
at dawn the next day.

To him it was a profound tragedy that India's moment of
triumph on attaining national freedom should be marred, and
indeed disgraced, by this outburst of destructive passion. His
spirit felt depressed, but not too daunted by pessimistic gloom. He
felt sure the evil would pass, that human common sense and goodness would prevail, and India would then go forward to a
peaceful, constructive future. He spoke interestingly about that
prospect, making remarks which indicated his opinion—in contrast to that of Nehru and other important Congress leaders—that
the country should not indulge in too much ambitious modern
industrial development in search of massive material wealth,
but should depend on its own humbler, indigenous economy
based on the agriculture, native handicrafts and domestic in-
dustries of the people.

Every now and then he turned our conversation to other topics.
His mood kept changing from the solemn to the gay. Several times
he burst into light-hearted laughter. He had a schoolboyish sense
of fun; and his jokes were simple and direct. In fact the old septuagenarian lazing in the sunshine was cheerful and sorrowful,
thoughtful and witty, brooding and alert, all at the same time.
He seemed extraordinarily hale and hearty.

When I rose to take my leave of him I remarked, "Gandhiji,
I've never before believed those whose devoted faith in you makes
them say you'll live to be 150 years old. But this afternoon I
begin to wonder. You're so vivid in body and mind and spirit that
I think they may be right!"

He gave me a beaming, appreciative grin, but shook his head
knowingly, and said, "I don't think I've got much longer to live."

Next morning he started his fast unto death; within a week the

Hindu/Muslim killings ceased; and on the following day he abandoned his self-imposed penance amidst tremendous popular rejoicings. The power of India's national hero had never seemed greater.

A few days later—in the garden where he and I had sat talking—he was assassinated by a crazy religious fanatic.

Cousinly Love

Early one morning in August 1964 I left Nairobi—where I had become the Governor-General of Kenya—to visit some distant cousins of mine who lived beside Lake Tanganyika. After motoring for the better part of two days I reached Kigoma, a small town on the edge of a sheltered bay. When I arrived there I abandoned my car and stepped aboard a motor-launch waiting to take me to my relations' home several miles away along the shore. For unrecorded ages they and their forebears had resided in the forest of the Gombe Stream Reserve.

After a pleasant voyage along a wide corridor of water between steep Tanzanian mountains on one side and Congolese highlands on the other, I reached my destination. By then the afternoon sunshine had faded into twilight, and dusk in its turn was overtaken by night. The lamps of a fleet of native fishing-boats glittered like a golden necklace far out in deeper water as I stepped ashore. My friends Jane and Hugo van Lawick welcomed me with lanterns to guide me to a rendezvous where my (and incidentally also their) cousins would meet us the next day. We stayed in tents among trees beside a murmuring stream which tumbled from high hills; and after an early supper we retired to bed, so as to rise at dawn.

I slept soundly in that quiet, remote woodland under a starry sky, not opening my eyes until seven o'clock in the morning, partially recovered from the exhaustion of months of ceaseless official labours. Looking through my tent doorway, I observed that two of our cousins had already put in an appearance. They were sitting munching bananas on the grass—a couple of wild chimpanzees. Jane and Hugo squatted on the ground a few yards away from them.

Feeling a thrill of excited pleasure, I slipped into my clothes and went to meet them. One of the apes was husky and old, whilst the other was smaller and evidently much younger. Jane told me that the elder animal was a male called Huxley and that the youngster was a female named Pooch. She added that their ages were about thirty years and six years respectively and that the relationship between them was rather intriguing. For a long time they had kept company together, seeming to feel a special affection for one another, and often being inseparable among all the other chimpanzees in the forest. Yet they were not lovers, for although Huxley was still not too aged to enjoy occasional liaisons with members of the opposite sex, Pooch was too juvenile to invite the act of mating. He seemed to have acquired a sort of protective attitude towards her as if she were an adopted daughter—in fact, to be a "sugar daddy" with only a Platonic association. Nevertheless it could not be denied that her bare posterior was now for the first time beginning to show signs of blushing pink—an unmistakable indication of approaching puberty.

Before long other chimpanzees strolled down the hillside behind the camp to join us. As they appeared one by one or in little parties of twos and threes Jane told me the names with which she and Hugo had christened each of them. A formidable looking old female called Flo came accompanied by her five years old daughter Fifi and her latest born infant Flint, now aged a few months. Soon afterwards her two older sons called Faben and Figan joined them. Many of the apes had surprisingly handsome hairy black figures. Faben, for example, was a fine-looking beast in the first flush of adult life, aged nine or ten years. Attaining a height of over four feet when he rose upright, he was long armed, broad torsoed and slim hipped, with the customary rather short legs. His round head had an aspect of blunt strength as the shrewd eyes in his dark face gazed from beneath their beetling brows. His sloping nose was flattish, his protruding mouth and jaw large, and his wide lips mobilely sensitive. When he stood erect his powerful chest stuck out like that of a human boxing champion showing off his physique in a ring; and the similarity was all the more vivid when he stroked it as if he were proudly challenging any rival to dare to come and hit him. The only ugly part of him (to human, though not of course to chimpanzee eyes) was his naked, fleshy backside.

Yet the most impressive individual among them all was his mother, Flo. It would be difficult to tell her exact age, but probably she had seen nearer thirty than twenty summers. Probably also she was the most productive matron in the chimp population throughout the neighbourhood. Definitely the parent of Faben, Figan, Fifi and Flint, she may have borne older offspring too. Her progeny treated her with the fond respect due to a mother; and her authority among them was as unquestioned, easy, and when necessary, absolute as that of some traditional queenly ruler. That was natural, for (as I shall describe later) the world of chimpanzees is a matriarchal society. There were many signs on Flo's person of her august age, such as her half-bald pate, her very wrinkled brow and cheeks, and the slightly faded, contemplative gaze in her eyes. Her face was reminiscent of that of a charlady, except that every now and then the dignified and indeed imperious expression of a dowager empress crept across it. One of her ears was badly torn, perhaps a relic of some lovers' quarrel in earlier amours, and her nipples drooped long on her otherwise flat breasts, extended by the still constant suckling of little Flint, the product of her latest romance.

She was one of the most distinguished looking old dames whom I have ever had the privilege to meet.

II

It is time that I explained the reason for my rendezvous with these interesting creatures. For two years my friend Jane had been living among them in the Gombe Stream Reserve, a Nature Sanctuary where no other members of the species Homo sapiens resided except for seasonal visits by native fishermen along the lake shore. Jane was studying the characters and habits of chimpanzees. I need not repeat here the remarkable story of her association with them, for she herself has already told it modestly and fascinatingly in her own published writings. But perhaps I should mention in passing that no greater difference of appearance between two females could exist than that between Flo and Jane.

Jane was in her early twenties, lovely of face, graceful in figure, and with a charming personality—in the fresh bloom of human youth. She was about the last person you would expect to find living in voluntary exile in remote, wild solitudes; at first glance you would rather expect to meet her in some gay party in a Mayfair night-club. Yet during the first eighteen months of her residence in the Gombe Stream Reserve her loneliness was virtually as complete as if she had been a nun in a Trappist convent. Through the initial five months only her mother and an African cook accompanied her as protective guardian and domestic help respectively; then her mother had to return to England, and she remained alone with the cook and his wife. The reason for all this was Jane's dedicated passion for biological research. However, it turned out later that she was not entirely indifferent to other, more usual feelings; for when in due course the *National Geographic Magazine* authorities, who financed her work, sent (with conspicuous good judgment) the expert animal photographer Baron Hugo van Lawick to join the party for a few weeks and take pictures of the chimps, she must have occasionally let her thoughts wander from their apish antics to his gentlemanly behaviour. Not long afterwards the two became engaged to be married, and their wedding was celebrated a little later.

During the first six months of her sojourn in the forest Jane never got near the chimpanzees. All day, every day she stayed out of doors by herself, quietly and discreetly trying to track and approach them—but they were shy of this strange primate who had suddenly intruded into their domain, and lolloped away whenever she came within 500 yards. She used to watch the creatures through field-glasses across great distances from one hill-top to another, scribbling notes about their behaviour, and so beginning her study of their lives. But often she felt frustrated and hopeless, thinking she would never get on closer terms. Nevertheless she persevered; and gradually they grew more accustomed to her. By the end of six months she occasionally crept within about 100 yards of a group before it became alarmed and scampered out of sight. Then they really started to accept her as a fellow inhabitant of the wilds, for every now and then she spied parties of them sitting in tree-tops or squatting among long grass at no great distance away, eyeing her cautiously—obviously ready to retreat at the slightest unfriendly gesture, but otherwise not unduly disturbed.

In her writings she has described the evolution of her relationship with the great apes. Their initial fear gradually gave way to curiosity, and later curiosity changed to defiance. Instead of running away or peering inquisitively at her, some of the chimps would climb into near-by trees and rock the branches, glaring at her in silence. At first those quiet stares were still tinged by nervousness, and more weeks passed before the chimpanzees were sufficiently unafraid to react with positive aggression. Then, as they squatted in trees and undergrowth close round her, they would suddenly break into a hullabaloo of (to quote her own words) "loud, savage yells that raised the hair on the back of my neck." *
But with the cool courage of a dedicated scientific student Jane sat unmoving through those performances.

That daring stood her in good stead on a later occasion which probably carried her relationship with the chimpanzees a decisive step farther. One day she was standing near a ripe fruit tree when she heard footsteps in the grass behind her. Not wanting to startle the apes, she lay down, hoping they would reach the tree without seeing her. But the footsteps stopped, and she heard small, high-pitched chimp voices murmuring, "Hoo! Hoo!" The inflection indicated that they were surprised or uneasy.

She did not move, and suddenly a mature male climbed into the tree and sat just above her head, peering down at her. He quickly worked himself into a rage, hitting the tree-trunk and

*An article in the August, 1963 issue of the *National Geographic Magazine.*

shaking its branches. His small hoots became ever louder until, with mouth wide open to display yellow canines, he was uttering high-pitched, choking screams of anger.

"Still I did not move," Jane wrote. "Through the corner of my eye I could see three others watching. All at once the male disappeared, and I heard him moving in the leaves behind me. There was a silence and then, with a loud scream, he rushed forward and I felt the slam of his hand on the back of my head." She made no sudden gesture of protest at the beast's assault, merely sitting up quietly and slowly. At that the ape moved away with his companions "still brave from his passion, calling out and drumming on the trees." If Jane had betrayed any motion of fright or anger, she might have invited instant, fatal retaliation by the attacker, and certainly she would have forfeited for ever the chimps' tolerant trust. After months of observing her curiously, the aggressor was probably putting her to the test, to see whether she was friend or foe. She had passed the test.

After that the apes' confidence in her good neighbourliness continued to grow. One day her association with them took another important step forward. It happened that the fruit ripened on an oil-palm just outside her tent; and the boldest of the chimpanzees (whom she had named David) came to refresh himself. His visits continued as long as the fruit lasted, and he raised no objection when Jane strolled around close by. Soon afterwards she won his friendship by providing him with bananas, a delicacy which the forest did not itself offer and for which he developed a taste under her tuition.

"After three days," she writes, "he actually took a banana from my hand. It was a wonderful moment. He was apprehensive when I held it out. He stood up and hit the trunk of a tree, rocking slightly from foot to foot. But when he took the fruit there was no snatching—he was amazingly gentle from the first."*

Some time after that two of David's companions plucked up

My Friends the Wild Chimpanzees by Baroness Jane Goodall Van Lawick.

courage to follow his example. Jane had become accepted as a useful member of local jungle society.

III

By the time I visited Jane and Hugo in their small tented camp more than forty out of some eighty-odd great apes scattered over several square miles in the surrounding country came now and then to enjoy munching bananas. The more familiar among them arrived regularly, some of them turning up every day. These two score habitués had all been christened with names, for their various physical appearances and characters were so individual that Jane and Hugo could recognise each and every one of them at sight.

During my couple of days at the camp twenty-two of them paid calls. Most of these seemed no more disturbed at the appearance of a new man than they were at the accustomed presence of Jane and Hugo, accepting me as a similarly harmless fellow primate. For example, after a few minutes a youngster called Gilka walked within a few inches of me on her way to explore a box which she knew to be a banana store, giving me only a momentary indifferent glance as she ambled past. No doubt their unconcern was helped by the fact that I stayed immobile for a time after their arrival, making no movement which might arouse their distrust. Nevertheless some of them were for a while uneasy at my being there. Thus, when an old fellow named Leakey (after the great anthropologist Louis Leakey, who had been Jane's inspiring teacher) first arrived he was distinctly suspicious of me, halting his advance when he caught sight of me, staring uncomprehendingly, and then withdrawing several paces and sitting undecided for five minutes before recovering confidence and approaching once more. And young Fifi remained for a long time shy of me, although she romped trustfully very close to the two Van Lawicks.

Sometimes on their arrivals the chimps greeted each other with glad enthusiasm. For instance, as soon as a certain young male caught sight of Faben sauntering down the hill he gave a loud shriek, ran towards the newcomer, patted him on the back and flung his arms round him in a warm embrace. Faben responded with equal affability. In other cases the genial creatures varied their gestures, adopting many human styles of salutation. Sometimes they slapped each other on the backs, at other times they put their arms across each other's shoulders, at yet other times they hugged one another, and quite often they even gave each other a kiss. In the latter instances the pair usually put their faces close together and pouted their huge, flabby lips until they briefly touched; but once during my visit Jane observed the most sumptuous chimpanzee kiss she had ever seen. One animal extended its lips invitingly to another, who promptly opened its mouth and enclosed them within its own.

The most extraordinary greeting that I personally witnessed occurred between a veteran called Hugo (not Jane's spouse) and a matron named Marina. Hugo was sitting greedily chewing several bananas when Marina appeared with her infant son Merlin clinging to her tummy. Hugo at once stood up and darted at her. She dodged behind a tree to avoid him, but he chased her round its trunk three times, trying to grab her. She attempted a diversion by running across a path, but he followed her, thrust out his arms, and gave her a vigorous push—at which she fell to the ground with a now screaming Merlin clasped to her bosom. Hugo rolled her over, and she obligingly lay flat on her face and belly with the infant grasped protectively beneath her. Gripping the fur on her shoulders, Hugo jumped on to her back, where he leaped up and down several times with bouncing skips as if he were a child playfully but energetically testing the springs of a mattress. It seemed to me an almost murderous assault but Jane and the other Hugo assured me that it was all a rather mild, affectionate affair. Merlin, however, seemed to share my opinion, for he continued to emit panic-stricken shrieks throughout the performance.

Immediately afterwards Hugo stepped off Marina and returned to the heap of bananas on which he had been feasting. Marina picked herself and Merlin up, followed him, and crouched close against his back, panting heavily and apparently kissing his fur with her lips. For a while he took no notice of her, continuing to swallow the fruits. Then she stretched out a hand, took a banana from his pile of food, peeled its skin, and bit it. He glanced approvingly in her direction and afterwards they ate their meal in perfect companionship.

Jane explained to me that the incident was probably caused by Marina having originally approached too close to Hugo's hoard of provisions without proper warning, thus arousing his suspicion that she intended to steal a lot of it. Therefore he registered his protest in that strong but (Jane assured me) thoroughly amicable, if extrovert manner.

IV

The greeting that made the deepest impression of all on me was one in which I myself was involved. It occurred during my second day in the camp. I stood observing Flo and a few other chimps lazing and grooming each other, when her eight year old son Figan suddenly disengaged himself from the group and stared at me. After a few moments hesitation he sauntered towards me purposefully on all fours, keeping his eyes intently concentrated on mine, as if seeking to discover some secret about me from my returning gaze. He did not halt until he had made a half circle round me and stood immediately at my back. I could see him out of the corner of an eye standing erect now on his hind legs, and scrutinising me still with an air of absorbed curiosity. Of a sudden he lowered his head, leant forwards, and thumped my buttocks with the top of his pate. I did not stir. A second later he slapped both my legs, first with one hand and then with the other. I stayed stock still, wishing to instil trust in him. He hit me quite hard several times.

Jane, sitting watchfully near-by, said softly, "You can touch him."

I stretched out a hand and scratched him on a shoulder. At

that he gripped my wrist in friendly, if firm greeting. I turned round, and sat down facing him. He promptly also squatted on the ground, and I resumed my scratching of his furry body. He smacked me on the head, patted my chest and legs, and then clasped both my arms, holding them tight and gratefully as I tickled him. It seemed like a reunion between two long lost cousins who vaguely began to recognise each other after a separation of many millions of years. All his handlings of me were strong and yet gentle. He evidently liked me scratching him, and more than once he whacked me appreciatively, and perhaps still rather enquiringly, on the head. Jane and Hugo remarked that he might be fascinated by my white hair, which he had never seen before on any anthropoid animal, and which he touched to test whether it felt the same as any other beast's fur.

After a while he rose and returned nonchalantly to the company of his nearer relatives.

V

None of the chimpanzees ever showed the slightest concern at Jane's or Hugo's close presence, having grown accustomed to them as fellow creatures of the wild who performed a useful function by providing them with bananas. The apes therefore behaved entirely naturally in the vicinity of those two human beings, paying calls on them whenever they felt like eating more fruit. Often they stayed around for hours afterwards, snoozing in the sunshine, conversing boisterously, playing games, or engaging in their favourite pastime of grooming one another before returning to their more native habitats. The Van Lawicks responded by conducting themselves quite normally amidst their visitors. Jane would sit on the grass scribbling notes about their behaviour in an exercise-book, whilst Hugo crouched a few yards away with his cine-camera ever ready to take significant photographs.

Thus the small tented camp in the middle of the spacious jungle was like a Chimpanzee Club for all those primates in the neighbourhood, with the Baron and Baroness Van Lawick as its manager and housekeeper. The first arrivals each morning appeared at about seven o'clock, and others came at various times throughout the day. Often as many as a dozen chimps were strolling, sitting or lying around the premises at the same time. It was an entrancing sight. When they had finished their banana breakfasts or luncheons they would turn to other occupations. Their principal hobby was scratching and grooming each other. One ape would squat motionless whilst a colleague sat beside it like a masseur busily working on its body. With restless, gently exploring fingers the latter searched its companion's fur for uninvited insects, loose bits of skin, specks of dirt or other foreign matters, nimbly plucking them off and throwing them away—or occasionally popping them into its own mouth for chewing. It left no part of the other's anatomy uninvestigated, examining with meticulous care the backs of the ears, the insides of armpits, the hairy length of chest, the groin, the backside, and every other nook and cranny of the figure. The animal being groomed usually stayed stock still with a bored, far-away gaze in its eyes, although every now and then it helped its friend by raising an arm or stretching a leg into some position convenient for examination. The groomer's face wore a look of solemn concentration throughout the operation. As often as not when its job was completed the two reversed their roles, the groomer becoming the groomed and submitting itself to a similarly thorough cleansing. Sometimes a group of four or five chimps would all huddle together and engage in simultaneous co-operative scratchings. Incidentally, as a result of this mutual duty, which is performed many times every day, chimpanzees are among the cleanest animals on earth.

When that conscientious, often very protracted labour was completed the apes lay down for a rest in the sunshine, stretching themselves in various positions on the ground. Propping their heads against hillocks or upon each other's bodies, they would fold their arms across their stomachs, cock one knee over the other, and close their eyes in sleep. The comfortable snoozing attitudes of these black-frocked chimpanzees taking their siestas made me think of a group of bishops enjoying post-prandial naps in the Athenaeum Club in London.

The chimps were always very disciplined in their movements. Sometimes they advanced with deliberate strides on all fours, whilst at other times they stood erect and walked on their hind-legs. They stepped nimbly over obstacles in their paths—such as Hugo's camera tripod, bits of photographic equipment and parcels of books—or side-stepped them without ever touching them, let alone knocking them over. If they picked up a bottle to inspect its contents, they handled it with the utmost care. They would sometimes invade the tents, and stroll through them inspecting this or that box, tin or package to see whether it contained food; but they never broke anything. Every now and then, however, one seized a towel, a pair of trousers or some similar article, and ran off to gnaw or play with it.

One of the interesting things about them was their distinctive individual personalities. Figan was, for example, an extrovert. A handsome young male by any chimpanzee standard, he seemed aware of his robust masculinity, and sometimes liked to draw attention to himself in violently self-assertive ways. On one occasion I saw him careering threateningly to and fro in front of a group of his companions, vigorously stamping his feet. He picked up a long palm-frond from the ground, raised it above his head, and waved it in the air like a flag. A few moments later he dropped that huge leaf, seized another, and repeated the same self-advertising motions. Twice he ran at Jane and Hugo, who were sitting on a path near-by, as if to assault them, but he sheered away each time when he came close to them. On a third approach, however, he gave Jane a strong sideways kick as he passed her—a provocation of which she took no notice other than a dedicated zoological student's objective observation. Then he went to a near-by tree which the chimpanzees used as a "drumming tree" when they felt excited, and gave its trunk a resounding whack.

On another occasion I watched him display superior intolerance at a couple of baboons who wandered innocently on the scene. He ran at them, then stopped as they retreated, grasped a leafy branch of a sapling and shook it at them, stamping his feet the while.

Jane thought that he might have acquired an inferiority complex because of his mother Flo's preference for his elder brother Faben, and that his jealousy of this favourite made him feel he must now and then demonstrate his own importance. If that theory was correct, Figan had only himself to blame for his parent's greater fondness for her other son, since he did not groom her body very often, whereas Faben frequently engaged in that filial duty. In return she scratched and cleansed Faben much more often than she did Figan, although she groomed Figan conscientiously when his brother was not around.

Other chimpanzees showed different traits—some being timid and others bold, some sociable and others stand-offish, some gay and others morose. Their individual characters begin to show quite early in their infancy. For example, Flo's latest offspring, five months old Flint, was already a distinct personality in his own right—charming, resolute and adventurous. A miniature model of a chimp, standing (when he managed to stagger up for an uncertain, wobbly moment) scarcely more than eighteen inches high, he still had the pinky-brown face of exceeding youth instead of the black face of maturity. Accustomed to being transported everywhere on his mother's back, or slung somewhere else round her person, he could hardly yet progress forwards, sideways or backwards by his own unaided efforts on the ground. Like a human baby beginning to learn how to crawl, he kept raising himself on all fours, taking one pace forward, tumbling over, rearranging himself on his limbs, advancing hesitantly again, overbalancing once more, and so proceeding slowly by a succession of stumbles. He was most at home on Flo's body, where he was experienced at gripping her fur in his fists and pulling himself into whatever position he desired whilst she aided him with firm maternal gentleness by holding one of his wrists and guiding him this way or that. Sometimes she would play with him much as a human mother plays with a human infant. For instance, she would lie on her back coddling him and every now and then lifting him into the air on her upstretched hands and feet, where he stayed precariously balanced, peering down fondly but perplexedly at her. His brothers and sister would also amuse him with games. They were always very careful with him, whilst he was bold with them, climbing on them and clambering all over their bodies. Many of his gestures were reminiscent of a child's. Thus he would often sit sucking one of his thumbs; and at other times he would stick a finger up his nose, pick a nostril, and put the contents in his mouth for chewing.

He was still almost wholly dependent on Flo's milk for nourishment, and often clung to her with his lips sucking her nipples. Yet he was beginning to learn from her example how to consume other fare, for on two occasions I saw her give him a strip of banana skin to lick and munch. However, when he tried to grab a bite of the fruit itself, she refused him, no doubt knowing instinctively that it might prove too much for him and give him indigestion.

The younger chimps enjoyed playing games, joined sometimes by their elders. One such sport seemed to be a form of touch-last, and another was mock wrestling. A couple would roll over and over on the ground locked in each other's embrace and pretending to bite one another. Often their playful exercises had a touch of gymnastics which was useful training for forest life. For instance, I once watched a two and a half years old female called Gilka performing an acrobatic act on a tall sapling. The part-grown, supple, thin-limbed treelet stood fifteen feet high beside a much larger, older tree. Gilka would climb up that veteran's trunk, scamper along a bough, and take a flying leap on to the sapling's upstanding summit, which she gripped in both hands. The flexible stem bent under her weight, swung swiftly downwards until it almost touched the ground, and then sprang upwards again—for Gilka's avoir du pois was just enough to carry it within a few inches of the grass before starting up again. The little chimp did not jump off, but kept dangling from the branch, descending and ascending again and again through the air as it bounced up and down several times before the original momentum triggered off by her arrival became exhausted, and the sapling resumed its stationary upright poise. Then Gilka leaped back into the older tree, climbed high on its trunk once more, and dropped afresh on to the sapling's top—to repeat the exciting performance all over again. She repeated it fifteen times in the next ten minutes before she tired of the game, and went in search of other sport. It was a joyous exhibition—which tiny Flint squatting on the ground watched enviously.

Indeed, Flint then tried to emulate it—with no success. His weight was not yet sufficient for such an enterprise. Nevertheless he climbed small trees with a certain naïve, halting skill, and jumped around among their branches with more competence than he showed in walking over ground. This was interesting evidence that chimpanzees are by nature more tree-haunting than earth-frequenting animals.

VI

As I have already mentioned, old Flo's authority among the members of her family was unquestioned; and she was invariably treated with the utmost respect also by the other apes. This was a mark of the fact that chimpanzee society is matriarchal. The reason is not far to seek. The younger chimps all recognise their mothers because of their dependence on them throughout their earliest years. It is their mother who feeds them, fondles them through the day, cradles them at night, transports them everywhere on her body, and in due course teaches them by her example to walk, find food, build tree-top beds, and generally look after themselves. In contrast, they have not the slightest notion who their father is. Nor do the fathers know which of the youngsters scampering around them are their own offspring; and so they feel and exercise no paternal responsibility. Male and female alike are entirely promiscuous in their sexual habits. When a young lady's bare-skinned hind-quarters periodically grow swollen and pink, indicating that she is "on heat," she is fair (and usually willing) game for any desirous sire. Her wooers sometimes literally queue up to gain satisfaction from her. Jane has seen as many as eight potent males waiting in line to enjoy the favours of a single female, who accepted each one of them in turn. Their embraces did not last long, all the eight acts of mating being accomplished within about five minutes.

The activities of the chimps so filled each day with fascination that I had little leisure to observe other animals living in their vicinity. Every now and then a party of baboons intruded on the scene, trying to snatch a share of the bananas. But they were usually kept at a respectful distance by the great apes, who gave them disapproving, threatening glances, and if necessary inflicted cuffs on their bodies. So as often as those smaller monkeys hopefully approached, they discreetly withdrew again. Their troupes were a perpetually charming sight, with the infant baboons sitting on their mother's backs as they scampered to and fro, like jockeys riding race-horses.

I observed a few of the other local inhabitants of the wild. Bird life was not very common. Occasionally a sunbird, bulbul, whiteeye or weaver flew into view, and once a majestic crowned hornbill perched in a tree close beside my tent. But I was told that birds' nests were few and far between in the neighbourhood, perhaps because the restless, inquisitive chimpanzees raided any such curiosities to explore what they might be.

The chimps' own "nests" were evident, scattered here and there through the surrounding forest. Every evening they built manytwigged, leafy platforms high in the trees as beds for their nightly repose. These simple structures take only a few minutes to create by expert bendings and interlacings of supple young branches over a convenient foundation, such as a junction of more solid boughs. The finished product forms a broad couch on which an ape can lie and sleep. Young chimps share nests with their mothers until they are about three years old, when they have learnt to make their own beds. One afternoon I saw Merlin, aged eighteen months, experimenting in the manufacture of such a resting place, bending several slim leafy branches of a small sapling, joining them together on the ground, and then reclining prostrate on

them. He did not find it comfortable, and soon rose and scampered
away to enjoy some other fun.

VII

Jane's patient, painstaking observations, supported by Hugo's
vivid films, have widely extended mankind's knowledge of chimpanzees. Probably the most important of her discoveries is the
revelation that chimps are tool-makers. Hitherto it had been
assumed that what distinguished Homo sapiens from all other
anthropoid creatures was his capacity to invent tools. Jane has
blown that theory to smithereens, for she watches Flo and her
companions making and using a few different types of crude, arti-
ficial implements. One such is the employment of sticks for ex-
tracting termites from their ant-hills, much as we use a fork to
extract lumps of ginger from a jar. At the season of the year when
young termites are ready to spread their wings and fly from home
the chimps are very partial to termite-meat. A hungry ape will
pluck a dried stem of grass, squat beside the ant-heap, and poke
the instrument into one of the subterranean tunnels to disturb the
insects. They resent this intrusion, run to the stalk to bite it, and
grip it with their fangs. The chimpanzee promptly withdraws
the straw, sticks it into his (or her) mouth, and enjoys the tasty
morsels clinging fatally to it. Sometimes, instead of using such a
ready-made utensil, the hunter picks a living twig from a bush,
rips off its leaves, and employs the bare stem as his tool.

Another primitive implement which Jane has seen fashioned by
chimpanzees is used for drinking. Sometimes in dry seasons water
is scarce in the forest. However, little "cupfuls" of it exist trapped
in holes in tree-trunks or other natural receptacles. The chimps
have learned by experience that if they poke a finger into the
liquid and then suck it, the number of drops so caught are too
few to slake their thirsts quickly; so they have devised an alternative method. Gathering a heap of leaves, an ape will crush them
together by chewing until they form a sort of sponge, and then

dip them into the water. When the leafy mass is soaked with the fluid the beast pulls it out again, puts it between his lips, and enjoys a goodly mouthful of drink.

These and other revealing habits of the Van Lawicks' neighbours establish the chimpanzee as Man's nearest surviving relative in the animal kingdom. Flo and her family are in truth our very, very distant cousins.